Nine Wingcos and the Lancaster

NINE
WINGCOS
AND THE LANCASTER

THE SECOND WORLD WAR
EXPERIENCES OF A BOMBER
COMMAND FLIGHT ENGINEER

PETER BAXTER

Published in 2018 by Fighting High Ltd,
www.fightinghigh.com

British Library Cataloguing-in-Publication data.
A CIP record for this title is available from the
British Library.
ISBN – 13: 978-1-9998128-3-6

Designed and typeset in Adobe Minion 11/15pt
by Michael Lindley. www.truthstudio.co.uk.
Printed and bound by Gomer Press.
Front cover design by www.truthstudio.co.uk.

Contents

by Mike Baxter

My father was a hero. He was a flight engineer on Lancasters and on a wing and a prayer he completed thirty-four operations over enemy territory and came out alive at the other end. After his first operational tour with No. 12 Squadron, he was given responsibility and made the engineer leader for the newly formed No. 153 Squadron. During his 400 hours in the air, half of which were at night, he flew with a succession of pilots and among them were nine wing commanders. A key item of his equipment that he took with him on each trip was a pipe containing a hidden compass, just in case he was shot down.

I am not a hero. I am just an ordinary chap, someone in awe of his father's achievements and who still struggles to comprehend how anyone could have gone through what he did. In pursuit of this understanding, in 2014 I was fortunate enough to be able to get a ride on the Canadian Lancaster 'VERA' when she was over in the UK. I took off from Humberside Airport, which was the original RAF Kirmington where No. 153 Squadron had started. I carried my father's pipe on that journey with me; it flew again in a Lancaster, seventy years on.

My father was a hero and, in his own words, this is his story.

Introduction

After reading a book entitled *Lancaster Target,* which featured life on a bomber squadron during 1943, I wrote to the author Jack Currie in nostalgic vein as I had indeed been on the same squadron at that time. During the correspondence that followed, Jack suggested that I also should write a book about my experiences as a flight engineer in the Royal Air Force.

This idea was initially greeted with some hilarity, but after being pressed by my two sons to explain what I had actually done, I was spurred on to put pen to paper. I was prepared to write a page or two of the highlights of my career, but just as great oaks from little acorns grow, so did my tale, and the outcome was this rather lengthy account. This was partly brought about by my terms of reference to include everything that I could remember, and partly through my own enthusiasm as the story unfolded. I do not claim that this is other than a homespun tale in simple terms, and I hope that it generates enough interest to compensate for its somewhat amateurish style. I have tried throughout to avoid the use of jargon, but where a term was used in common parlance, or was a technical expression, I have considered it appropriate to include it.

I have endeavoured to describe not only my experiences, but also the environment in which I lived. I have been guided primarily by my logbook, sundry documents, and notes that I made at the time, but I have had to rely on my memory to fill in the gaps, which means that I cannot vouch for all the facts being correct after such a lapse in time. This is particularly true of events appertaining to the front-line squadrons, where a week on an operational station was a very long time, and many changes could happen during those few days!

I have tried not to let hindsight alter the views of the scenes that I had at the time, and in this respect I must especially mention the bombing of the towns in Germany. We ordinary airmen accepted this policy without hesitation, and if it later became controversial, at the time it was all part of the national struggle for survival – I make no apologies for the part I played in it.

Finally, I must particularly thank my elder son Michael for his encouragement while I was writing the script, and the subsequent tasks of proofreading and typing – essentials without which the story would not have been completed.

March 1985

Chapter One

Halton

After passing the entrance examination in November 1937, I was informed that I had gained entry to the Royal Air Force Technical Apprentices School at Halton, near Aylesbury in Buckinghamshire. The course upon which I was about to embark was of three years' duration and was designed to produce technicians of the highest standard for the maintenance and servicing of aircraft, and had been originated by Marshal of the Royal Air Force, Lord Trenchard, back in 1919, at the end of the First World War. At the end of my apprenticeship I would be expected to complete a further twelve years of full-time service.

So it was that on 25 January 1938, at the tender age of fifteen, I caught the train to London from New Street station, Birmingham. After transferring to Marylebone station, I completed the journey to Wendover (the nearest station to Halton) in the company of a throng of my fellow sufferers-to-be that I had met on the train. Our suffering actually started at Wendover when we were assembled in columns and marched the mile and a half to Halton. Our cases etc. were thankfully being conveyed by a station wagon!

At first, Halton appeared very forbidding, but in time I developed an affection for it (if not for the routine). The camp was in a very beautiful setting, with the Chiltern Hills in the background, and had been presented to the nation by the Rothschild family. The family mansion was taken over as the officers' mess.

A proportion of our 834-strong entry was divided off to be trained as fitter armourers (by request) and the rest of us were divided alphabetically into wings, with the top half (including myself) becoming airframe apprentices and the bottom half being engine apprentices. Whether this designation was known to us beforehand I do not know, but one had no choice in the matter, and the only loophole was that one could leave Halton entirely within a specified number of weeks if the rigours of the course could not be faced. To distinguish between the various wings, we wore hat bands of different colours – our No. 5 Wing colours were red and green checks, which we always considered very superior to the others!

On day one of service we were kitted out, shown how to salute correctly, and given our apprentices' wheel insignia to sew on our uniform. The kitting out took place in a large wooden gymnasium at the side of the drill square. It was one of the few wooden buildings I remember at Halton's main camp, as the majority were built of brick and stone. The worst feature of these were the linoleum floors of the barrack blocks, which had to be kept in pristine condition at all times and twice as good on the weekly 'bull night'! The workshops, about half a mile away, were substantially built but in shabby condition. When I revisited the camp in 1982 I was told that they were still there, used regularly, and still had the same leaking roofs!

Our time was divided into three main activities: workshops for basic metal working; and schools (held in another Rothschild building) for theory of flight, history of the RAF, general studies, mathematics and European history. The third activity was sport and drill, including physical training (PT) on the square at 6.30am rain or shine! We were marched everywhere; to the workshops we had to form fours and then eights (the camp had very wide roads) and were accompanied by bag-pipes of the wing band. It may be thought that bagpipes make a very discordant sound, but we found their music excellent for marching. One activity we did not like was to be paraded round the camp boundaries, the main object of which was to give us no excuse if caught out of bounds. I was never apprehended in such a fashion, though I expect I transgressed like everyone else. Neither did I take part in some of the stunts that went on, e.g. jumping out of upstairs windows, or sleeping all night hanging by one's trouser braces from a coat hook! These activities were motivated by monetary reward and inter-wing rivalry.

One event that we had mixed feelings about was our first flight. It was mandatory that we went up once at Halton for air experience, and on the big day we all put on parachutes and tried to get to the back of the queue. Realising that it was inevitable, however, I pushed my way to the front to get it over and done with. The aircraft was an Avro Tutor of the stringbag type that seemed to take ages to get airborne, bumping over the uneven grass airfield, but when we eventually left the ground my fears subsided and I began to enjoy the experience. I can well remember the aforementioned gymnasium, which from our height resembled a matchbox, and the flagpole (which had been lowered to the ground for painting) looking like a match!

I must describe the beds on which we slept. These were built from iron slats made up into a frame that was then attached to the bed ends by being pushed through a slot and pegged with small pins. The result was a solid mass of iron that did not 'give' whatever load was put on it. They were nicknamed 'MacDonalds'! In place of a mattress we had three padded cushions known as biscuits and also had two blankets and two sheets. (We were fortunate in respect of the sheets at Halton as they were not universally supplied throughout the RAF, and I subsequently spent many nights of discomfort between blankets at other stations.)

All of these items had to be neatly folded and placed with precision at the ends of the beds immediately after rising in the morning. The beds themselves were then lined up by holding a string from one end of the room to the other. Only after all this positioning were we then allowed to visit the ablutions, and proceed outside for the PT already mentioned as a prerequisite to breakfast. Sundays were rest days from the working routine, but church parades were compulsory and, needless to say, highly unpopular. Unless one was officially unfit for duty the only way to avoid the church parade was to attend the sickbay to have a throat swab taken; this was quite an accepted practice, as it was laid down for two persons from each billet to have this done weekly as a health precaution. When this routine was first established I managed to secure one of the places, but unfortunately, on the first occasion, the session took place some time before the church parade started, and my colleague and I returned to the billet to find that our beds had been dismantled and the component parts widely distributed around the block! It was no joke spending the rest of the day searching for the bits and pieces to assemble the beds again, and when our disgruntled room-mates repeated the performance on the following Sunday we suddenly realised how much we liked going on church parade and applied for a release from our sickbay duties! The powers that be would not countenance any change in the arrangements, however, but did alter the time for our attendance so that we stayed behind until the church parade had started.

We were paid one shilling (5p) per day, of which three shillings were paid out each week. The remaining four shillings were kept back to accumulate and the savings were given to us each time we went on leave. The leave periods were a week at Easter, three weeks in July/August and a week at Christmas.

In early April I fell foul of a minor epidemic of mumps, and actually spent my sixteenth birthday in the isolation hospital that was part of the Princess Mary's Hospital complex at Halton. The rigorous routine followed us into hospital, and as soon as we were fit enough to get up we had to scrub the floors and also the walls. In addition to this we had to take the gargles round to the fortunate patients who were still in bed. During my isolation period everyone else departed on Easter leave, but I did manage to get out in time to enjoy an abbreviated first holiday at home. I was taken to Tring station personally in a Service transport, to catch the train to Birmingham, and thus early in my career I had a demonstration that, in spite of all, the RAF were very welfare conscious.

During my short stay at Halton there were many things going on and plenty to occupy the mind. There was a thriving model aircraft club and a first-class rifle range among other things. Each wing had its own NAAFI, and I recall listening to the 1938 Cup Final on the NAAFI radio. Empire Air Day that year brought a fine air display to the airfield; this was given by the Hendon team, and the highlight was an acrobatic display by three aircraft coupled together with elastic ropes. Not quite as spectacular as some seen at today's air shows, but exciting stuff just the same. There were also numerous impromptu events, and one of the most interesting concerned 'Tich' Flett, one of the smaller lads in my billet who maintained that he could run around the square ten times in half an hour. We all thought that this was impossible and took him on, putting a few precious coppers in the kitty. Needless to say, he flogged himself into the ground and made it with two minutes to spare. As he was also one of the persons who had hung from his braces, he made a fair amount of money out of us. Is it surprising to know that he was a Scotsman?

During 1938 the government realised that there was a distinct possibility of war breaking out against Germany. On hearing the distant guns, it decided on a crash course to prepare the country for defence. New RAF camps were built and many of the existing procedures and routines were disrupted, naturally affecting the apprentice scheme as a consequence. The course was reduced from three to two years and the wings were condensed into one unit and divided into squadrons. To make more room for an increased intake, No. 5 Wing was to be posted to No. 2 School of Technical Training at the newly built RAF Cosford, to form a nucleus for the new station. The armourer apprentices were also involved in this move. So as things turned out, my sojourn at Halton had lasted just half a year, although to my young mind it had seemed like a lifetime!

Chapter Two

Cosford

On our entry into Cosford on 4 August 1938, after summer leave, our attitude was much different to that on our arrival at Halton. We were not marched there, but arrived at the purpose-built railway station situated within the camp area, and generally we regarded ourselves as old sweats by this time.

The camp buildings were all wooden structures except for the four main hangars, which were steel-framed brick buildings and housed the cinema, gymnasium, swimming baths and workshops. The workshops had large steel doors opened by a hand-operated winding mechanism. (I was a victim of this winding gear when on one occasion I had my fingers trapped between the handle and the door. Fortunately, apart from losing a couple of nails, no great harm was done.) The living quarters were huts built in parallel rows and interconnected by corridors. They were centrally heated, the water being conveyed from the boiler house by overhead pipes lagged with fibreglass. On entering our huts we discovered that we had proper beds – with springs! However, the biscuits were still there and so were the sheets. The floors were a replica of those at Halton, subsequently to become the object of many hours of polishing.

At first we were designated No. 1 Wing and had red and green hat bands (as at Halton), but when the numbers grew, our entry was transferred to No. 2 Wing and the hat bands were then green and black. Each wing had its own musical band, comprising bagpipes, flutes and drums. With the combination of corridors and wooden buildings, band practice was heard far and wide, and the members had a nil rating in the popularity stakes. Eventually they were banished to another building and peace reigned thereafter. There was also a station silver band; the noise of both bands practising together was unbelievable!

The working routine was much the same as at Halton, i.e. workshops, schools and sport with liberal inspections, parades and periods of PT thrown in for good measure. Having done our basic training at Halton, the workshop emphasis was now drastically changed. As this was the next step anyway, and also with the contraction of our apprenticeship to a two-year course, we were now working on actual aircraft and related trades. These trades consisted of hydraulics, pneumatics, electrics, carpentry, welding and brazing, hulls and floats and wire-splicing. We practised on numerous redundant aircraft including Fairey Battles, Bristol Blenheims (which were the latest thing in those days), and the older-type biplanes such as Gloster Gladiators, Bristol Bulldogs and Hawker Harts.

On these aircraft we took out the hydraulics and pneumatics and assembled them back again. Out came all the control cables and trimming mechanism; we made new cables to replace them. The same happened with the electrical wiring. Off came the wings, undercarriages, wheels and brakes, and back they went. We punched holes in the sides of aircraft and repaired them again. We bled this, painted that, and riveted the other, not to mention the fabric-covered aircraft that gave us plenty of work with needles, thread and beeswax. As can be deduced from all this, it was hectic going but we enjoyed it and the time passed very quickly.

Several incidents stand out from this time. We had a sergeant instructor for the splicing course who was never satisfied with our efforts, and no matter how perfect was the finished job, his criticism was always the same: 'I could drive a coach and horses through that splice' or 'I could get my week's pay through there!' On another occasion one lad climbed into a seaplane float (a standard procedure when repairing the skin), but he got trapped inside (which was not the standard procedure) and the float had to be cut in half to release him. Likewise, someone lowered an aircraft down on to a trestle that should not have been there, and had to jack it back up again smartly on hearing a cracking noise – but not before the back of the aircraft had been broken. I recall this providing a good exercise for the following class as a repair! In addition to all this we had to produce test pieces constructed of bits of metal precisely bent (by hand) and riveted. I also made a cold chisel at Cosford, which I used for many years afterwards.

One of my instructors at Cosford was Harry Ward, who had been well known as a 'birdman' in pre-war days. He had a pair of wood and linen wings made and flapped about at 11,000ft making several success-ful flights. As well as this he also made 1,100 parachute jumps, and he was registered by the Air Ministry as a light aircraft! As can be imagined, he had many tales to tell and he was a great hero-figure to us. He instructed us, not on parachutes or theory of flight, but about aircraft wheels, tyres and brakes.

From time to time we had practical instruction in handling aircraft on the aerodrome. This part of the course was quite popular but had its drawbacks as part of the time was spent washing the aircraft down. I well remember, during the winter of 1939/40, having to dig the aircraft out of the snow before commencing a prop-swinging exercise. There were two ways of doing this – the normal method of swinging with one hand for light aircraft, and a method of rope swinging for the heavier types. To do this, a canvas sling was positioned on the prop and attached to this sling was a rope; on the other end of the rope were two or three airmen. On the call 'Contact', the airmen had to race away, the sling sliding off the prop on the downward stroke – a hilarious thing to watch as the men very often fell over each other when the sling was released.

Other elements of this aerodrome course included refuelling, the picketing down of aircraft (the pickets being screwed into the ground and the ropes attached to the undersides of the wings), the laying of flares (this was before the days of universal aerodrome lighting), handling an aircraft during taxiing, salvage (including the use of shear legs), and learning the aerodrome ground signs.

During my time at Cosford we had two commanding officers – Group Captain Guilfoyle, OBE, MC, and Group Captain Budgen, who succeeded him. While most of the officers were remote figures to us, the CO was almost a figment of the imagination rather than a reality. I did, however, see Group Captain Guilfoyle occasionally in the distance as he was wont to ride a white horse around the camp. Group Captain Budgen was the first officer of his rank that I had seen who was an observer rather than a pilot.

As at Halton, there were camp boundaries to observe. At Cosford these were a bit more liberal and we were allowed into nearby Albrighton, Codsall, Shifnal and Tettenhall at all times. Wolverhampton was out of bounds, though, except to senior boys (with, I believe, one and a half years' service), who were allowed a pass to visit there twice a month. During my first year I was friendly with an armourer apprentice named Smith, who, being somewhat senior to me, had this important facility to visit Wolverhampton. Smithy had an auntie living there, and on her birthday invited me to the party. Of course I was not officially allowed further than Tettenhall, but yielded to Smithy's persuasion. 'Keep in the background,' he said; 'if we are challenged I will show my pass and do the talking.' Off we went on our cycles (I had brought my old one from home on a previous leave), and we had a very enjoyable day out, there being a carnival in the local park at the same time. The inevitable happened, however, and on returning to Auntie's house we were stopped by a couple of RAF policemen. Smithy showed his pass and tried to do the talking, but unfortunately there was no background available for me to keep in, and I was asked for my pass also. Not having one to show, I was immediately ordered back to the camp, and Smithy was also, for collaborating with me. The upshot of this was that we both had to do seven days' 'jankers'. Jankers was a punishment that involved parading three times daily and doing fatigues each evening, usually in the cook-house. Needless to say we were confined to camp for this period, and had to wear a yellow armband to show that we had transgressed. The worst aspect was that it was recorded in our records as a very unwelcome black mark. Smithy's name was mud for quite a time, but eventually relations healed up, and after he was posted from Cosford I kept in touch with him by letter for some time.

Smithy had another pal, a fellow armourer named Brown, whom I also liked (a very unlikely pair Smith and Brown, but I assure you that this was quite true). When I went on holiday to Bournemouth during summer leave, I met Brown who lived on a nearby farm. He came to pick me up in his father's MG sports car and took me to meet his parents at the farm. The only thing I remember of that occasion was the ride there and back in the open car, with the wind rushing by and the loud exhaust.

Having thankfully completed my period of jankers, I found myself in line for another one! In the forces it is customary for the orderly officer to enquire whether there are any complaints during mealtimes, and one day a group of us stood up in unison to protest about the lack of sugar in the tea (this had been a long-standing grievance). Rather than cause a commotion at the time, the officer ordered us to attend evening parade when a tasting would be made of the offending tea. We then ran into difficulties, because for some reason the colder tea gets, the sweeter it tastes. So when we were paraded with our tea mugs the officer did not get the true picture and, being a shirty type, put us all on a charge of making a frivolous complaint. Fortunately, the wing commander had plenty of common sense and dismissed the charge. There was also a sudden improvement in the tea, so it had been worth the grievance, even though, as at Waterloo, it had been a close run thing! The Wolverhampton affair remained the only time I received any punishment at Cosford, although we all committed minor offences that usually ended with a ticking off.

There were facilities for many outdoor sporting activities at Cosford, most of the enthusiasm being for football and cricket. Those of us who were not much good at these formed a cross-country running group on the compulsory sporting half-days. This usually degenerated into a glorified ramble, complete with long sticks! We were known to climb trees and swim in local streams, and to visit well-known places such as Tong Church, Shifnal waterworks and even the model shop in Albrighton. That I did actually play football on occasion is very well remembered from an incident during a game in the autumn of 1938. I was playing full-back and ran forward to clear the ball up field at the same time that two of my opponents kicked it in the other direction. The ball became a solid object and I tumbled forward over it, putting my arm out to break the fall. Unfortunately the arm didn't bend as nature had intended, and I was carted off in the 'blood wagon' with a dislocated elbow. I was treated in the hut that served as the hospital, thereby gaining the dubious distinction of being one of the first patients in what became one of the best-known hospitals in the RAF.

A Parents' Day was held on 15 July 1939, and the workshops and schools were opened to visitors. The living quarters were also available for inspection and a flying display took place on the aerodrome. Our entry was among the senior echelons by this point, and we acted as guides. At about this time we had a visit from Queen Mary who was staying at nearby Patshull Hall. The only part of her visit that I can remember was when we lined the station road as she drove past in her car. On her approach we had to lift our hats and give three cheers. I can see her now, all in black holding her parasol, staring straight ahead as though we didn't exist.

Mention of the station reminds me of the rail ticket queue. When we went on leave, we were paid the accumulated portion of our pay, as at Halton, and were also given free railway warrants. These were distributed in the mess hall, and each one had to be written out or stamped with the destination. We received these in alphabetical order of destination and this caused long queues to form; even Birmingham seemed a long way back. I had the brilliant idea, however, of booking to Acocks Green, which was morally correct as I lived there at the time, and it could be reached from Cosford by changing at Snow Hill. I often contemplated cycling home, but for me the distance was just too far.

Church parades were also compulsory at Cosford and the services were held in the gymnasium. On Sunday 3 September 1939 the padre had a wireless set rigged up and the service was interrupted for us to listen to Mr Chamberlain's speech. On hearing of the outbreak of war our reaction was to give a hearty cheer. I cannot really explain this, unless it was in anticipation of the expected excitement to follow, but when the 'excitement' came it was a different matter. In fact we were very quickly deflated as the gates were closed and everyone was confined to camp. Worse was to come, and for the next week or so we were hard at it, filling sandbags and digging trenches near the entrance gates. Sand bunkers were constructed and piles of sand were left at strategic points; underground shelters were dug near huts, and respirators had to be carried everywhere in case of a gas attack.

We had recently started rifle drills, and these were now stepped up in earnest and included intensive firing practice on the range. My results were just average, but I was consistently very much better when wearing a respirator! Bayonet practice was also carried out and we had numerous lessons on military tactics. After the initial scare, life returned to normal with the exception of observing the blackout regulations and carrying out ARP (air-raid precautions) drills.

Although we were once more allowed out of camp, in reality we did not go out all that often – mainly only on cycle rides when the weather was fit. There wasn't much to do otherwise as we were fairly isolated being in the country and could not do much patronising of the local hostelry on three shillings a week. Most of our leisure time was spent in the huts writing notes and making model aircraft, or in the NAAFI where we could listen to the wireless and join in a sing-song around the piano. There were numerous technical posters around the walls, and a surprising number of people carried out their studies there. I can remember finishing off a workshop drawing in the NAAFI, and also taking part in a serious discussion on engine oil systems (although we were airframe fitters, we did have a lengthy course on engine theory as part of the school's syllabus). As well as this there were several societies that one could join, philately, model-making and wireless being among them.

During 1939 the camp grew in size with the addition of more huts, which were occupied by direct-entry trainees on courses lasting about eighteen months. A large brick barrack block was also built and known as the Fulton Block. A detachment of naval personnel were posted in; these were naval aircraft apprentices seconded to our school for training along the same lines as ourselves, and were eventually to be posted to the Fleet Air Arm.

As I have previously mentioned, the time at Cosford passed quickly, and at the beginning of 1940 we were suddenly faced with our final examinations. I will not mention the state of panic that prevailed, except to say that during intensive swotting up I grasped more about airframes in the last two weeks than in the previous two years. As a preliminary to this, and in anticipation of our passing out, we were allowed to indicate two units to which we would like to be posted. Most of us were anxious to be near our homes, so I chose Castle Bromwich and Coventry. In due course I learned that I was to go to Penrhos in North Wales, about 150 miles from Birmingham, and reached by one of the most tiresome rail journeys in the British Isles. Perhaps if I had put Land's End on the form I might have ended up in the Midlands!

When the examinations started we were required to make the inevitable test piece. This was a complicated affair of bits of mild steel bent round a tube with the flanges riveted up, the whole thing being on the skew. It was necessary to determine the exact allowance for bending the metal before wielding the hacksaw, as we were not allowed to make a guess and file the surplus off. A further difficulty arose when the drawings were issued to us and we found that some of the dimensions were in inches and some in millimetres (metric measures were very un-common at the time). I must have fluked my test piece because I eventually passed out with quite reasonable marks.

We had to sit written papers in our school's subjects, of course, but the big one was the Trade Test Board, which took place on 29 February. I am unable to recall the precise details, but there were two or three oral examinations that took up the whole of the day. I can remember being asked questions on all types of basic metalworking including heat treatment and anodising. On the aircraft side, I was questioned on rigging biplanes (plenty of them about in those days) and subjected to a lengthy inquisition on Dunlop braking systems and Lockheed hydraulics. Fortunately I knew my stuff regarding these and was fairly confident that I had done enough to pass. Sure enough, of the three grades to be attained (LAC – leading aircraftman, AC1 – aircraftman first class, and AC2 – aircraftman second class) I was promoted to AC1, which was the result expected of us. Two or three of the bright sparks achieved the LAC rating and a goodly number were AC2s, so I was well satisfied with my lot.

The thirty-seventh entry of apprentices held their passing-out parade (bayonets fixed and all) and their passing-out dinner on 14 March 1940, and on the 15th had a final party at the Bell Inn, Tong. We were now fully fledged 'erks' about to enter the real world, and would henceforth have to look after our own interests. For the first time we would have no set routine and timetable – there was a mixed atmosphere of both relief and apprehension! We were posted to our new units without first accorded leave, for I remember us all gathering on the small platform of Cosford

Aerodrome halt. Two or three of us were going to Penrhos and we travelled on the mid-Wales line via Barmouth to Pwllheli. We were met at the station by RAF transport, and arrived at the camp about seven o'clock on a wet and windy night.

Chapter Three

Penrhos

RAF Station Penrhos was a relatively small unit with a grass airfield and a compact group of wooden buildings. The airfield was on high ground and had a fairly steep incline on three sides. From the north-western edge of the field the ground sloped upwards on just a gentle gradient, and it was on this rising ground that the camp was situated. Although there were no runways, there was a concrete perimeter track that ran about halfway round the airfield. The station had been built in 1935/36 for pilot training, and was partially burned down in September 1936 by Welsh nationalists. After being rebuilt it was realised that it was unsuitable for pilot training after all, owing to persistent sea mists, and it was used instead for bombing and gunnery training. The official title when I arrived was No. 9 Bombing and Gunnery School.

This, then, was the camp to which I reported on that wild night a fortnight before my eighteenth birthday. The road up to the camp had a guardroom at the bottom, and another at the top where we were dropped off. It was not a real surprise to find that we weren't expected; that this was a regular occurrence (throughout the Service as a whole) was substantiated by the existence of a transit hut to which I was dispatched. In this hut I met a motley collection of erks who had all arrived within the previous two or three days. They included a drogue operator, a tractor driver (straight from Ramsey on the Isle of Man where he had been the lifeboat driver), a cook, an Army private and many more.

I was soon sorted out, however, as I was collected the following morning by an orderly and taken to the Maintenance Department. Later that day I transferred my belongings to a hut that was occupied by airmen of my own trade, the majority of whom worked in the same department.

The maintenance hangar was the biggest building on the camp and was indeed a world of its own; once inside, all else was forgotten. I have never seen a hangar so full of so many types of aircraft since then – it was reminiscent of the RAF Museum in latter days. Although not exactly in their prime, these aircraft were certainly not museum pieces, and it was our job to keep them in flying condition. In one corner stood a Handley Page Harrow bomber (No. K6939), a huge thing for those days, which had force-landed on the airfield and was damaged in the process. The fact that it had landed at all was a marvel on our small aerodrome, and there was a great deal of speculation as to whether it would be able to take off again after being repaired. That Harrow was with us for over twelve months, and eventually got so much in the way that it was pushed outside and securely picketed down. I was destined to work on it several times, as was almost everyone in the department! More of this anon.

Other aircraft in the hangar at this time included Westland Wallace and Hawker Demon biplanes, and a permutation of the Harvard, Battle, Blenheim, Whitley and Anson monoplanes. Later on we were also to have the Defiant, Henley and Lysander. All of these were second-hand machines, having been handed down from the front-line squadrons. The Maintenance Department was concerned with all major inspections, overhauls and repairs, with the routine minor inspections and running repairs being dealt with out on the flights. A major inspection would often entail taking the mainplanes and tail unit off the aircraft to inspect the securing bolts and also check for corrosion. The undercarriage would be dismantled and examined for wear and tear, with attention being given to the brakes, tyres and oleo legs. The oleo legs (compressed-air shock-absorbing struts) were the bane of our lives, with leaking oil glands that had to be replaced. This leaking oil would get on to the brake shoes and the tyres and this was compounded by oil leaking from the engine up above; altogether a messy business!

With the biplane types it was mandatory to replace all the control cables – this is where our splicing expertise (?) came in! Long lines of cables were to be seen being stretched so that they would be the correct length afterwards, as no adjustment was possible. These aircraft were fabric-covered and often the covering had to be replaced. Although we had had instruction on this procedure, it was seldom that we did the actual work as it was handled by men who specialised in fabric work (they were colloquially known as the 'dope bashers' from their use of the special cellulose aircraft varnish called dope). The dope bashers were allowed to drink several pints of milk during working hours to counteract the effects of this varnish, but we who were working nearby were breathing the same atmosphere, yet were not afforded the same consideration!

We had a great variety of work to do when considering the different types of aircraft involved, and also the fact that we had to make up new assemblies to replace worn-out ones (the rudder bar pivot was a good example of this). Numerous components also had to be changed (flap jacks, brake units, etc.), while at the same time electrical and instrument mechanics were at work and getting in our way. Fortunately we were not hampered by the engine fitters, as the engines were usually removed and taken to the repair shops at the end of our hangar when the aircraft were first bought in.

It was always a big day when the finished plane was wheeled out on to the large apron outside the hangar. The inspection had to be signed for, of course, but to ensure that the aircraft was correct in all details, the senior fitter had to fly on the air test.

The department was run by a small hierarchy comprising Warrant Officer Hole, Flight Sergeant Richardson and Sergeant Fielding, aided and abetted by several corporals. Sergeant Fielding was a rigger and was our mentor. Flight Sergeant Richardson was a father-figure, grizzled, with many years of experience, and who wouldn't stand any nonsense. Warrant Officer Hole was indescribable, a beast of a man with a vile temper, and who we naturally kept clear of as much as possible. One incident will suffice to show his nature. One day, an old chap by the name of Arthur Gandy arrived in the hangar. He was an ex-fitter who had retired years previously but had been recalled to the colours as a 'Z'-class reservist. Mr Hole asked him his name and Arthur naturally replied 'Gandy'. As Hole had a slight resemblance to the Mahatma, he thought he was being made a fool of and went purple in the face. It was soon established that this was Arthur's real name, but had he been fooling, he would have been for the high jump as Mr Hole could not stand a joke against himself and I cannot recall ever having seen him laugh. By a great coincidence, it turned out that Arthur Gandy lived in Acocks Green, Birmingham, and on one occasion I went on leave with him and we had a drink in the New Inn.

On 14 June 1941, the title of the unit at Penrhos was changed for the second time to No. 9 Air Observers' School, but I cannot think of the reason for this as I seem to remember that navigational exercises had always been on the curriculum. Nor can I recall the exact status of the pupils under training, but in rank they went from sergeant upwards. During the early part of the war, the observer (later to be re-titled navigator) was a general dogsbody who was expected also to drop the bombs and man the guns; hence the reason for the existence of schools to teach them the basics of these jobs. Later in the war, with the advent of specialised crew members for bombing and gunnery, the emphasis of training at these schools such as ours, was probably switched to navigation.

In whatever way the change may have affected the flying staff, it did not alter our routines except for the increased demand for serviceability of the aircraft; the great idea was to pack the flying hours in! Owing to already mentioned weather conditions, there were inevitable hold-ups, but on the fine days flying took place from dawn to dusk. We had no facilities for night flying, but later on this was carried out at a neighbouring airfield.

A Fairey Battle was kept in constant readiness for duty if any enemy attacks took place from the sea. It was positioned at the edge of the airfield and could be seen clearly from the road leading up to the camp. This duty Battle, as it was called, gave a certain psychological assurance as it stood there, a silent sentinel for all to see, but heaven help us if anything had happened with only this antiquated and underpowered machine to guard us; reconnaissance maybe, but defence no!

It may be appropriate here, to give a short résumé of the bombing and gunnery routine. Small bombs that were painted white were used for bombing practice on the range in nearby Hell's Mouth Bay. The aircraft normally used for this purpose would be Whitleys, Battles and Blenheims. The gunnery practice was more adventurous and consisted mainly of firing at drogues, which were towed by other aircraft. Most of the aircraft types were used for gunnery, but the Henley (adopted from the

Hurricane) was the specialised drogue-towing plane. To elaborate on the adventurous angle, it was not unknown for the pupil gunners to hit their own tailplanes, and more than one aircraft crashed for this reason. The towing aircraft also had a few near misses, even though it was at a fairly safe distance. The drogue-towing cable was frequently severed by a chance shot. When this happened, the local farmers rushed out to collect them as a reward was given for their return.

My first flight at Penrhos, in September 1940, was in a Fairey Battle as a passenger during a gunnery exercise, and what a flight it was! It has to be remembered that I had only flown once before on that famous occasion at Halton when all was quiet and serene, so naturally I was very apprehensive to start with. We had all been encouraged to make the odd flight 'just to see how it works', so I decided to take the plunge. If I was nervous before being airborne, this soon paled into insignificance. To start with, the pilot was a Pole who could not speak English, and if he had had reason to order us to bale out we wouldn't have understood him! We could hardly have heard him anyway over the clatter of the engine and the chatter of the guns, and for this reason a klaxon was installed to warn the gunner when to commence firing. There was I, cowering (no exaggeration!) on the bottom of the fuselage in semi-darkness with an ear-splitting din going on, being showered with empty shell cases from above, with the klaxon horn blaring forth, praying that the engine wouldn't pack up. I see from my logbook that the flight took forty-five minutes – arguably the longest forty-five minutes I have endured. Suffice it to say that while I flew again at Penrhos (the next occasion being the very next day in fact), I never ever took to the skies again in a Fairey Battle!

My flight the next day was in a Whitley bomber, which stooged around for almost two hours, though I cannot remember what exercise it was on. The only thing I can recall about the flight was being airsick most of the time. Having suffered nearly every agony there was to endure on two consecutive days, it was to be a year and seven months before I flew again!

In an attempt to keep to the correct chronology, I must mention an event that had two amusing consequences. This was my contracting chicken pox in May 1940, and of course being put in isolation. The only buildings far enough away from the camp for this purpose were a block of married quarters, which had been built just prior to war breaking out but had never been occupied. I had a room to myself in one of the houses, the only other occupant being a medical orderly who had measles and was in an adjacent room. This chap had never had chicken pox and so didn't want to catch it. To this end he organised everything to his advantage and had first sight of the newspapers and was seen first by the MO (medical officer) on his rounds; he even had his temperature checked before me. I can now confirm what has been obvious from the beginning of this episode – on the day of my discharge he went down with chicken pox! I can well remember sitting outside in the glorious sunshine during my convalescence, thinking about my colleagues sweating it out in the hangar, and reading in the newspapers about the desperate evacuation from Dunkirk. I went home for a while after this and was treated like a hero when I casually mentioned I was on sick leave, but was honour-bound to explain that I had not been in France, but merely North Wales!

At intervals of approximately three months (depending on the amount of work on hand), we were allowed a week's leave, which I always spent at home in Birmingham. The rail journey via the North Wales coast was abysmal and involved changes at Afonwen, Bangor, Chester and Crewe, with frequent stops at (and between) many other stations on the way to let priority trains through. Owing to the wartime timetables, trying to get home via the mid-Wales line was even worse.

Stationed where we were, the world seemed very remote and it was only while going on leave that the war came into focus. I was involved in air raids on numerous occasions when in Birmingham and saw the results of The Blitz as soon as I arrived at New Street station. On walking to Snow Hill station one had to avoid fire hoses and debris littering the streets, but I cannot recall seeing any bomb craters; it seemed that most of the damage was caused by fire from incendiaries. The bombings also affected the trains as they were often brought to a halt at the height of a raid. My stay at home was very pleasant, of course, and as I had to wear uniform at all times I was easily recognised by neighbours and friends. It was embarrassing at times to be asked what we did at camp when we were living there in near peacetime conditions while the war had arrived in Birmingham. During The Blitz period (on later leaves) it was a relief to go back to camp, much as we had looked forward to being at home. If only we didn't have to face that journey.

Back at Penrhos, although we worked hard and long during the day, most of the evenings were free as there was no night flying. Being ingrained into camp life by this time, I often stayed in the hut and wrote letters or played cards etc., frequently repairing to the NAAFI about eight o'clock for a plate of egg and chips to augment our frugal meals. There was a station orchestra that played there two or three times a week, and of course the inevitable piano, which drew the inevitable crowd! Sometimes games of Housey Housey (Bingo) were held, this being the only gambling game allowed by regulations; there were also one or two snooker tables. The NAAFI closed at 9.30pm, except when Churchill was making a speech whereby we were allowed to listen to it.

If we went out, we would normally visit Pwllheli about two and a half miles away. The main attractions there were a couple of cinemas, a snooker hall, a WVS (Women's Voluntary Service) canteen, a dance hall and a few pubs. We visited all these places in turn, particularly the pubs, but the WVS canteen was very well patronised and we could play numerous board games there, including Mahjong if one had the patience to learn. What little bit of snooker expertise I have was gained in the Liberal Club where we played against the locals. There didn't appear to be any membership formalities to observe, and each game cost 3d. On a visit to Pwllheli in 1983 I saw that this club was still going strong although the 'Liberal' part had been dropped. On Sundays the town was dead, with only the chapels and clubs open. We normally chose the clubs, and for some unknown reason cider was the most popular drink. Dances were held on Saturday nights at the British Legion Club and were usually packed out. At these dances the standard of behaviour was very good, which was just as well because the club premises were alongside the harbour although I cannot recall anybody falling in. How values have changed – by today's standards the harbour would be half full! On these occasions we would return to the camp in relays in Mr Williams's taxi, but once when he was short of petrol about ten of us piled in at once. Both doors were half open and the chap in the middle had to change gear while Mr Williams worked the clutch; oh, happy days! Mr Williams's garage on the corner of Station Square later became a Co-op store.

We did have one incident concerning the harbour when one of our aircraft crashed into it. I think the aircraft was a Demon and may have been on gunnery duty. Whether the crash was caused by shooting off its own tail or not I don't know, but it must have been something drastic as it was within gliding distance of the airfield. However, the Maintenance Department swung into action, ably led by Flight Sergeant Richardson who was an old hand at this sort of thing. We went out in launches and somehow manhandled the plane to the harbour wall where it was raised up by shear legs (and perspiration) on to a lorry for conveyance back to base. The whole scenario was made much more dramatic as darkness had fallen during the operation and temporary lighting was rigged up, including car headlights – this when we were supposed to observe a total blackout!

Something even more dramatic happened at about this time (still 1940) when the Navy arrived. A Butlin's holiday camp, built between Pwllheli and Criccieth, was taken over by the Navy and given the name HMS *Glendower*. A large contingent of sailors were drafted in for training, presumably in seamanship, but it would have been a good idea for them also to have had a course in statesmanship as a lot of friction cropped up in Pwllheli! There are, of course, two sides to any argument, and no doubt our chaps were just as much to blame for any incidents that occurred. This is not to say that the town was knocked about, and in comparison with today's violence one would have imagined that we were in a kindergarten. There were a few clashes, though, especially after closing time, so to obviate as much trouble as possible naval and RAF piquets were formed to patrol the streets at these times. The dictionary definition of 'piquet' delightfully sums up the situation as 'a guard kept in readiness in case of alarm'. I had to take my turn as a 'guard in readiness' because this duty was farmed out among the lower ranks and usually came round about every six weeks or so. Six of us were marched round the town by an NCO and we had to report to the provost marshal at regular intervals – his office was in the High Street where the public houses were at their thickest! We were not armed, but had to wear white belts and an armband.

We all learned to live with the situation but had to put up with the fact that the naval people nursed what they thought was a genuine grievance against the RAF. On numerous naval operations in the early part of the war there had been a conspicuous absence of air cover, and in consequence they had suffered high casualties. This feeling of betrayal filtered right through the naval ranks and was particularly high at the time of the Narvik operation. As an example of the harassment we were subjected to I would mention an occasion when I visited the dentist in Pwllheli to have a tooth out. A group of us arrived in an RAF transport to have dental treatment, and I, having been first in and waiting for the others to take their turn, wandered into the local cafe for a cup of tea to ease my aching jaw. This was a grave mistake as the cafe was full of Navy personnel. They all stood up as I walked in and foul language issued forth. I turned about and was chased back to the dentist without ceremony. Fortunately I won the race, otherwise I would have been even more toothless!

No description of Pwllheli would be complete without mentioning the beach, which is the best feature of the town. The sand stretches for about half a mile from the harbour to the golf course to the west, and during the summer months it was very well patronised by the local population plus RAF contingents from Penrhos and Glendower. On the far side of the harbour lies Abererch beach, which I always thought slightly better than Pwllheli's sands although more awkward to approach. We saw the beach in the winter as well, of course, and a very wild place it could be indeed, especially when covered in thick snow.

There were other places within easy reach to visit from Penrhos, notably Llanbedrog, Abersoch, Criccieth and Morfa Nefyn. All of these were very small in comparison with Pwllheli and did not have much appeal except to visit briefly during the summertime. We had a regular RAF transport run to Abersoch on Sundays for us to take part in a rather good whist drive organised by the WVS. The ladies were always very tolerant of our frequent late arrival and fitted us in without any hassle. They gave us an average score for the hands we had missed, and occasionally we won without starting from scratch!

Llanbedrog was visited rather more frequently because it was only half a mile from the camp, but it only had a beach and a solitary large build-ing to attract us. The building, called the Glyn-y-weddw, was rather a mystery to me as, although it appeared to be occupied as a private house, it was also used for public dances on special occasions. Nowadays it is a smart hotel frequented by the yachting fraternity. Llanbedrog beach is nothing to shout about, but is rather a suntrap with large rocks to lie on. Several of us overindulged in sunbathing on one occasion and we got badly burned. Unfortunately on the following day we had to clamber in and out of the aircraft to effect some repairs, and an agonising time was had by all. As a self-inflicted wound was a court-martial offence in the Services, we had to grin and bear it!

To return to the subject of camp life, there are several other items of 1940 vintage to recount, some amusing, some surprising and others tragic. In late June and July we had an influx of tradesmen from among those who had escaped from Dunkirk, and many were the tales we heard from these chaps, most of whom had got away by the skin of their teeth without any of their possessions, and in some cases very few clothes. I can remember replacing some Perspex panels on a Blenheim together with a Canadian who was so badly affected that he could hardly hold his screwdriver, and he told me that he had had the shirt torn off his back in the rush and ended up on the boat wearing just a collar and tie. My friendship with this Canadian grew stronger when he began having food parcels from home and I had a share of his cigarettes and bacon cake – by this time cigarettes had become almost unobtainable and his 'Sweet Caporals' (a Canadian brand) were highly appreciated!

Another lad in the department was a mechanic by the name of Pringle, who was quite a character and the butt of many jokes. Pringle had two very fortunate escapes, one from the result of his own foolish action, and the other from someone else's stupidity. To explain the first incident, it is necessary to describe the engine starting procedure of the Wallace aircraft. The engine was fitted with an inertia starter, which was basically a heavy flywheel which had to be rotated by a hand-operated crank on the starboard side of the aircraft. When the flywheel was turning at the correct speed (judged from the sound) one pulled a cable to engage it with the engine gearing, immediately stepping to one side to miss the now rotating propeller. By now the outcome of this story will be obvious, but just in case further elucidation is needed, I need only say that Pringle was starting one of these engines one day and stepped in the wrong direction, and in so doing was clobbered by the propeller blade. Fortunately for him the engine drive did not engage properly and he only received a glancing blow. After a short spell in the sickbay, he returned as dotty as ever.

The other occasion was when Pringle was shaving with a cut-throat razor. Suddenly somebody shouted out his name and he involuntarily turned his head while forgetting to lower the razor, causing him to cut his cheek to the bone. It was by great luck that he missed his eyes, but once more we were deprived of the pleasure of his company while he was incarcerated in the sickbay!

The sickbay was always a very busy place, and so was the mortuary alongside, which from time to time held the bodies of the unfortunate victims of the occasional crashes that took place. Most of these episodes happened away from the airfield and were usually fatal as they were caused by flying into mountainsides during sudden bad weather, or by engine failure over the sea etc. The airfield incidents included several forced landings; during this period I remember one by a Blenheim and one by a Hurricane from which I managed to 'rescue' the propeller blade. There were also one or two instances of aircraft landing with their under-carriage up – it must not be forgotten that retractable undercarriages were a novelty then, and most of our aircraft had fixed wheels. While there were no injuries occurring from these escapades, the same could not be said when two people had the misfortune to walk into spinning propellers. Both of them were killed instantly, one of them being a pilot who was about to fly the aircraft.

Referring back to the Maintenance Department again, as already mentioned it was the customary practice for an air test to be carried out immediately after an aircraft was overhauled, and on one occasion this was done by a very peppery flight commander who was somewhat hard to please. 'Port wing low' was his first complaint, followed by 'Starboard wing low' on the next flight after we had carried out the adjustments. After the third flight the port wing was supposed to be low again, and by now we were so exasperated that we adopted the time-honoured procedure of wheeling the aircraft in and out again without altering the trim at all. 'Much better this time,' he said, 'but it has a tendency to fly nose up'. In and out of the hangar it went without a finger being laid on it and after the next flight he pronounced it 'all right at last'!

There was a sequel concerning this most awkward pilot who had been so critical of us – he was one of the first people to land a Fairey Battle with the wheels up, having forgotten to lower them and wondering what the devil the horn was blowing in the cockpit for. Now there was a regulation stipulating that if a damaged aircraft was unserviceable for more than twenty-four hours, the incident had to be reported, and we were treated to the spectacle of this fellow appearing post-haste in white overalls to help with the repairs. All hands were put to the pump and the poor aircraft was repaired so quickly that had it flown port wing low, nose down and hardly able to climb, for some reason or other he would have passed it fit without comment!

I have not yet mentioned the disciplinary way of life at Penrhos, and it has to be said that after our experiences as apprentices there was a welcome relaxation of rigid procedures, but we still came under the military code, of course (more strictly, King's Regulations), and offences had to be punished accordingly. Strangely enough I cannot remember instances of anyone being outside the law apart from being late back to camp or similar minor indiscretions, but there were two areas where discipline was rigidly enforced. We were always marched to work and back, and once a week had an inspection parade that was held between the maintenance hangar and the engine workshops, which had a large forecourt. Wing Commander Scoley, the officer commanding the wing, would bear down on us and woe betide anyone who was unshaven or improperly dressed. The parade days were varied so one could not take any chances with one's appearance. In the other instance we had to be on our mettle when leaving or returning to camp and having two guardrooms increased the chances of being pulled up if our dress was not in order. In practice, we had to report to the top guardroom on leaving camp and the bottom one on return but both of them were active and one could be caught out twice. Shiny buttons and boots were the order of the day and I was once castigated for not doing up the hook at the neck of my greatcoat, this being at the bottom guardroom when going out. Respirators had to be carried everywhere in those days, and while a check was made to see that we had them strapped round our shoulders, the case was not always opened to ensure that the respirator was inside. This was just as well because often the case contained scarves, books or dance shoes etc.

The Service police were usually very understanding and at the worst if we were caught without the right article in the case we were merely sent back to collect it.

In referring previously to the various pubs and clubs in Pwllheli, I would not like this to be construed that we were all a bunch of seasoned topers! We were a gang of lads roughly the same age and hadn't a great deal of choice where to pass our leisure time. There was a limit to the number of nights spent in the NAAFI or the hut, so the cry went up 'Who is coming out for a drink?' Usually we sat in the pub with half a pint, which was replenished occasionally, and we couldn't really afford anything more exotic. Naturally there were a few hardened drinkers who spoiled things for the others, but speaking for myself, there was only one occasion when I had one over the eight and that was on a birthday celebration.

Christmas 1940 was spent at Penrhos as I do not think that special leave was granted to anybody, but the authorities did their best to make up for that. On Christmas Eve, flying finished at midday and the aircraft were picketed down and the hangars locked up in time for festivities in the evening. Transport was laid on for us to have a drink in Pwllheli, and we were then whisked to Llanbedrog as a special dance had been arranged at the Glyn-y-weddw. We were conveyed back at midnight (no guardroom inspection this time!) and a good time was had by all. On Christmas Day a special dinner was laid on when we were served by the officers in accordance with tradition, and then came the surprise referred to earlier – the cinema at Pwllheli was opened especially for us, and we saw Noel Coward's Bittersweet, which was all the rage at the time. The evening was rounded off with an impromptu concert in the NAAFI, complete with station band. So ended 1940 – a hectic year, but no more so than the following year was destined to be.

At the beginning of 1941, a reorganisation of the technical departments took place and several of us were transferred to a new Servicing Department dealing with the more day-to-day inspection requirements of aircraft on the aerodrome. Although being in Servicing Flight took us nearer to the actual flying, we normally did our work in the two servicing hangars at the side of the airfield just beyond the sickbay. The total area of these hangars was about the same as the main Maintenance Department, but we were not so crowded with aircraft and had much more room to manoeuvre. Some of the Whitley aircraft (which seemed to need more attention than the other types) took up a tremendous amount of space, and it was just as well that they were only in for a day or two at a time. Owing to the passage of time I can only recollect working on Whitleys during my months in this flight, and cannot recall any other type being in the hangars. I only once remember the hangars being empty. On this occasion the station band went past, practising the RAF March, and we connected the two events together, imagining them to be celebrating the only occasion that all the aircraft were serviceable at the same time.

This state of affairs did not last, however, and in no time we were hard at it again. We were constantly pushed to rush the jobs through, and because of the shortage of time, we would sometimes have to lie on the floor to carry out a repair, or put up with poor lighting arrangements, whereas in the nearby maintenance hangar they would have their aircraft up on trestles, walk on a spotless floor, and have the doors closed with no draughts. The grass was definitely greener there in the wintertime, but we had the advantage in the summer!

A particularly thankless job we were saddled with was to change the glands in a Whitley hydraulic control unit as they were constantly leaking. Normally this would be done while the unit was in situ as it was even worse to take it out and then replace it. Unfortunately they were positioned underneath the cockpit floor and only accessible from below. A very brief description of this operation would read: 'lead light, illumination still not sufficient, grin, struggle, hot bath'!

Towards the end of March 1941, several of us were sent on detachment to our satellite station at Hell's Mouth about ten miles south-west of Penrhos and right on top of the cliff overlooking the sea. This was a very small unit with a cluster of well-built wooden buildings, plus two brick Bellman hangars. A small force of Whitleys were based there, and these were used for bombing practice. I remember this because the white practice bombs were well in evidence, although I cannot recall why the aircraft were there as we had plenty of them already at Penrhos! It is also a mystery to me why they wanted us there at all in view of the fact that a permanent maintenance staff were already stationed there. But we were there for two or three weeks before our eventual return to base.

Two things stand out in my memory, both connected with the location of the station. Security was uppermost in the minds of most people at that time, and the small airfield was covered with wooden obstacles to thwart an airborne landing by the enemy. This necessitated an obstacle removal operation whenever our own aircraft were flying, and replacement afterwards. Given this elaborate arrangement at Hell's Mouth, why not the same procedure at Penrhos? More to the point, although most unlikely, were the patrols that were mounted on the cliff edge at night looking for enemy submarines. I was collared for one or two of these duties, which were most unpleasant. Picture us walking along the cliff with a loaded rifle and our eyes trained out to sea looking for lights or any other suspicious movements, bearing in mind that we were not used to working at night, and that it was very eerie and cold. Thankfully we never saw anything and were very pleased to get back to Penrhos and a more orderly life. If only we had known what was in store!

May 1941 was a time to be remembered, and our lives were to be considerably changed before the month was out. First of all a War Weapons Week was held at Pwllheli from the 10th to the 17th. Basically this was a drive on savings, and several functions were held to this end. I bought a ticket for the gold watch competition (based on the time the watch stopped at), but I had no luck at this and although I still have the ticket, the watch went elsewhere! A grand gala dance was held at the West End hotel on the seafront, together with another one at the Pavilion, which was directly opposite. One was allowed to wander from one to the other as the fancy took; a very novel arrangement, especially as three different bands were involved. We all turned up in force, as did most of the locals. What a good job it was that the Pavilion, especially, was a large place, otherwise they would have had to station an orchestra on the promenade! I have no doubt that it was a financial success and probably helped to pay for yet another Whitley.

Shortly after this we were in the hut one evening talking to Johnny Pass, our tame instrument mechanic and watch repairer, when at about seven o'clock an almighty bang rent the air. One of the hut walls parted company with the rest of the building and the components of two or three watches went flying simultaneously into the air. We were thrown to the floor amid all the confusion, and our first thoughts were that the boiler house had exploded, but on picking ourselves up and rushing outside, we were met by the sight of a German bomber overhead with its machine guns rattling away! We dived for cover, but by this time the intruder, a Dornier Do 217 'flying pencil', was sheering away with the damage already done. Practically everyone in the camp was running about by now, and it took some time for the panic to die down before an assessment could be made of the damage.

It transpired that the officers' mess had suffered the worst of the attack, with two officers being killed. One wing of the building had been completely shattered by several bombs, and the contents strewn over a large area. Two other bombs that had fallen on a different part of the camp had not exploded. One of these had hit the face of the maintenance hangar with a glancing blow and had then ricocheted a considerable way round the camp before stopping just outside station HQ, its course being shown by skid marks on the roads. Both of these bombs were later defused and mounted on a plinth outside the HQ building as a grim reminder of our entry into the war. Besides these bombs, a lot of damage had also been done by the machine guns, including several lorries being destroyed by fire, and two Henleys wrecked on the airfield.

To say that the atmosphere at the station changed after this episode was to put it very mildly, and we were all dreading a repeat performance. Orders were given to sleep in the air-raid shelters behind our huts, but this wasn't a complete answer as there was no telling when another raid might happen, bearing in mind that the original attack had taken place in daylight. A distinctly uneasy peace hung over the camp, but conditions had gradually returned to normal when some time later we were attacked again at about six o'clock one evening. This time the aircraft was spotted first before it opened fire, and we rushed out towards the shelters. This frenzied activity was seen by the raider, who dived down on us with machine guns chattering while we ran in all directions to escape the gunfire. I found myself charging along a path leading from the edge of the hutted area and distinctly saw bullets striking the ground just ahead of me. I eventually threw myself into a ditch and remained there until the raid had finished, although I was constantly concerned about the bombs dropping all around me. One fellow went streaking past stark naked –

he was one of the Poles who had been taking a bath when it all began!

When all went quiet, a group of us debated what to do, as we were much too scared to return to the camp. We ended up walking in the opposite direction until we came to a farm where we laid up for the night on a cold stone floor in one of the barns. Apart from scaring the living daylights out of us, the raid had been a failure as, except for five people being slightly injured, no further damage was done, the bombs having dropped mainly outside the camp area and only spoilt some of the fields. We all trooped back to camp the following morning, and from then on we always retired to the shelters directly after teatime each day. The shelters were damp and musty, and after a while we were pleased to get back to our beds in the huts – this being the signal for Jerry to attack again! There was a variation the next time, as the raid took place about five o'clock in the morning and consisted of the machine-gun routine plus a few small anti-personnel bombs and a quantity of incendiaries. Our huts were the target on this occasion and the Dornier flew along the row, peppering them with shells. The first huts in the row bore the bulk of the attack, so fortunately when my hut was reached it had largely petered out, although we were hit, the aim being right down the centre line. This actually saved us as the beds were against the walls, but as we slept head to toe, the people with their heads out had a fright they would never forget. Five chaps were badly injured this time but the incendiaries were poorly aimed and dropped only on the edge of the camp.

After this latest episode the authorities had to act, and this they did dramatically by having most of us billeted out in Pwllheli. Before describing this move I would point out that Pwllheli itself had also suffered slightly during the bombings. Several buildings had in fact been set on fire by incendiaries, particularly the cinema, but of course the mere fact of an enemy aircraft flying over was enough to scare the residents. Although I wouldn't say that it sparked off resentment against a military camp (Penrhos) being in the vicinity, it certainly stirred a few fifth columnists to take action. One rumoured incident was a man on top of the town hall at the height of a raid waving a torch to attract the attention of the aircraft. He was eventually hauled down and prosecuted, so it was said. Another action that was most obvious was a ring of lights at night in the hills a few miles distant and surrounding the camp. This was too blatant to be anything else but a deliberate act to outline the camp as a target for a raid, but to the chagrin of the perpetrators, the camp was never bombed again and had never actually been attacked at night-time.

As can be imagined, the billeting-out idea was very popular, mainly to get away from the camp, of course, but also for the novelty of it. We were dotted about all over the town, and I found myself forced upon the previously mentioned dentist in Lleyn Terrace. I wasn't very pleased about this as I had to pass a dentist's chair on my way up and down stairs; evidently the dentist was not enamoured with the arrangement either, for after a short time he managed to get me sent elsewhere.

My second home was in Bay View Terrace, a rather exaggerated description as although the house faced the right way, one couldn't see the bay owing to the fact that the railway station blocked the view. Perhaps the name had originated many years ago, before the railway arrived. The place itself was nothing to shout about, and two of us had to share a medium-sized bedroom, with the bathroom being the only other room we could use. We had all our food in the camp, which was just as well as our boarding-house proprietor was not very well disposed to us. One example of this was the solitary light bulb in our room. When this broke we had considerable difficulty in getting it replaced as he maintained we had misused it. No extras ever came our way and we had to console ourselves with the small mercies that we had, mindful that we were at least away from the camp. How long we were there for I cannot say, but it must have been a few months, for when the colder weather came I recall having a ding-dong over the coal! At the time I was surprised at our host's attitude as he was an Englishman and one would have thought that he would be in sympathy with us. All was explained just before we left, though, when we discovered that he was an ex-naval man and did some occasional work as a storeman at Glendower!

Conditions were far different for the lucky few who were billeted along the promenade, especially as they were there during the summer. We used their rooms to change in when we went bathing, and it was just like a seaside holiday for all concerned. One of our number, Harry Warburton (of whom more later), had a front room to himself, and being well heeled, had laid himself a good stock of drink in. Most of us who were billeted nearby were invited in to sample the goods on a regular basis and for a short period of time lived like lords. We had to make our way to the bus station each morning, from where we were taken to Penrhos by station transport and returned likewise in the evening. An interesting episode occurred one morning before we boarded the wagon, when an announcement was made that Operation Barbarossa, the German invasion of Russia, had just taken place – this was on 22 June 1941 and helps me date this period of billeting.

As I have already said, I cannot remember the actual date of our return to camp, but with the lack of enemy activity at Penrhos and the cost of billeting weighing on their minds, the authorities eventually had us back in our huts. It may be wondered how we had passed our time at Pwllheli during the evenings, and the short answer is that I can't recall in detail, but apart from the time spent on the beach (and in Harry's 'bar') I did make a model Spitfire from an old piece of wood, and, as promotion was a distinct possibility in the near future, I spent a good few hours cramming for the pending Trade Test.

An outstanding question in our minds was the reason for the enemy attacks on the camp, which had given rise to our being billeted out. There were various theories on this, and one that may have been feasible concerned the bombing of Liverpool. It was apparently well known that aircraft raiding Liverpool and the north-west were flying over the Irish Sea from bases in France, and turning at Anglesey to proceed parallel with the coast of North Wales. Several of these had been intercepted at Anglesey and had been forced to jettison their bombs and turn back. It had been suggested that one of these aircraft had spotted our camp and had unloaded their bombs on us instead. I thought differently, though, and believed that our raids were deliberate and intended to be of nuisance value coupled with intimidation to keep our aircraft (and those at RAF Valley in Anglesey) on the ground. Be that as it may, the raids stopped as abruptly as they had started, which may have been due to increased activity from the fighter squadron at Valley. To end this saga, I must go back to the beginning and report that unfortunately the watches being repaired by Johnny Pass were never reassembled and the component parts are probably still there buried in the ground!

I applied to take an examination for promotion after I had been an AC1

for twelve months. This request was granted and I faced the music at
the end of May 1941. First of all I had to make the inevitable test piece,
complicated by the fact that I also had to produce a drawing for it as well.
This completed, the next move was a local Trade Test, which was a sim-
plified version of the one at Cosford, but made more difficult as most
of the questions came from Warrant Officer Hole. Not a person to inspire
confidence, he compounded matters by asking trick questions among
the genuine ones, and it really was an ordeal. Just when I thought that I
had scraped through, I was picked up for not mentioning a trivial item
regarding the heat treatment of light alloys, and he announced that I had
failed the exam but could re-sit it in ten days' time. The next attempt I
finally made it, and in no time at all was elevated to the rank of leading
aircraftman (LAC). It happened that I was going on leave a day or so
afterwards, and I took my insignia of rank with me so that my mother
could sew it on. Imagine my astonishment when returning from leave,
I was informed that I had been promoted to corporal in my absence.
My pleasure at this move was mixed with annoyance that I had to cut
off my new LAC badges and sew the stripes on by myself. In fact I had
only worn these badges while on leave, which must be a record!

Coupled with my rapid promotion, I was now transferred to 'E' Flight,
right in the thick of the flying schedules, but in spite of the hectic
time we were to be faced with, I was very happy with the move as I had
never really settled down in the static Maintenance Department. By now
I was aged nineteen and very pleased with my position, as promotion to
the rank of corporal tradesman would have taken five to six years in
peacetime.

Harry Warburton came with me to 'E' Flight, also recently promoted
and transferred from the Maintenance Department. We joined forces
with two other corporals, Graham Gwynne (who was to become a close
personal friend), and one whose name escapes me. Sometimes it was a
dog's life being a corporal, sandwiched as we were between the higher-
ups and the lower-downs, but fortunately there was very little friction
among our small group and we all got on together fairly amicably. We
were in charge of ten to twelve mechanics, and had something in the
nature of fifteen aircraft to look after, all of them being Avro Ansons,
used for navigational training.

The senior NCO in command of our servicing group was Flight Sergeant Bates, known to us as Chiefy (all flight sergeants were Chiefies!), and actually called by that name unless there were any officers around. Chiefy Bates had a fascinating Service history, having been a tradesman before becoming a pilot. As a pilot, he was among the 'top flight', and was a member of the Hendon Air Display Team, which gave regular displays similar to (though in more genteel fashion), the Red Arrows of today. On being forced to cease flying due to a medical condition, he was awarded the BEM (British Empire Medal) and reverted to his ground crew status, eventually ending up at Penrhos. As a former pilot, he was the only ground crew member who was allowed to taxi the aircraft on the airfield, and was in constant demand to perform this service. It is interesting to note a comparable restriction regarding the running up of aircraft engines – this could only be done by an engine fitter of corporal rank upwards, or by an airframe fitter of sergeant rank or higher. There were various reasons for this, including potential damage to the engines themselves, the risk of tipping the aircraft on to its nose, or the possibility of the machine running away. It was considered that NCOs of these various minimum ranks would have the sense to avoid the pitfalls. In view of this it will be deduced that I wasn't allowed to run any engines up, although in the not too distant future, on our beloved Lancasters, I was the only person in the crew authorised to do so, apart from the pilot.

On 'E' Flight, we were accommodated in a large hut that was partitioned into two, the other half being the crew room for the pilots who were presided over by Flight Lieutenant Tobyska, the flight commander. The hut was positioned halfway round the airfield from the hangars and we had to make our own way to it, usually by walking or cycling. It wasn't that we were more privileged than the maintenance marchers, but more a reflection of the odd hours we worked, and the fact that there were never sufficient people available at the same time to form a column! Obviously enough, the work we had to do was to maintain the aircraft in flying condition, which involved routine servicing as well as more complicated repairs. The Ansons were gentle aircraft to maintain, but owing to their age needed constant attention, particularly with regard to the flying controls and the brakes. It seemed to me that the engines gave more trouble than the rest of the aircraft put together, for the mechanics were forever changing magneto leads and oil filters etc. Overnight the machines were left on the airfield facing into the wind, and if the weather forecast was bad they were picketed down in a similar fashion to the guy ropes of a tent. If the following day was unfit for flying, the planes would have to be turned around if the wind had shifted. On flying days, there was a constant stream of aircraft movements as one landed after the other, and each had to be checked over before the next flight. Even on non-flight days many jobs had to be done, and the opportunity was taken to attend to various odds and ends that were outstanding.

To again digress beyond my mainstream work activities for a while, I will start by mentioning two acquisitions that I made at this time. One of the mechanics on a nearby flight was posted abroad, and he advertised his bicycle for sale. Graham Gwynne brought this to my attention, and on looking it over I decided to buy it. It was a pre-war Raleigh that had had very little use, although the tyres were rotting and needed replacing. It was otherwise in very good condition and I considered it a bargain for the £3 that I paid for it. I was now mobile again, and the bike went into immediate use in being ridden to the flight hut and back, and to Pwllheli and other points of the compass. Graham was a pre-war cyclist of repute, and he and I formed a cycling club that drew a membership of twelve to fifteen people riding bikes of all types and sizes. During the evenings when we were off-duty, we burned up the roads in the vicinity and became well known in the WVS canteens for miles around. Morfa Nefyn was a favourite spot as it was a comfortable ride of about eight miles, and we also frequently went to Criccieth and Abersoch. Sometimes we had races around the perimeter track, but they always ended up with finding out who would come second to Graham!

The other item I acquired was a small wireless set, which my grandfather bought for me while on leave. It was an American set with five valves and an inbuilt aerial, and it ran off the mains supply. I used it for some years, but it then wore out and ended up on the scrap heap as I couldn't obtain replacement valves for it.

I had not been with 'E' Flight very long before I left it again, the reason being that I was sent away to attend a corporal's course at, of all places, Cosford! I was very surprised at this as I had always associated Cosford with technical training, but when I arrived I found out that they had been running disciplinary and related courses for some time. I was accommodated in the new Fulton Block, which I had seen being built, and needless to say it was back to the old spit and polish. The course entailed endless drill practice under the supervision of a sergeant instructor who truly put us through the mill; when we finished we would have been a credit to the Guards! Our sergeant continually harped on about this comparison with the Guards and I really think that he actually brought us up to their standards. After the course was over, and as was the custom, we bought him a present. This gift was an alarm clock, which he said he was very pleased with as it would ensure that he wasn't late for parade when dealing with our successors on the course. He wasn't a bad guy, and gave us all a hearty handshake when we left, saying that we had done him proud. This was obviously his routine with every programme run, but we did wonder what he did with all the alarm clocks! In addition to the physical side of the course, we had numerous lectures on discipline and codes of practice, which were probably of much more practical use than the drill. All in all I was glad to get back to Penrhos for a rest after that gruelling fortnight.

In case I seem to be rambling on unduly through my adventure at this time, I would now like to present a short story just to break the routine. A notice appeared stating that cameras could not be used on the station unless permission had been granted, and forms for this purpose could be obtained from the station HQ. My application was turned down. I still used my camera. End of story. Now back to the rambling!

In the autumn of 1941 I was incarcerated for about ten days in the sick-bay, having been infected with scabies, a very unpleasant disease caused by a mite that burrows under the surface of the skin, causing extreme discomfort. Most of my chest and back were covered with small scabs, and the remedy at that time was to scrub them off after having had a hot bath, and then to apply a horrible green liquid that stung like blazes. This routine was followed each day, but after a while sulphur ointment was applied instead, this being much more soothing. Scabies is highly contagious, so I was kept in isolation and all my kit was fumigated. It cleared up in due course, but broke out again shortly afterwards, and back in I went for more torture. I had apparently caught this from sleeping with infected blankets, even though we had sheets, and so all the blanket stock had to be fumigated as well. While in the sickbay, I met a Welsh soldier from Anglesey who had never left there until he joined up, and he couldn't speak a word of English!

Ever since I had joined up I'd had a latent desire to fly and be among the action, so when an opportunity arose, I volunteered to take a pilot's course. The first step on the ladder was to obtain the station commander's recommendation, which necessitated an interview. This meeting was very short and sweet and the outcome rested on two questions. I was asked if I played golf, and also to quote the headlines in the *Daily Telegraph* of that morning. Unfortunately, I didn't play golf and certainly didn't read the *Telegraph*, and in view of my negative answers my application was rejected. I was very indignant over this and considered that the questions were not at all relevant to the subject. It was only afterwards that I realised that I was being tested to see if I was potential officer material. Unfortunately this was an attitude that prevailed among a lot of ex-peace-time officers, and owing to this snobbish outlook a lot of potentially brilliant pilots were lost to the cause simply because they didn't play golf etc. I like to think that I would have been one of them, but my chance had gone and I had to buckle down to my normal routine again. It is laughable to think of the *Daily Telegraph* appearing in the airmen's mess or the NAAFI, so to have satisfied the CO, I would have to have had my own private copy sent specially from Pwllheli each day!

Returning to aerodrome matters, it was decided in the summer of 1941 that we had seen enough of the Harrow aeroplane, which it will be remembered was manhandled out of the maintenance hangar to grace a corner of the airfield. Some priority was given to make it airworthy again, and this even involved changing both engines to a new more powerful type. During the time the Harrow had languished at Penrhos, new identification marks had come into force, so it had to be partially repainted and have red, white and blue stripes marked on the fins. Eventually this great machine, almost as big as a Lancaster bomber, was ready for the air, and so intense was the interest that the whole population of the camp turned out to see whether it would make it. All the aircraft were cleared from one corner of the field to give it as long a run as possible, and then came the great moment when the pilot (who had never flown this type before) opened up the engines. It lumbered forward, gathering speed, but then suddenly the engines shut down and it ground to a halt. On taxiing back, it was discovered that the pitot head cover had been left on and so no airspeed had registered on the dial. (The pitot head is a tube facing forward outside the aircraft, which bleeds air to the air-speed indicator.) The cover was duly removed, and on the second attempt the Harrow pulled off the ground before the end of the run, made a couple of circuits, and then landed again with very little room to spare. On being pronounced suitably airworthy, arrangements were made to have it flown away, and once again we all turned out to see it depart. It took us some time to come to terms with the disappearance of our landmark!

The Avro Ansons we had out on the flights had a remarkable history on two counts. They were the first monoplanes to be used by the RAF and were also the first Service aircraft to have retractable undercarriages, which in those days had to be cranked by hand. As they were the main aircraft that I worked on for the rest of my service at Penrhos, a few words about them would not go amiss. The Anson was first introduced into the RAF in 1936 on reconnaissance duties with Coastal Command. After the outbreak of war it was used considerably by Flying Training Command and on training schools in Canada. It was in continuous production for seventeen years, and was officially retired in 1968 with about 11,000 having been built. With a maximum speed of 170mph it was not particularly fast, but its special virtue was that it could carry six passengers (sometimes more, as I can vouch), and had a range of 660 miles. It was fabric covered and had two engines that had to be hand cranked to start. I can never remember a new Anson, so the ones we used must have been ex-Coastal Command. They were very reliable aircraft and indeed needed to be, for they were flown continually from early morning until dusk each fine day, and even in Wales we had many of these in the summertime!

The summer months spent out on the airfield were very enjoyable, and this feeling was enhanced by the superb location of the camp with its views of Llanbedrog Head, and more distantly across Cardigan Bay, Harlech Castle and the mountain of Cader Idris. The war seemed very far away. Our first job each morning was to round up and disperse the sheep and horses that had invariably strayed on to the airfield from the surrounding fields; having done that, work could commence. The pilots and trainee observers would arrive while we were checking the aircraft over, and soon the roar of the engines being started would rent the air. As each engine was fired it was allowed to tick over for a short time to warm up, and then it was run up to be tested by the pilot, switching each magneto off in turn. If the revolutions dropped off to an unacceptable level it was panic stations for the engine mechanics to change the leads or make other adjustments. Similarly, we would swing into action if the brake pressure had dropped or a tyre was flat. There was always a sigh of relief as each aircraft took off, but there were usually one or two left behind having developed some fault that needed to be worked on. We used to think that gremlins had been active during the night, because an aircraft that appeared perfectly in order the night before was quite often unserviceable the following day!

A period of quiet would ensue after the confusion of the morning start, and the routine jobs would then be dealt with. Equipment would be cleaned, trips made to the stores, oil tanks replenished and so on. There was no rest for we corporals either, as we had to juggle with the rosters to cover for missing people to ensure adequate attention for the aircraft as they landed. 'Missing people' covered those mechanics who were sick, going on or returning from leave, plus those who had been on fire piquet or guard duties the night before. A proportion of our staff were detailed off in rotation to form a duty crew who dealt with visiting aircraft, and there were routine matters such as gas drill, which could involve the whole staff coming and going in turn during the same day. It wasn't unknown for one or two naughty people to be absent as they were 'on the peg' or involved in fatigues, and not to be forgotten were those who were late, deliberately or otherwise, or those who would do very little work even though they were physically there! Naturally on many occasions we did a large proportion of the work ourselves just to keep things going. It was no sinecure out there, but I must say that we thoroughly enjoyed it as we were always involved in the action, and the time flew fast like wildfire. In spite of the comments I have made about our personnel, most of them cooperated well, but we had to rule with a firm hand or things would begin to slide. I never had occasion to put anyone on a charge, although there was a very thin dividing line every now and again.

No sooner had we finished our numerous tasks, than the sound of returning aircraft could be heard and the routine would begin all over again. As flying continued until dusk (sometimes nearly ten o'clock at the height of summer), we had to organise a form of shift work whereby a section of staff would work from say 8am until 3pm, and the remainder from 3pm until close of play – another reason for the depletion of staff in the mornings. The landing of the last group of aircraft at night was fun and the procedure merits description.

The first task, just before they were due back, was for us to charge round the aerodrome on the lookout for sheep etc., and also to frighten the plovers that always seemed to congregate in the evenings. On landing, the aircraft were surrounded by men pulling on engine and cockpit covers and filling up the oil tanks. We would be checking tyre pressures and, the biggest chore of all, building up the brake pressure, which had to be done with a foot pump. While this was going on the bowser would arrive and start refuelling. (Refuelling was always done directly upon landing to avoid condensation in the tanks.) The bowser was towed by an ancient tractor, which would have been on the scrap heap years before if not for the war. It could only be started by one man, an ex-farm hand who happened to have the knack; if he wasn't about, it had to be pushed. Gear changing was hilarious as it could not be done while moving or else the engine would stall, so it had to be driven in bottom gear or changed by stopping on a favourable slope. To complete the picture, it only needs me to say that the gear lever was half broken off! The last thing to be done was to detail the state of each aircraft on a large blackboard at the end of the hut so that the morning contingent would know the exact situation on arrival. After this we stumbled our weary way back to the mess for a meal, and then to bed.

Flying training went on every day and there were no such things as Saturdays or Sundays, although we did have a day off just occasionally to recharge our batteries. Even though we worked together for a long period, I find it difficult to recall the names of the staff members of 'E' Flight. Apart from Flight Sergeant Bates, I can only recollect Corporals

Gwynne and Warburton with any certainty. Graham Gwynne and I became soulmates, and we both worked out the duty rosters and lists of people for the gas drill and other unlikeable chores. We usually collaborated together both in work and play, and he eventually changed his hut and moved into mine.

Harry Warburton was a different character, and he is remembered mainly from the odd ventures that he initiated, such as his 'bar' in Pwllheli. I have already mentioned that he wasn't short of money, but he also had the propensity to obtain commodities that were normally difficult to come by owing to wartime shortages. He had been well educated and was definitely upper class, but at the same time was a bit of a spiv! When none of us had cigarettes, Harry was there with seemingly un-ending supplies, and he kept us chosen few going as though the shops were full of them, only charging us at cost price into the bargain. On one occasion he came back from leave with a deluxe box of fishing flies and inveigled Flight Sergeant Richardson (Maintenance Department) into going fishing with him. He soon had Chiefy hooked on the sport and eventually sold him the flies at a handsome profit! Another NCO had an Austin Seven car for sale owing to the difficulty in obtaining petrol, and this was snapped up by Harry for £100. I was present when this transaction took place, and he paid in cash from an immense roll of fivers produced from his pocket. Soon he was seen travelling everywhere in this car while petrol was still unobtainable by ordinary mortals! Rumour had it that he owned a garage in Llanbedr, and there must have been a grain of truth in this because he certainly got his petrol from somewhere. An addition to the rumour described the day when he was filling up from one of his own pumps and was smartly apprehended by the police for stealing petrol. Naturally they refused to believe his story and he had to take them to the local bank to prove that he owned the garage!

During 1941 we had the usual spate of aircraft crashes, most of which were relatively minor and caused by burst tyres or heavy landings etc., but there were one or two of a more serious nature. One Blenheim failed to pull up in time while landing and smashed into a hut near the servicing hangar. It caught fire, but luckily the crew managed to scramble out in time before the machine blew up. Up to that time I had never seen an aircraft fire and I was quite amazed at the ferocity of it. In no time at all the whole thing was melted down to nothing; if anybody had been injured, they wouldn't have stood a chance.

Something even more spectacular happened one summer's day when a nasty accident befell an aircraft taking off. A loud explosion was heard at about 3pm, and our immediate reaction was to dash for the air-raid shelters, but it soon became apparent that one of our own aircraft had gone down on the other side of our flight hut. Dashing across, a scene of devastation met our eyes with a panorama of aircraft pieces spread far and wide. The explanation for this was that a Whitley on take-off had failed to clear a Fairey Battle parked on the edge of the airfield. One of its wheels had hit the top of the Battle's wing right above the fuel tank, which had exploded with dramatic effect. The Whitley had been thrown upwards and had practically cartwheeled down the slope, catching fire after its own fuel tanks had been ruptured. The Battle had disintegrated and the explosion had severely damaged several other aircraft parked nearby. The fire tender arrived within a short time and managed to contain the fire before it gained a firm hold.

The crew of the Whitley (which was damaged almost beyond recognition) all managed to escape, except for the observer in the nose who had been killed instantly at the moment of impact. All the crew members were suffering from shock and were severely cut and bruised – one of my clearest recollections of Penrhos was seeing these poor chaps huddled together on the ground in such a state. They were quickly whipped off to the sickbay for attention, and although nothing could be done for the unfortunate fellow who had died, his body still had to be brought out after the MO had certified him dead. The officer in charge of the servicing wing, who had by now appeared at the scene, asked me to perform this task! At this I suddenly felt as bad as the crew who had climbed out, and wished I had run in the opposite direction instead of towards the crash. There were no medical personnel in the vicinity (they were too busy tending the survivors), and it was obvious that someone had to do it. Being a junior NCO I would have lost face if I had not made an attempt, so taking the deepest of deep breaths, I clambered into the wreckage and managed to haul him out by the shoulders. Pulling him through the shattered cockpit, I got him as far as the ground outside the door, by which time I could stand it no longer and dropped him there.

He had suffered appalling injuries during the explosion, and the fact that his body had been burned during the fire made this the most sickening job I have ever done in my entire life. It was time for tea by now, and although I didn't feel like eating much, I went into the mess for a drink – but when I discovered that there was meat pie on the menu, I came out quicker than I went in.

Of course, there were to be many inquests into this crash, which was obviously caused through pilot error, although there were several coincidences of bad luck. The undercarriage was already retracting when the impact happened, and a second or two later the Whitley would have been clear. Misfortune also struck when the wheel hit the petrol tank instead of some other part of the Battle that would have given rise to much less damage. On the other hand, the fellow in the nose should not have been there at all during take-off, as clear regulations were in force that he should have been further back in the cockpit until the aircraft was safely in the air; he had therefore contributed to his own death by ignoring the correct procedure.

As the autumn drew on and winter approached, the flying hours became restricted due to fewer hours of daylight, and this coincided with the demand from Command HQ for an even greater output of trainees. As with the case of the bombings, the authorities were forced to take action, the outcome of which was that night flying was introduced. Penrhos airfield was too small for capers of this kind (the longest run was only 860 yards), as the pilots would not have a large enough safety margin. This, coupled with the presence of the surrounding high ground, made such operations much too hazardous. To solve the problem, arrangements were made for us to function at night from RAF Llandwrog, an airfield some twenty miles north-north-east of us and fairly near to Caernarvon. Llandwrog was situated on a broad flat peninsular next to the sea, and the aerodrome had been provided with proper runways – an ideal place for any type of flying, with only the weather to worry about. A training unit similar to our own No. 9 AOS (Air Observers' School) was already stationed there with Whitleys etc.

The arrangement was that six of our Ansons would be stationed permanently at Llandwrog, and a group of mechanics and associated personnel would transfer from Penrhos to service and refuel the aircraft.

In addition, these people would have to lay out and maintain the flarepath as there was no airfield electric lighting. Initially, the scheme operated with the mechanics having to travel each night from Penrhos until the snags were ironed out, after which they stayed on a permanent basis. I can only remember being on two or three of these duties – but then there were more mechanics available than NCOs. We travelled in canvas-covered lorries furnished with bench seats, and a mighty uncomfortable journey it was, broken by several stops to enable us to stretch our legs. On arrival we would fill and light the gooseneck flares and position them at intervals along the runway, before erecting the battery-lit 'T' sign to indicate the direction of the wind. The scene was then set, and flying would commence.

The pilots remained attached to Llandwrog, and no doubt the pupils were stationed there during the period of their night-flying exercises, being replaced at intervals with other groups. The aircraft flew on various details, some on long cross-countries taking a couple of hours or so, and others on shorter exercises of up to an hour, so there was usually plenty for us to do. We reckoned to turn each Anson round in about fifteen minutes if refuelling was necessary.

Flying went on until about midnight, which gave about five to seven hours of night flying, according to the month and weather. When there was a lull in the proceedings we dashed off in turns to the NAAFI for refreshments, our main meal being provided at Penrhos when we returned in the early hours. In one sense we enjoyed these trips to Llandwrog as it was a novelty and took us away from our normal routine. The NAAFI visits were memorable, too, as they had a resident accordionist there, and on one occasion he gave an admirable rendering of Suppe's *Poet and Peasant*, which I have been hooked on ever since! Reflecting on the necessity for this night-flying operation, it was of paramount importance to increase the flying hours, as already explained, but the practice was also essential for the aircrews as, after all, most of their future operational flying would be at night.

On the return to camp from our billeting out in Pwllheli, it was de-cided to introduce a makeshift airfield defence in case we were attacked again from the air, and also to guard against infiltration from the sea. A crash course was set up to teach us the art of rifle firing and grenade throwing, and we had to undergo training in the methods of unarmed combat. All this was long before the formation of the RAF Regiment, and the whole thing was rather amateurish. To add to our enjoyment of the situation, the rainy season came upon us, and gumboots and capes were the order of the day. Two different patrols were organised: one around the camp perimeter, including the hills, and the other around the airfield itself, which also incorporated the safeguarding of the aircraft. The camp patrols were under the command of Arthur Gandy, who had previous experience of airfield defence in the Middle East, and as he had actually fired a rifle in anger, he was considered the ideal person for the job.

I was involved in the airfield patrols, which were extremely unpopular. It does not take much to conjure up a vision of these duties. All the ingredients of a horror film were there; more often than not there was pouring rain, pitch darkness (a torch was only to be used in an emergency), and the creaking of many aircraft agitated by the wind. On one occasion, I heard a stealthy movement ahead. This was it – should I fire at him, or shout, or shine the torch? Rooted to the spot I suddenly recognised hoofbeats, and realised that it was a straying horse that was obviously just as scared as I was!

The situation was often further compounded by bumping into aeroplanes and tripping over objects on the ground, added to which there was a real danger of meeting a shadowy figure at any time, as another poor soul was doing a similar patrol on the opposite side of the airfield! Remembering the previous raids on the camp, I am not ashamed to say that I was really frightened; how glad we were when winter was over and we were able to stand down.

There was a genuine fear in the camp that anything might happen, and we tended to get away from the place as much as possible during the winter months. A favourite place at this time was Caernarvon, which we visited frequently when duty permitted. We used various methods of transport and, surprisingly, considering the dearth of traffic in the area, we had much success with hitchhiking. There was a choice of several boarding houses at which to stay, and sometimes eight or nine chaps would pack into one of these at a time, mostly for only one-night. But just one night in Caernarvon did wonders for our nerves, as it was very pleasant to sleep in peace away from any possible danger. In this way 1941 drew to a close, morale plunging even deeper with the news in December that two of our battleships, HMS *Repulse* and *Prince of Wales*, had been sunk off Malaya by the Japanese.

Our working routine in 1942 remained along the same lines as before, but even greater pressure was put on us to turn out more and more trained aircrews at this critical stage of the war. In April, a memo was issued from Wing Commander Scoley congratulating us on our great efforts in keeping sufficient aircraft serviceable to fly 3,400 hours in the previous month. This was a tremendous figure by any standards, and rather miraculous when considering the ancient aeroplanes with which we were saddled. Perhaps he deemed it imperative to circulate this letter in order to keep us from flagging – we were pleased that our work had been recognised, but thought that it was rather a cleverly disguised pep talk for the future!

Mention has been made of the duty crew who stood by each day to attend to visiting aircraft. About a dozen men were detailed for this task each week and had to stay in a hut next to flying control. If things were quiet, some of these men would be sent back to their own flights, being liable to recall if necessary. Things were often quiet, but conversely sometimes they were very busy, with a great number of 'foreigners' coming and going; indeed on one or two occasions the duty crew were overwhelmed. I well remember them having to cope with a flight of American Mitchell bombers that arrived one afternoon from Gibraltar. They had landed mainly to refuel, but also had to stay awhile for the aircrews to rest, this causing chaos on the crowded airfield with our own aircraft attempting to work normally. Extra men had to be drafted to the ground crew to deal with this situation, and the Mitchells were dispatched with as much haste as possible.

Another incident of a similar nature happened one summer's evening when I was in charge of the duty crew. We had about five minutes' notice that a squadron of Fairey Fulmars (the naval version of the Battle) were on their way from an aircraft carrier, and soon the air was filled with noise as they came in to land. About twenty of them eventually lined up for attention before nightfall. Into action we went, with all the petrol bowsers we could muster; I drove one of these, or to be more precise, the ancient tractor pulling it. I had had experience of driving this on the flights, but had never mastered the art of getting it started. How we coped I do not know, but we had the visitors finished in due course, and they managed to get airborne again in the gathering gloom. As can be guessed, we spent the rest of the week twiddling our thumbs in inactivity!

During the summer, another Harrow landed (with difficulty), and narrowly missed a hangar when taking off again after being serviced. It should be borne in mind that we had no servicing manuals for all these different types of aircraft, and had to cope as well as possible, always under extreme pressure, of course. We could easily manage the Fulmars as they were similar to a Battle, but had no experience of Mitchells or Hurricanes, let alone a squadron of Spitfires that landed on one occasion.

Unfortunately, there was no end to the toll of aircraft accidents, and at least three Blenheims crashed during 1942, all due to engine failure on take-off. One of these hit the ground just after getting airborne, but although the Blenheim was written off, the crew luckily escaped without injury. Far different, was the plane that fell and hit an upward slope near Penrhos church – all the crew were killed and it was a devil of a job salvaging the aircraft from among the trees. The third Blenheim crash was a very poignant affair involving a popular pilot who I got to know well while he was duty pilot on flying control tasks. In this case, the aircraft was airborne when an engine packed up as it cleared the perimeter track, and it nose-dived down the slope not far from the scene of the Whitley crash, killing all on board. I was again roped in to help with the salvage work and it was rather a gruesome affair because, although the bodies had been removed, the cockpit was covered in blood. It would have been just slightly better if I hadn't known one of the poor aircrew so well. After this I managed to keep clear of salvage operations.

As we were in daily contact, we were very familiar with the pilots on the flight. They were a mixed bunch, approximately half being Polish, including the flight commander, Flight Lieutenant Tobyska, a very courteous man who would go to great lengths to iron out any difficulties. His command of English was good, which was more than could be said of most of his compatriots! We got along very well with all of them, except a certain Pilot Officer Jones, who was never satisfied with the state of his aircraft, and would insist on every minor detail being correct before a flight. I remember him berating me on several occasions about some supposed defect, and it got to the stage where he insisted on myself or a fellow corporal doing the work ourselves as he could not trust anyone else. As my logbook shows, I flew with seven different pilots during 1942, but never with Pilot Officer Jones – I wonder why?

Most of the flights I made during this period were air tests of short duration, about fifteen to twenty-five minutes, and all were made in our Ansons. While most of these flights were genuine tests, it was in a pilot's interest to carry a passenger to wind up and down the infernal undercarriage, and for this same reason, there was a great reluctance among the ground crews to participate. According to my records, I flew twelve times between April and August 1942. Nine of these trips were air tests, but the other three were rather more interesting. One of them was to Hell's Mouth to deliver some practice bombs. The total duration of this flight was approximately thirty minutes, including both landings, so we must have just thrown the bombs out on arrival! Another flight was an air-sea rescue search for a missing aircraft, which meant that I had to stand by the door holding several lifebelts, ready to cast them out if necessary. After a short time we had a radio message to say that the aircraft had actually crashed on dry land, so back to base we went. The third flight was made as a result of an accident to one of my fitters. He was winding the starting handle of an Anson when the engine kicked and he sustained a broken arm. Unfortunately his arm was too badly injured to be treated locally, so he had to be flown to hospital. The nearest RAF hospital was at Cosford, so once again I landed there, literally. It will be remembered that I had helped to pioneer this hospital, so I suppose it was fitting that I should be involved in accompanying this poor chap on his journey. It also meant that I had in turn arrived at Cosford by road, rail and air, but this was to be my last visit until I attended an athletics meeting there many years later.

One feature of the flights made from Penrhos was the scenery. They were all undertaken during the summer months at an altitude of about 2,000 feet, and we had a bird's-eye view of the Menai Strait and numerous other landmarks, including, of course, Penrhos itself. When flying with Flight Lieutenant Tobyska, he once took me down to below 1,000 feet over Pwllheli on a sight-seeing excursion.

We had a different type of sight-seeing trip in the middle of 1942. In the early hours of 20 July we heard the unmistakable rattle of machine guns, and naturally feared the worst, but on rushing outside we were greeted by the spectacle of a dogfight at a high altitude, lit up by brilliant moonlight. This went on for some minutes until one of the aircraft dived down out of control to crash out of sight in the general direction of Pwllheli. Eventually word filtered through that it was a German aircraft that had been shot down, and that it had ended up on the town's beach. How we managed to obtain permission to leave camp the following morning is beyond my recollection, but a large group of us ended up on the beach to see the wreckage, which was strewn over a considerable area. The aircraft, a Heinkel III bomber, had been bagged by a Beaufighter from RAF Valley while it was presumably on its way to bomb the Liverpool area. Two of the crew were killed, but the others managed to escape by parachute. They were subsequently rounded up and held under armed guard at Penrhos. The dead men were buried in the churchyard next to our camp, with full military honours including a firing party of which I was a member. The occasion was very depressing and was made worse by torrential rain that soaked us to the skin. I had two souvenirs of this incident – a bad cold, and a small nameplate off the aircraft!

Although we weren't aware of it to begin with, there were actually regular streams of enemy aircraft in the vicinity, and eventually we had our own fighter unit at Penrhos. This consisted of a Polish Spitfire squadron, which had been sent to our area for a rest from the front line. The crews were very active, and in the course of the next few months obtained several 'kills', each one being celebrated in the appropriate time-honoured way. The Poles were fearless airmen who had a deadly hatred of the Germans, and they would take off in weather that was unfit for ducks if there was the slightest hope of an engagement. At the same time they were mad-headed when the occasion didn't warrant, and numerous complaints were made by the local farmers against them flying too low; indeed, it is on record that they flew under the Menai Bridge more than once! They were a self-contained unit and we had very little to do with them, our contact being restricted to occasionally helping out with servicing. It was a bit different dealing with a Spitfire after being involved with our Ansons for so long, although it was a pleasure to work on a new machine instead of our museum pieces.

Mention of Ansons reminds me to refer to the navigation exercise (NAVEX) training flights. The normal practice was to fly a prearranged course with one observer map-reading on the outward leg, while the other one worked on the plot. On the homeward leg they would change round, but there was no real fear of them being lost because the pilot was so familiar with the route. The observers were all keen to plot the outward course, as the map-reader had to wind up the confounded undercart, it being a much easier task to wind it down again on return to the airfield. Eventually the Ansons were converted to hydraulic power.

Leaving aviation matters aside, there are one or two other items from this period to comment on. For a change from the normal round of places, we decided to spend a weekend at the mining town of Blaenau Ffestiniog. Six of us went on this jaunt, for which we had to have forty-eight-hour passes. We travelled by bus, changing at Pwllheli. I recall only that we stayed for bed and breakfast in a cottage (or two cottages) and spent the evening in the Cross Keys pub. Although all this sounds a bit hum-drum, we thoroughly enjoyed the journey there and back, and on Sunday morning visited the local open-cast slate mine. In those days, this area was in its natural state, before it was commercialised, and we were content to savour the peaceful atmosphere. In addition to this trip, I went on an organised bus tour to Snowdon, but the mountain and the weather being what it was, one could hardly see anything at the top. Fortunately, I had seen the view from the air so I wasn't too disappointed.

One evening in the early summer, I was standing outside Pwllheli station waiting for the bus, when the doors behind me started to rattle. Thinking that someone was locked inside, I turned to investigate and at that moment the whole station appeared to move. At the same time, a fearful banging and rattling noise was heard, and turning again I saw the shops across the square actually rock. People started to rush into the streets, and I heard one man shout 'It's a ... land mine!' This was no land mine, however; what we were experiencing was an earth tremor of fair proportions. It went on for what seemed an eternity, but in reality it was only about a minute later that it suddenly subsided. I have no

recollection of my reaction, but I probably ran round in circles like the
rest of the townsfolk, for it was a time of absolute panic. Afterwards I
joined one of the group of people standing in the square trying to calm
each other down, unfortunately with little success as we had all been
considerably shaken. People were still rushing about and a good many
of them failed to grasp what had happened, especially as very little damage
was evident. I found it hard to understand why the effect was not more
severe as the buildings had actually moved, but on touring the streets,
the only things I could see were some roof tiles on the ground. Slowly
things returned to normal, and I decided it was time to return to camp.
By this time I had missed the last bus and had to walk, but I was at least
in the company of several others who had undergone the same ordeal.
We all agreed unanimously that it was the most frightening experience
we had had on the ground.

At about the same time of year, a Warship Week was held in Pwllheli,
but on this occasion few special events were organised, and reliance was
placed on the people to give voluntary donations. Also at this time, an
RAF Transport Driving School (No. 3 (WAAF) M/T School) took over the
pavilion on the seafront, thus swelling the number of Service personnel
in the small town. One advantage we gained from the arrival of this
unit was that we were allowed to use their NAAFI, and among other
things we bought from there was our soap, as it was cheaper than in the
shops. (Throughout the war, soap was rationed, and could only be
obtained by exchanging coupons, which were issued to us periodically.)

I have written previously about the bicycle rides we took during the
evenings. These still continued in 1942, but the club numbers had
dwindled, and more often than not, the 'club' consisted solely of Graham
and myself. On one of these rides, along the Nevin Road, we were pushing
our bikes up a hill when we encountered two young ladies out for a stroll.
Not unnaturally, we stopped to chat them up, and soon discovered
their names to be Mary and Florence. After giving them the pleasure of
our company, we escorted them home and arranged to meet them
again on the following day. This meeting led to several others, and a
serious relationship very quickly developed between Graham and Mary,
which flourished to such an extent that it seemed no time at all before
Graham burst in on me one night to say that they were engaged. I was

not really surprised, even when I heard that they planned to marry a few months later, but then fate was to take a hand.

The next group of events were triggered off when a notice appeared that invited technical tradesmen of the rank of corporal to apply for training as flight engineers. This was decidedly interesting and a buzz went around the camp. Graham and I discussed the matter, and we finally joined up with five other corporals in putting our names forward. There were several reasons for me to take this step, paramount of which was my lost opportunity to become a pilot after that disastrous interview, but in addition I fancied a change of scenery by this time. Whatever the upheavals Penrhos had produced, I had enjoyed the sea and country-side and had been content to stay as long as I had. The idea of a change from Wales appealed to me, but in the event I was actually posted to a different part of the same country, albeit for a relatively short period of time. The prospects for advancement to sergeant were, in addition, a long way ahead as promotion of ground crews to the higher echelons was inordinately slow, even allowing for the wartime increase in tempo. Further-more, winter was approaching again, with all its attendant difficulties, and there was a little matter of an increase in pay if I made the grade!

After a wait of a week or two, we learned that we had all been accepted subject to medical fitness, so one day in the middle of August, the seven of us reported to the sickbay to undergo the local examination. We all passed this, even though most of us had difficulty in holding our breath for one minute, and now we had to wait patiently for further orders. They soon came through (it turned out that they were very short of flight engineers!), and we were instructed to report to RAF St Athan, near Cardiff, on 2 September.

Graham was now presented with a problem. In view of the fact that Mary could not leave Pwllheli, and that he had to leave within a few days, the proposed wedding plans had to be altered. In the end, drastic action was taken, and a special licence was obtained for the ceremony to be held on the day before we were due to leave. The marriage took place at two o'clock on 1 September at St Peter's English church in Pwllheli, with myself in the role of best man.

After the wedding pictures, we repaired to Mary's home in Lleyn Street for a meal. This magnificent feast had been conjured up by much dubious dealing at the local shops that very same morning, and included chicken, fancy cakes and a bottle of whisky. Not bad going for wartime! This was followed with a drink at the Tower Hotel, and celebrations continued in the evening, when we were joined by Mary's office colleagues at the Penlan Fawr public house. As can be imagined, it was with great reluctance that I tore myself away from the festivities to get back to camp in time to finish packing for our early departure for St Athan the following morning.

When the next day dawned, the Penrhos contingent arrived at Pwllheli station at seven o'clock, complete with all their kit and worldly possessions (I had dispatched my bike home several days previously), and we now awaited the arrival of Graham and the train, hopefully in the right order! Graham eventually appeared, running down the street clutching his case with Mary hotfoot behind. He made it to the platform to the accompaniment of our lusty cheers just as the train came into view. With very few other passengers, we were able to settle into our carriage very comfortably, and soon we were off. I have no recollection of the route we followed, but I travelled with very mixed feelings, on the one hand contemplating the bittersweet relationship I had had with Penrhos, where I had spent the best part of two and a half years, and on the other hand not really looking forward to our arrival at the unknown station in South Wales.

Chapter Four

St Athan

It was long after nightfall when we arrived at Cardiff General station after a tremendously weary wartime journey, thankful that we were not expected to catch a bus to complete it. Station transport was waiting nearby, and we even had help to carry our kit; our first impression was therefore very favourable. The journey to St Athan remains a mystery as I was asleep for most of the time, but I can remember that after dropping off our kit on arrival, we went to the airmen's mess to be given mugs of cocoa. Until this time I had had a violent dislike of cocoa, but this was different and I went back several times for more. In fact, I drank cocoa whenever possible while I was at St Athan and always thoroughly enjoyed it. It is hard to explain why this local brew should be so good; perhaps it was something to do with the water. Soon we were shown to our billets, and after unpacking the bare essentials of our kit, it was heads down and off to the land of nod.

RAF St Athan was a very big station, the largest in the United Kingdom, and was divided into two separate entities – the main camp and the aerodrome. The aerodrome was also used as an aircraft park, similar to that at Cosford. The main camp, designated No. 4 School of Technical Training, was host to a good number of various courses, of which ours was a small cog in the wheel. The station had been built before the war, and the workshops and hangars were brick-built, although the majority of the living quarters were wooden huts, which were actually quite comfortable with central heating. The public buildings comprised a cinema, gymnasium and swimming baths, again comparable with

Cosford. In fact both camps were probably built at the same time, to the same standard RAF plans.

On day two, the whole course (several hundred strong), was marshalled into a large hangar for a very essential purpose – we had to be divided up into five groups in line with the type of aircraft we were to be instruct-ed on, namely Sunderland, Catalina, Lancaster, Halifax or Stirling. Another favourable impression was made on us when we found out that we actually had a choice, and that alphabetical considerations did not come into it. The idea was that we were to line up in the appropriate column in front of a row of desks. I had a hankering to be in Coastal Command and wanted to work on Sunderlands if I could, so I joined that queue. My chagrin can be imagined when eventually I reached the desk, only to be told that the chap in front of me had taken the last vacancy, and that I would have to settle for my second choice. I had not actually got round to having a second choice as I thought there wouldn't be any difficulty with the first one! 'You will have to put up with Lancasters,' said the officer in charge; 'all the others are filled up.' Obviously I now had no alternative, so I reluctantly went to the Lancaster desk to record my name. It will be seen, therefore, that it was pure chance that I was eventually to fly in the best aircraft in the RAF, and it didn't take me long to consider myself lucky that I had not ended up stooging around in a miserable Sunderland!

It must be emphasised that the Lancaster vacancies were not due to any particular aversion to the type, but merely that they were being built in much larger quantities than the others, giving rise to a larger demand for engineers to be trained for them. At the same time as this selection process, we were given white flashes that had to be worn at the front of our Service caps to denote that we were trainee aircrew. With that, the meet-ing dispersed and we were marched off to meet our new instructors.

The whole of the course was conducted on the ground and did not involve any flying. There was a static aircraft that we used on frequent occasions, but the bulk of the instruction took place in the workshops and schools. In the workshops we were divided into groups of about twenty-five, each group being under the control of a staff corporal. Although we were all corporals, we were subordinate to our instructors during working hours, and had to do as we were told. Off duty, we were free to exercise the dubious privileges of our lowly rank! It had been deliberately arranged that the course was made up of equal numbers of airframe and engine fitters who now had to learn the other person's job, and this was the basis of our group segregation. For me this meant engines, engines and even more engines, and they had plenty at St Athan. We started with the basics and had to strip down and rebuild old de Havilland Gypsy engines, including replacing the cylinder linings and regrinding the crankshafts. When we had used up our allocated time at this, we transferred to carburettors, and then to magnetos and finally airscrews. Only after all this preparation were we allowed to get near a Merlin engine, used on the Lancaster, but now the emphasis was on ignition and valve timing, engine controls, supercharging, oil coolers and radiators, etc. In parallel with this, time was spent in the static aircraft running up the engines and diagnosing faults. We then followed up with a short course on electrics, and finally we spent about two weeks on Lancaster familiarisation, together with a refresher on hydraulics and pneumatics. School periods were held several times a week, when engine and electrical theory were drummed in. An important part of the school curriculum was engine handling and fuel conservation – subjects we would dream about in the near future!

Throughout the course we were continually being assessed as to whether we were likely to make the grade. This resulted in a few people being weeded out and dropped as time went by. We had been there for six weeks, approximately halfway through the course, before we were medically examined, and the reasons for this delay are hard to understand. The aircrew medical was, of necessity, very thorough and detailed, and there was much more chance of failing this than there was of completing the technical course. It would seem, therefore, to have been logical to have had it on arrival at St Athan to save the time and effort of those who subsequently did not pass fit. Whatever the reason for this arrangement, quite a number were found medically unsuitable and had to leave. One fellow was very unlucky in being too big, bearing in mind the cramped spaces in even the largest aircraft. The medical itself was quite an ordeal and lasted all day; everything that could be tested was tested, and we were in a permanent state of undress – thank goodness for the central heating!

It was at this stage, after actually passing the medical, that Graham had second thoughts about becoming aircrew. He mulled over the situation for some time but eventually decided to drop out, and having made his mind up, would not yield to our (or officialdom's) persuasion to stay. The forthcoming trade examination could have had no bearing on his decision to leave as I am positive that he would have romped through, but I am sure that it was made somewhat reluctantly in regard to his newly married status. Be that as it may, I had lost the company of a staunch friend, and had rather a lonely time during the rest of the course. Incredibly enough, Graham was posted to a Lancaster squadron in his ground-crew capacity, and when we met up again some years later we were able to converse about Lancs almost as though we had been together as aircrew.

I passed the medical A1 and went on to complete the course, at the end of which we had a searching examination. During the exam I was referred back for a day over a question on Lancaster hydraulics, but subsequently managed to satisfy the examiner, and then I was through!

The intense pace of the course had left us very little time for relaxation, and in the eleven weeks that we were there, I went out on no more than nine or ten occasions. There was a fair amount of entertainment staged in the camp, including exhibition boxing matches and ENSA (Entertainments National Service Association) concerts, and there was always the camp cinema. By way of variety, we had the unpleasant tasks of fire piquet and camp guards to perform. I did at least one guard duty round the transport compound, but all I had to report concerned a lorry with its lights left on. I often wondered whether this sort of thing was done deliberately to check whether we were awake!

When we did go out, it was either to Cardiff, Barry or Bridgend. Barry, being the nearest place, was fairly straightforward to reach by bus, but the attractions there were minimal, the one bright spot being a dance hall called Bindles. I went there twice, the second time being a passing-out celebration when the majority of the course survivors packed the place out. Barry was memorable for another occasion, however, when on arrival by bus for the first time, all the passengers were lined up by the police and were required to show their identity cards. This was the only time during the whole of the war that I had to prove my identity other than at various camp guardrooms. I rather liked Bridgend, but it was a difficult place to reach and involved a walk of over a mile to the railway at Llantwit

Major. It was only feasible to go there on a Saturday, and there was the added snag that the last train back left at 10pm, with no alternative means of transport. (I suppose that one could have spent all day Sunday walking back!) As with Barry, a group of us went to the local dance, but it was also a reasonable town to walk round, with pleasant shops. The main attraction was Cardiff, again only reachable at weekends by train or bus. On the few occasions we went there, we usually arrived about two o'clock and wandered around sightseeing until it was time for tea, which we had in a rather large cafe in St Mary's Street. After this, a drink in a local bar and then off to the cinema to see the latest epic. Just one event at Cardiff remains in the memory, when some fifteen or twenty of us went to a special dance at the City Hall, the music being played by Victor Sylvester. This may not sound very exciting to the present generation, but it was something very special at the time!

After the trauma of our final tests, things moved very quickly. On the following day we reported to the workshops as usual, and lists were circulated advising us of our operational postings. This done, we had a makeshift passing-out parade and then went to the stores to draw our air-crew brevets and sergeant's stripes. As we were to be leaving the following day, we had to collect our travel warrants and get clearance certificates signed. All this took until teatime, after which we repaired to Bindles in Barry to celebrate. We knew beforehand that we would be posted to the Lincolnshire area, as that was Lancaster country, but when I heard that I was going to No. 12 Squadron at Wickenby I was completely lost as I had never heard of it before. The travel warrant, however, said 'Snelland Station, change at Lincoln', so I knew I would end up correctly, although once again I was in for a lengthy journey, this time via London. Fifteen of us were posted to Wickenby, and on 16 November we left on station transport for Cardiff, and were on our way. It is interesting to reflect that although we had not flown at all at St Athan, we were now full-blown members of aircrew, and whereas I had had a fair amount of experience in the air, I was sitting in the train with several other flight engineers who had never been airborne in their lives. It must be a record of sorts, to have qualified as aircrew without leaving the ground!

Chapter Five

Wickenby – Part One

We duly arrived at Lincoln's St Mary's station and, having some time to spare before the train for Snelland drew in, we went for some liquid refreshment at the nearby Queen Hotel. Our teetotaller lookout soon came to report that the local train was pulling in, and we dashed across to jump on board. There was one stop before Snelland, which we reached in the gathering gloom. The station was deserted, but this was no real surprise as it was really no more than a country halt. There was a public telephone available, though, and soon we had contacted Wickenby for transport. Not long afterwards, we piled aboard a covered lorry and rattled our way to the camp.

During the latter stages of the journey there was a sense of apprehension among us when we realised that we would soon be treading this unknown territory with its attendant dangers, and on entering the camp this feeling was increased. I am sure that if someone had stopped us at that moment and said that through some mistake we were no longer wanted, a heartfelt cheer would have rent the air. Unfortunately, however, no saviour appeared and we were forced to stifle our thoughts. Soon we were bundled off to a transit hut and, having sorted out our kit, we were taken to the sergeants' mess for a meal before turning in for the night.

RAF Wickenby was a real wartime camp, having been opened in September 1942. The camp site must have originally been part of a wood, as there were plenty of silver birch trees still there. These trees took some of the bareness away, for otherwise it would have been very bleak and barren. Naturally the site was completely flat, as was most of Lincolnshire.

The roads and paths were very good but one couldn't always avoid the mud, making gumboots an essential item during the winter. Most of the administrative buildings were wooden, but there were a few brick-built structures such as the ablutions, control tower and bomb dump. The living accommodation was provided in Nissen huts. The airfield was of irregular shape, with three excellent runways and a 50-feet-wide perimeter track from which concrete dispersal pans led off at various intervals. Three steel hangars catered for aircraft maintenance. All the aircraft were left at the dispersal points to minimise the chance of damage if an attack was made or if fire broke out.

While I was at Wickenby, the only flying unit there was No. 12 Squadron, which had a long history as the number signifies, having been formed in 1915. In 1926 the squadron was equipped with Fairey Fox aircraft and had great success flying them, winning all the competitions that it could enter in 1930. Due to this achievement, a fox's head became the squadron badge, and it acquired the nickname 'Shiny Twelve' because of the highly polished aircraft. This name lingered on, and we all regarded ourselves as the 'Shiny Dozen'! At the beginning of the Second World War, during a raid on the Maastricht bridges in Belgium, one of its aircraft deliberately rammed the bridge, and the pilot, Flying Officer Garland, and the observer, Sergeant Gray, were awarded Victoria Crosses, the first of the war. Their portraits in oils hung in the officers' mess. In March 1941, Wellington bombers were supplied to the squadron, which was then stationed at Binbrook. They transferred to Wickenby when it opened and the first Lancasters arrived about ten days before we did, although the Wellingtons stayed for some time.

We were involved in a flurry of activity right from the start. Firstly we were dispatched to RAF Binbrook (our parent base), where we acquired most of our aircrew kit including battledress, silk under-clothing, flying helmet and, in my case, a portable tool kit. Back at Wickenby we were given lockers for this kit, and we were additionally issued with a parachute harness and Mae West. (Parachutes were always kept in a specially heated packing room, and had to be collected from there for each flight.) Then came the day when we were allocated to crews. Many accounts have been written of various aircrew members wandering round a large hangar attaching themselves to each other to make up crews.

Sometimes this came about by being introduced by a friend, or maybe, for example, through a desire to fly with an Australian pilot, and so on. In our case it was cut and dried, and we had to conform to a pre-arranged list. There had been a rejuggling of the existing crews (which were each made up of six men before we engineers arrived), and it only remained for us to be included. This was done at a simple ceremony in the crew room where the whole squadron was assembled. A very stern-looking flight lieutenant stood on a chair and commenced to read our names from a list, and we had to join our new pilots as he went along. All the names were read out except mine, and on enquiry I was informed that 'You are my engineer; report to me afterwards.' I had been involved with some awkward superiors in the past and my heart sank in contemplating this man, who had all the appearances of a martinet. It was thus with reluctant footsteps that I duly reported after a few other preliminaries had been carried out.

When I got there, I met my other crew members who, on the whole, seemed a friendly lot, and I began to think that things were not so bad after all. I was also to revise my opinion of Flight Lieutenant Villiers, whose bite was slightly better than his bark; indeed, I was to count myself exceedingly fortunate to have been in his crew as, of the original fifteen of the new engineers, I was the only one to complete my tour of operations at Wickenby. All the others were lost as time went by, although undoubtedly a number of them would have been taken prisoner.

After this session of 'getting together', there was a general change-round of sleeping accommodation as it was much more convenient for members of the same crew to be billeted together, and I ended up in hut 13 together with my rear gunner and bomb aimer. Joining up with Villiers and moving into hut 13 on the same day was not a combination that filled me with any confidence at the time, but as events were to turn out, it was probably the lucky omen that was to save our bacon! For the record my fellow crew members were as follows:

- **Pilot** – Flight Lieutenant Villiers; he had already completed one tour of operations with No. 87 Squadron at Scampton.
- **Navigator** – Flight Sergeant Orchard; he had also done one tour of operations.

- **Wireless operator** – Pilot Officer Dear, DFC (Distinguished Flying Cross); he had also achieved a previous tour.
- **Rear gunner** – Sergeant Prowse; he was on his first tour, but had already flown on one operation in a Halifax on a previous squadron, and I had to bow to his superior experience most of the way through our tour.
- **Mid-upper gunner** – Pilot Officer Saunders; he was on his first tour.
- **Bomb aimer** – Sergeant Thomas; he was on his first tour.
- **Flight engineer** – yours truly; ditto!

None of us had completed any operations at Wickenby and were embarking on a fresh tour. Due to sickness etc., though, we slowly got out of line with each other and eventually finished at different times. My companions in hut 13 were Fred Prowse and George Thomas, and we soon became excellent friends. The remainder of the occupants were a mixed lot from various crews, and included Sergeant Driver, a gunner who had won the first DFM (Distinguished Flying Medal) of the war in 1939; Sergeant Straker, who was an actor; and Sergeant Thompson who was a bomb aimer – of whom more anon.

The date of 20 November 1942, four days after my arrival at Wickenby, was a red letter day because we became airborne for the first time! We clambered into Lancaster W4372 and took off on an aircraft familiarisation flight that lasted forty minutes. Details of the flight escape me, but I was understandably nervous as this was my first trip with proper duties to perform, and I didn't fancy falling foul of Villiers either. I was rather taken aback by the noise level as well, but this was somewhat muted as we were wearing headgear. Helmets had to be worn on all flights because the intercom microphone was an integral part, as was the oxygen mask.

Having mentioned my duties, I feel that I should detail these to give a better understanding of the job. According to an Air Ministry order dated 1943, the duties and responsibilities of flight engineers were as follows:

- to operate certain controls and watch appropriate gauges;
- to act as pilot's assistant to the extent of being able to fly straight and narrow on a course;
- to advise the captain as to the functioning of the engines and the

fuel, oil and coolant systems;
- to ensure effective liaison with the maintenance staff;
- to carry out practicable emergency repairs during flight;
- to act as standby air gunner.

In other words, a Jack of all trades – Mr Fixit! Apart from the bare bones of this statement, I was also involved in keeping a log of engine temperatures and pressures and fuel tank readings. I had to synchronise the engine revolutions, change the fuel tanks over periodically, carry out numerous pre-flight checks, operate the flaps and undercarriage, turn on the oxygen and feather the airscrews if necessary. I suppose I would have had to go in a gun turret in an emergency, but I never had any formal instruction in firing the guns, and we may well have been shot down before I fathomed it all out!

We flew again the following day, this time in W4371, and I then had plenty of opportunity to study the aircraft as it was a cross-country flight of three hours' duration. While on this trip we experimented with feathering the airscrews so that the pilot could get the feel of the aircraft with various engines out of action. To stop an engine by feathering was a simple operation involving the touch of a button after the fuel and magnetos had been turned off, but one had to be aware of the consequential effects of this as numerous services were dependent on engine power, including the turrets and the vacuum pumps for the instruments. The practice I was able to get during this flight was also invaluable as, later on, during my first bombing raid, I had to feather an engine in earnest while over the maelstrom of Essen. It had to be done quickly, and I had to change the vacuum pumps over to compensate. Afterwards I was congratulated by Villiers, which was almost as good as being promoted! How did a Lancaster fly with engines stopped? On three engines it made hardly any difference, and it would fly quite happily on two in level flight, even if they were both on the same side (hard work for the pilot, though, to keep it straight). It would stay airborne on only one, but would lose height fairly rapidly, and landing would be very dicey indeed.

On 25 November we flew another cross-country lasting three and a half hours, this time in W4368. Nothing to report about this flight, but some small item required adjustment after we had landed, as according to my records we took her up again at 17.30 hours for a night-flying test. A certain amount of night flying had commenced by this time, and it was customary procedure to test an aircraft in the late afternoon to make sure it was serviceable. This would apply not only if the machine had been repaired, but also if it had been standing at dispersal all day.

My next flight was a 'solo'! I was detached from my crew on the evening of the 27th to fly with Sergeant Featherstone on night circuits and land-ings. Sergeant Featherstone, an Australian pilot, belonged to RAF Lindholme, but was temporarily stationed at Wickenby to help train our crews. The aircraft, R5667 also from Lindholme, was an old banger that had seen better days on a previous squadron, and was filthy dirty. The duty we had to perform was to circle the aerodrome and make frequent landings with a pupil pilot at the controls, under the supervision of Featherstone. It was a dual-controlled aircraft, and things were pretty well in order, but at times the situation was a bit uncertain when the pupil was in charge! In addition, there were several other factors to be considered. It was my first flight at night (indeed, it was only the fifth time I had flown in a 'Lanc'), and I was with an unfamiliar pilot whose requirements I could not always anticipate. To offset this, however, as we were in sight of the airfield I had no need to keep a log, and I could use my torch on full beam as we were not under operational conditions. In spite of all the odds, I was determined to do a competent job, not only for the sake of my own skin, but also in case any minor indiscretion might reach the ears of Villiers! In the event, my efforts must have been up to standard as we all walked away from the Lanc at the end of the 1½-hour stint (any landing was reckoned to be a good one if one walked away from it), and I was able to make the first red (night flight) entry in my logbook!

On the camp itself, we soon got used to our unfamiliar surroundings, and during the training period drifted into a fairly settled routine. Wintertime was approaching and we had our fair share of rain with its muddy aftermath. Coal for the hut stove was in short supply, so we gathered some logs to help eke it out. With regard to our accommodation, the only semblance of central heating was in the bath hut, which I seem to remember was an annexe to the sergeants' mess.

The daily round started at about 7.15am, when we were required to wash in stone-cold water at the ablution hut some distance away. These factors gave birth to the so-called 'squadron wash', which was one inch of water, one wipe of the face and one minute door to door! After this refreshing interlude we would finish dressing and make our way to the mess for breakfast, after which we had to fall in for a parade outside the squadron headquarters at 8.30am. Squadron HQ was one of a group of buildings at the edge of the aerodrome (the other buildings were the crew room, locker room, parachute room, gunnery workshops, transport garage and intelligence library), and was about a nine- or ten-minute walk from the billets. This was the only instance of rigid discipline that we experienced at Wickenby, and even this diminished when we started operations as we were then up and about at all odd times. On this parade we were checked over rather than inspected and a roll-call was made, after which we went our various ways, some to squadron briefings, some to dispersals for flying, and others to the aircraft for ground testing.

It was usual for the engineer, the wireless operator and gunners to take part in the aircraft test, but very occasionally the whole crew would go out. For my part, I would have words with the ground crew to see if any faults had been discovered on routine inspection (shades of Penrhos!), and if all was reported in order I would do a visual inspection of my own. So many items had to be checked that it would be impossible (and boring) to list them here, so I will content myself with mentioning a few of the most important ones. Externally, there was checking that the pitot head cover was off, the hinged wing leading edges were secure, the tyres in order, and there were no engine oil leaks; internally, pressures of emergency air bottles (for the undercarriage) were inspected, the hydraulic accumulator was examined, and checks that the fuel cross-feed cock was off, the brakes were the correct pressure and functioning, and the master electric switch was set to 'ground' (to use outside accumulators for starting the engines). There were many more items still to be looked at when preparing for actual flight, which I will mention in due course.

This may, however, be the appropriate time to briefly explain the internal layout of the fuselage. As one clambered through the door one would notice the Elsan toilet just in front of the rear turret, and one would have to avoid banging one's head on the Direct Reading Compass nearby on the starboard side. Following this was the flare chute, and further on the flap jack. This flap-operating jack rates a mention of its own as it was a large cumbersome cylinder placed across the aircraft floor in the darkest part of the interior; truly a great hazard. Even more perilous, though, was the next large object, the main spar; again this stretched across the floor, and as it was about two feet high it had to be climbed over. Directly forward of this were two bulkhead doors. These were normally closed in flight and served several purposes: the prevention of draughts, the inhibiting of noise and (as they were armour-plated), the stopping of enemy projectiles! Next came the rest bed (to accommodate injured persons) with the crate of oxygen bottles beneath it. The forward crew positions started here, with the wireless operator and his equipment. The wireless op was most unfortunate in that he sat near the incoming hot air vents and had to control the degree of heat. He was hot while we were frozen, and many heated words passed over the intercom on long trips; occasionally we had to approach Villiers to arbitrate! The navigator's table came next, and then the pilot's seat with my position alongside. I had a folding seat that I found so uncomfortable that I normally stood up, and I am sure that this helped to keep me awake in the early hours. The bomb aimer's position was in the nose, directly above the escape hatch, and he also doubled up as front gunner.

Another important part of my routine was to test the engines. Naturally it was essential to check that the engines themselves were in order, but they also had to be run up to provide power for the gunners to test their turrets, and also for the wireless operator to check his equipment. The normal arrangement was to start the starboard outer first, followed by the others across the aircraft, but as only one engine at a time could be opened up while on the ground, it would be a long time before the port outer was dealt with. This engine drove the rear turret, and Fred wasn't very pleased with the system! If I started with his engine I would be upsetting the others, as each turret was driven by a separate engine, and indeed if I did not start up an inner engine the wireless op would complain. The only solution was to work to a roster and change the order on every occasion. Each engine was idled to warm up and then progressively opened up to full power, and at various stages the supercharger gears and magnetos were checked and the airscrew controls exercised. It was a tremendous thrill to me to run up each of these powerful engines to +12lb boost. The noise was terrific, and this heightened the sense of power, but even though the chocks were on the wheels and the brakes were on, I couldn't help but feel that the aircraft would suddenly break loose and start swinging round in circles!

After feeling our way during the early flights, we now carried out a more advanced training programme, and on 3 December took W4792 on a daylight point-to-point cross-country trip of just over four hours' duration, our longest flight to date. There was a proper briefing before this flight, and we had to circle each turning point at a precise time, giving essential practice to the navigator and the bomb aimer who was up in the nose map-reading. The route was Base–Aylesbury–Harlech–Douglas– Darlington–Base. For my part this was a purely routine exercise, but it was made that extra bit interesting by two highlights. The first was to see the Isle of Man spread out below me even though we were at no great height, and we fairly swooped down on Douglas, enabling us to see the promenade quite clearly. The second was that on the leg to Darlington, I had the thrilling experience of seeing both the east and west coasts of England at the same time. Admittedly we were flying over the narrowest part, but I was very impressed just the same.

This outing was followed by a night-flying test on the 5th in W4794. The significance of this flight was that it was our first one in this particular aircraft, which then became our own. We flew in it by right and only used others when it was unserviceable. Eventually we did wear it out, and reluctantly had to exchange it for a new one. What was its code letter? With a pilot named Villiers, it was naturally 'V' Victory! On the question of code letters and names it is appropriate to mention that the squadron code was PH, and so the legend 'PH V' appeared in large letters on the side of the aircraft. The squadron call-sign was ORAND and the aircraft sign was PINTO, thus PINTO 'V' Victory to ORAND rent the air loud and clear! Unfortunately a nearby aerodrome with the call-sign 'BONFIRE' frequently intruded, and on many occasions we had difficulty being heard. We often said that if we could find out which station it was we would make it live up to its name and burn it down! These call-signs and names were a security measure to confuse the enemy, but they often fooled us as well.

Our next trip was on the 6th, again in 'V' Victory, and was a cross-country following the same route as before but missing out the turn at Darlington. It took us four hours, and part-way round the navigator and bomb aimer changed places. After this we went on leave, which was well earned in my case after the traumas at St Athan and our energetic start at Wickenby. I always went home when on leave, so each one was much the same as before and the method of travel was very similar on each occasion: bus to Lincoln and thence by train. It was normally a dreary journey that involved a change at Derby, but on one occasion a bit of interest was raised when the train was routed via Leicester owing to floods.

Back at Wickenby we had a break from routine when on 17 December we took off on an air firing exercise to give the gunners some practice. This consisted of them firing at a drogue, and took me right back to my Fairey Battle experience of a couple of years previously, although this time I had a much more comfortable ride! We were airborne for one hour and twenty minutes, and two hours after landing we were up again for a night cross-country, our first flight in darkness as a crew. I have no record of the route flown, but we had trouble when the starboard inner engine developed a bad oil leak and had to be feathered. This put us so badly out on our point to point timings that we gave up and returned to base, having been up for two and a half hours.

Item 2 of the Engineer's Charter states that he should act as pilot's assistant etc., and on 20 December it was deemed that I should have practice in the art. The occasion was a cross-country that commenced in daylight, and we were in W4792 as 'V' Victory was still undergoing engine repairs. Again I cannot recall the route, but as I flew part of it the timing could not have been very important! The great moment came when we were at about 3,000ft and Villiers had 'George' in control while we changed seats. I had some idea of what to do as I had had a watching brief during our previous flights, and I had also had several sessions on the Link trainer. There was no substitute for the real thing, though, and I had to accustom myself to the 'feel' of it. I was somewhat uncertain about the response time of control movements and tended to over-correct at times, but I gradually sorted myself out and was soon flying very creditably straight and level, even if I had no idea of the speed or direction!

After a while, skipper Villiers introduced several new factors to disturb my peaceful routine, and I had to learn to cope with such things as the undercarriage being lowered (the nose going down after forty seconds), or being raised (the nose going up after twenty seconds), and also the movement of the flaps, which had a similar but opposite effect on the trim of the aircraft. During all these goings-on in the cockpit, the rest of the crew, although alert to the situation, didn't have much to say. All this was to change, however, when Villiers suddenly asked me to land on a cloud! With my vast experience of a few minutes, I was expected to lower the undercarriage and flaps together, and manoeuvre the Lanc in line with an imaginary runway so as to make a pinpoint landing. I had to do all this against the background rumblings of my colleagues elsewhere in the aircraft, who by this time, while not exactly standing by the escape hatches, were distinctly uneasy to say the least. The bomb aimer in particular was very vocal, and imagined that he could see high ground straight ahead of us all the time. Undeterred I went on to make a fair landing, and subsequently an adequate take-off before all the imagined rising ground appeared, and the crew subsided into acceptance of my new skills (which might conceivably be used to their advantage in the coming months). We eventually reached base and landed in darkness after what had been a long flight of three hours and forty minutes.

It was the turn of the bomb aimer to practice on the 22nd when we went on a short trip to the bombing range at Donna Nook. We only needed to be airborne long enough to drop the bombs, and we were back again and landed within forty minutes. The only results I have of George's efforts are by inference – it was the only time we had bombing practice, so his aim must have been satisfactory.

Our next jaunt was another night cross-country on the following evening. This was a relatively local affair of two hours' endurance and was flown in W4366, our sixth Lanc to date, but from now on we were to be more consistent as, after the Christmas break, 'V' Victory was serviceable once more.

Wickenby at this time was a rather chaotic place, and very little was laid on over the Christmas period, although we had a two- or three-day break. It would seem that we were left to our own devices, and so in the absence of a formal Christmas dinner, four of us went to Lincoln to eat at the Great Northern Hotel. The hotel had been decorated up for the occasion, and we had an excellent lunch in spite of the wartime rationing.

I remember that there was a delay in serving the pudding due to shortages of staff, and had we been in the mess at Wickenby we would have banged our spoons on the table, but in the luxury of the hotel dining room we were forced to show a little decorum and twiddled our thumbs instead! Unhappily, my three companions were all killed within a month, two of them in a crash on the airfield circuit, so I look back on that very happy episode with mixed pleasure and sorrow.

Our own aircraft was now back in action, complete with a new engine, and on 28 December we took it up on an air test. After flying round for an hour, including putting the new engine through its paces, we returned to Wickenby to find that we could not lower the undercarriage! The procedure to attempt to get it down was to throw the aircraft about a bit, including some shallow dives, but all this was to no avail and as it wasn't practicable to pump it down, the emergency air system was used. To our great relief it came down with a resounding crack, but the delight was tempered by the anticipated displeasure of the ground crew who would have to bleed the system through. I had plenty of this at Penrhos and it was one of the most thankless tasks possible. Time has erased my memory of their kind remarks I am glad to say! The fault lay in the hydraulic system, and had no connection with the new engine as a separate pump was provided on both inboard engines. It took a day to put things right, and when we went up again on an air test on the 29th, all was well.

The advent of the Lancaster, with its splendid performance, opened up the possibility of mounting daylight raids on Germany, and by the end of 1942 several daring operations had already been carried out. With this idea in mind, we were now required to practise formation flying at low level, and the whole squadron took off on 30 December on a two-hour cross-country. For this flight the low-level qualification was 2,000ft (against 20,000ft normal operational height), which meant that we could forget about ground obstructions and concentrate on formation. As it was our first exercise of this nature, it wasn't surprising that it was far from successful, but it was a start and a welcome break from our hitherto mundane programme. We were up again on the 31st carrying on where we left off and, after a further fifty minutes of flying, we must have made some progress!

At the end of this trip I made my logbook up for December to find that I had flown twenty-three hours to add to my total of nine hours in the previous month, and so in accordance with regulations I handed it in to Squadron Leader Bell, the 'B' Flight commander, for his signature. Squadron Leader Bell had been on No. 12 Squadron since August 1942, and was to finish his tour at the end of February 1943. When he left, several of his crew remained as 'spare bods' and his engineer, Sergeant Chapman, looked after flight engineer affairs while flying occasional operations with other crews. At the end of my tour he was to replace me as a permanent crew member.

Another prominent officer of the squadron was the CO, Wing Commander Wood, DFC, a very understanding person who later on helped my career along considerably, as will be seen. While on the subject of personalities, it would not be out of place to mention a man who was the station commander for the three months from February to April 1943. He was no less a person than Group Captain Hughie Edwards, VC, DSO (Distinguished Service Order), DFC, an Australian who had won his Victoria Cross on a death-defying raid leading a squadron of Blenheims. We used to see him limping around Wickenby with the aid of a stick, and these 'war wounds' somehow added to his stature. I was amazed to read many years later that the limp had actually been caused by a childhood accident. I had one official encounter with him that I shall describe in due course. In later life he became governor of Western Australia with the impressive title of Sir H.I. Edwards, VC, KCMG (Knight Commander of the Order of St Michael and St George), CB (Companion of the (Order of the) Bath), DSO, OBE (Officer of the Order of the British Empire), DFC – a far cry from Wickenby in the mud of 1943!

The Link trainer has been mentioned with regard to my stint of pilot training, so a few words about it might be appropriate. Basically, it was a mock-up cockpit mounted on swivel joints that would respond to the actions of the pupil sitting inside. The cockpit was 'blind', but had instruments as in a proper aircraft, and one could carry out any manoeuvre as dictated by the instructor. The track of the trainer was indicated on a large table alongside so that a proper course could be flown, and standard beam approach signals enabled one to make a realistic landing. I was usually able to make reasonable landings, but they were frequently several feet below ground level! I think that the Link Trainer was of inestimable value, especially to aircrew other than pilots, but there was a strange apathy towards it, and it was not used to maximum efficiency.

With the close of 1942 I had completed five years' service, but did not rate my chances of doing another year very highly as our transitional period at Wickenby had now ended and we were about to become operational! There was one more training flight to make before we were blooded, and this was on 2 January when we went local formation flying for an hour and a quarter.

The big day now dawned, and on 3 January 1943 we trooped into the briefing room to be told our fate, but it was with some relief that we learned that we were to drop sea mines off La Rochelle in the Bay of Biscay. This relatively easy trip had been laid on to give us confidence in our new role, and it was indeed very straightforward. My logbook confirms that we dropped 6 x 1,500lb mines and that we flew for six hours and forty-five minutes to do it; by far the longest time we had been airborne. For some unknown reason (but probably a request from Group HQ), we were then required to fly on a height test during the following day, and we managed to reach 25,000ft where the outside temperature was -35-degrees centigrade. This was not an exceptional height for a Lancaster (although we rarely exceeded it), but I am surprised that we did not do better on this occasion as we were unladen and the weather was cold, which enabled the engines to run more efficiently. Perhaps there was something the matter with the trim of 'V' Victory, but otherwise she flew very well so we did not complain.

Our operational tour commenced in earnest on 8 January with another mining sortie, but this time on a more heavily defended route to the Frisian Islands off north Germany. En route we strayed too near to Texel island in the Netherlands and ran into a stiff flak barrage – my baptism of fire! This incident led to a further discomfort for me as well when I instinctively ducked to avoid being struck, causing Villiers to round on me. 'You clot,' he said, 'if you were going to be hit you would be hit, and bending down won't save you. Pay more attention to looking out for night fighters!' With his great experience Villiers was obviously unmoved by this minor show of belligerence from the enemy, and in castigating me he had killed two birds with one stone. Not only had he shown me up in the full hearing of the rest of the crew, but I was also the first recipient of the 'clot' accolade that he had threatened to bestow on any of us who warranted it. In time, though, all the others were honoured in the same way and some more than once! This episode was the most noteworthy part of the trip, and we went on to drop our six mines and return to Wickenby after four and a half hours in the air.

We were operational again the next night, and this was a trip with a difference! The target was Essen, the home of the Krupp armament works and numerous other industries. Many towns resided in this part of Germany, making up what is known as the Ruhr, including Düsseldorf and the other manufacturing centres of the Wupper Valley. For this reason it was the most highly defended part of the enemy territory, and was well patrolled by night fighters. We had a very portentous name for it – the 'Happy Valley'.

Take-off was at 17.35 hours, and about an hour later we were crossing the enemy coast. I tried to appear as nonchalant about it as Villiers was, but in reality my knees were knocking. To buoy myself up I remember shouting (with my intercom off) 'Right you so and sos, look out now, 12 Squadron are back again!' This probably helped my confidence, but I doubt whether the Jerries would have taken much notice, even if they could have heard! On we went, and soon George began to query our route as he had seen no sign of the towns that we were supposed to pass. This led to a conference with the navigator (Flight Sergeant Orchard), and he had to admit that he was completely lost. Consternation reigned at this, and Villiers immediately turned the aircraft round in the general direction of England, there being no future in stooging about by ourselves without the protection of the main force, and it would have been suicide to attempt to find the target and bomb by ourselves, even if we had had enough petrol to do it. At this point we had to consider jettisoning the 4,000lb 'cookie' that we were carrying as it was much too dangerous to land with it on board. Although we wanted to get rid of it as soon as possible in case we met night fighters, it was important to drop it in the right place. Anywhere in Germany was OK but not in occupied France, so in our doubtful orientation we kept it until we re-crossed the sea and consigned it to the depths. The navigation department managed to sort out a route back to base, and we landed after three hours. Understandably, Villiers was furious, for not only had we been exposed to great risk in flying the wrong course and therefore being on our own, but we had flown over enemy territory for some time without it counting towards our operational total. The whole thing reflected badly on Villiers as the captain of the aircraft and he absolutely refused to fly with Orchard again. For my part it was most galling as I had keyed myself up for this great occasion and had inwardly even warned the Jerries, all to no avail!

Villiers stuck to his guns and Orchard departed to a new squadron. Some months later when stooging along over Germany, another Lancaster joined in formation with us and Villiers brought the house down with his remark, 'I bet that bloody Orchard is in that crew and they are following us to make sure that they are going in the right direction!' Whatever happened after he left us, he must have found some credence in some other crew as he was shot down and killed early in 1944.

Our new navigator was another second-tour type, Flying Officer Bill Allinson, DFM. I didn't see a lot of him except when we were on duty and he was in the officers' mess, but he was generally liked and he did at least keep us on the right course. Bill arrived with us in time for our next operation two days later on 11 January, the target again being Essen. We took off at 17.10 hours with our load of a 4,000lb bomb plus incendiaries, and we managed to reach the target correctly this time. On arrival I was amazed to see the ferocity of the anti-aircraft fire, which was much greater than I had imagined. Searchlights were everywhere as well, and the scene was compounded by the fires already on the ground and the various coloured flares hanging in the sky. The flak appeared as a sheet wall of bursting shells with no way through, and it was here that we benefited by Villiers's experience and calm manner. The bomb doors were opened and George was in position to sight the marker flares and guide Villiers in the right direction. By now we were in the thick of it and the noise was deafening – a veritable vision of Hell! We heard George giving corrections, and shortly afterwards it was 'bombs gone'. It was hardly necessary for him to shout this as the aircraft leaped upwards when they were released and I was nearly knocked off balance.

Far from the danger now being over, the next few moments were potentially the worst of the raid, for there subsequently came a photographic session! Simultaneously with the bomb release, a flare was dropped that lit up the ground sufficiently to show on a photograph taken by a special camera so that the target area could be confirmed. The film was exposed for several seconds as the bursting of the flare, planned to occur when the bombs were halfway down their descent, could not be predicted to a second. The object was to obtain a record of where the bombs were likely to have fallen, not necessarily the explosion itself. So in order to allow for this variation in the operating time of the flare, it was crucial for Villiers to hold the aircraft straight and level for a period of eleven seconds. As can be imagined, they were almost unbearable as there was an irresistible temptation to spin away and get out of it. Villiers usually contained himself for this vital period of time, although afterwards he would actually confess to being as terrified as the rest of us.

Having endured this agony, and with our thoughts on the homeward journey, we were suddenly hit by shrapnel and the port inner engine packed up. For a few moments pandemonium reigned, but I managed to feather the propeller very smartly before the engine caught fire, and then changed over the vacuum pump when the flying instruments ceased to function. The whole episode must have been over in seconds, and with a calm word from Villiers, allied to a diving turn away from the target, we all started to breathe again! As we flew home with only three engines functioning, this sortie took us nearly five hours to complete – much longer than usual for a visit to Essen. We naturally wouldn't have minded if it had taken even longer, though, as the vital thing was that we had returned safely from our inaugural bombing raid.

Returning from any operation was always a pleasing experience as one's mind registered that the worst was over, and the idea was to get the hell out of it and back to bed! Our instincts still had to be tempered, though, by the need to ensure that we would actually complete the journey. Several remaining hazards faced us, not least being the night fighters, and while we were lucky enough to avoid actually being attacked, we saw plenty of them during our tour. There was usually also more than enough flak to contend with, and the possibility of collision with our own colleagues was always present. In fact we had several near misses, one with a plane going in the opposite direction (Orchard again?!). Paramount also was the need to conserve fuel, and there must have been many an argument between a pilot who wanted to press on and an engineer who wanted to land actually at base instead of ditching in the sea! Villiers was quite amenable to dashing along when conditions were suitable, but he was cautious enough on other occasions to follow my advice to eke out the dwindling petrol supply and allow me to set the engine controls to fly for range rather than speed.

The standard procedure to enable us to spot fighters was to weave the aircraft from side to side while rolling it around the longitudinal axis, and many were the hours that we endured this movement, which gave us frequent attacks of airsickness. I had to do my share of looking out, and it is fair to say that the engineer spent about ninety per cent of his airborne time with his eyes out of the cockpit. It was usual to reduce height gradually on the return journey, and this gave us a big advantage in speed, especially as we no longer had the cookie on board or the full weight of fuel. We were thus able to fly at about 190–200mph instead of around 140–160mph going out. There was no organised timing on the homeward leg so we were always on our own, and while there was always someone trying to get back first, conditions had to be right for him to do it.

On approaching the English coast we would switch on the IFF equipment (Identification, Friend or Foe) and usually fire off the colours of the day, although sometimes even this did not help and we had to elude our own flak, which in my experience was more accurate than the German variety. Just before arrival at base we would call up for landing instructions, which usually elicited the order to orbit at X thousand feet and await our turn (note that I do not mention the word Angels – that was reserved for the blue-eyed chaps in Fighter Command!). During this waiting period, on confirmation from control, the altimeter was set to the correct barometric pressure to enable us to avoid landing below ground level (shades of the Link trainer), and when the all-important instruction '"V" Victory you may pancake' came over, it was like music to our ears.

As if we hadn't had enough, it was Essen again on 13 January. This time we flew in W4791 as 'V' Victory was undergoing an engine change, and for the first time we completed a bombing raid in a relatively peaceful manner. Taking off at 17.05 hours, we climbed over Wickenby at 10,000ft before setting course to Southwold on the east coast where we were to rendezvous with the rest of the pack before heading for the target. On this second leg we climbed gradually to our bombing height of 21,000ft, and after facing the music once again at Essen, made for home at a smart pace to land after just over four hours. The main reason for climbing over base was that on a sortie such as to Happy Valley, it was not really suitable to climb all the way on course because of the short distance involved. Another consideration was that having spent some time climbing initially over England, the rest of the journey could be flown at a greater speed for more safety, and also with the rendezvous we would travel in a more concentrated bunch. Against this, though, there was much more chance of a collision taking place, especially while orbiting over Southwold, and we experienced numerous occasions when we were buffeted about in someone else's slipstream – very dicey it was too. In this instance I have mentioned Southwold, but there were numerous other meeting places such as Beachy Head or Selsey Bill. If the weather was overcast, a vertical searchlight would be deployed to guide us.

The practice flights we made at low level were still not finished with, and were to continue on and off for some months until someone at Bomber Command made a decision regarding the viability of operating on this basis. Perhaps this decision was finally settled when the Dam Busters flew out in May, or maybe earlier than this, or later; who knows? In the meantime we were kept nibbling at it, and typical was the trip around Lincolnshire on 15 January when we had our old faithful 'V' Victory back again. Although we were up and down within the hour, we had enough fun for a lifetime, enjoying such escapades as swooping down on a farmyard to catch the chickens in the slipstream – sometimes they went up higher than we did! We also flew at wavetop height over the sea and trailed a rabbit's foot in the water from the rear turret! The incident that took the biscuit, however, was our shooting up a train on the line between March and Spalding. We flew level with the engine and I shall never forget the driver's face when he first saw us. Convinced that this was an enemy attack he ducked down out of sight. 'Clot,' said Villiers, and we howled with laughter. I expect the driver saw the funny side later on, and he ended up actually waving to us as we flew round and round the train. Oh happy days, this was one flight we were sorry to be back from!

If our tensions had been relaxed by this interlude, they were to be rudely tightened again the following day when we were called to an ops briefing in the late morning. The red line on the map seemed to go on and on, finally ending at Berlin, commonly called the 'Big City'. This was to be a maximum effort, and strenuous attempts were made to get our twelve aircraft serviceable for take-off. All the crew members were naturally very excited at the prospect, but there were mixed feelings about it. It was a long trip over Germany, and we expected to receive a very hostile reception on arrival; on the other hand, though, we were going to Berlin – which was the target that everyone was keen to visit at least once. In the event, all the aircraft were OK and we clambered aboard. On taxiing out, we were about halfway round when the undercarriage warning lights suddenly went red, indicating a strong possibility that it was about to collapse. Not wishing to be on board when the aircraft dropped on to our load of incendiaries, we all made an extremely hasty exit and put plenty of distance between ourselves and the aircraft. Both Villiers and I had slammed the magneto switches off, and so the aircraft stood in the middle of the perimeter track while we waited and watched, but nothing happened. It turned out to be an instrument fault, yet we couldn't take a chance on it and had to abandon the flight. Even if we could have taken off, we would have been too late for our timing, and so with great chagrin we disconsolately trooped back to the crew room.

Six of the remaining eleven aircraft reached the target, but the other five returned early owing to weather conditions, and these five plus ourselves were detailed to try again the next night. As 'V' Victory was out of action, we flew in another Lancaster, W4373, and owing to the lengthy flight we climbed en route. The outward journey was uneventful and we reached Berlin after about four and a half hours. My main memory of the raid was the clear view of the snow-covered ground in the moonlight, and over the target the streets could be seen without difficulty. In comparison with Happy Valley, the opposition was very light, although of course Berlin was a big place to defend and would have required an enormous number of guns to achieve any concentration. The weather clamped down on the homeward leg and unfortunately we strayed slightly off course, which took us into the vicinity of Kiel, a great mistake as we soon found out. A colossal bombardment suddenly erupted and buffeted us all over the sky, leaving us most fortunate in not actually being hit. A near miss, though, put us into a dive that Villiers could not control, and with the airspeed at over 300mph he called on me to assist him. Together we pulled back on the control column, and after an eternity the Lanc gradually levelled out. The effect of this dive had taken us clear of Kiel, but we were severely shaken and far from happy after what had been a very close shave. If the flak had been a few feet nearer to us we would have been candidates for the Roll of Honour! How ironic it would have been, surviving the target and then being shot down over some other place.

Having luckily cheated the Grim Reaper, our first consideration was to get our bearings and head for home again. The navigator got us sorted out, but before we got very far a radio message was received diverting us to Grimsby as the weather over Wickenby had closed in. The airfield at Waltham, Grimsby, was the home of No. 101 Squadron who were also in No. 1 Group, and here we landed in the early hours of the morning after another eventful operation, which had taken eight and a half hours. In spite of the relatively light opposition, the official report on the sortie showed that of the 187 aircraft that took part, as many as 22 of them were shot down. The staff at Waltham must have been hurriedly called on duty, but they had a meal ready for us, and after being debriefed we settled down to snatch what sleep we could in the mess armchairs. It was a simple matter to fly back to Wickenby the following day, by which time the weather had cleared and we were then able to reflect that although it had taken us almost exactly three days to do it, we had been to Berlin and achieved our main ambition!

Leave, for operational aircrew, was granted every six weeks, and as our time was now due, off we went. The week at home helped to soothe our jangled nerves, but it seemed like no time at all before we were back at Wickenby and in action again, this time to Düsseldorf, a near neighbour of Essen in Happy Valley. 'V' Victory was now fit for use after disgracing itself on the perimeter track, and we took off on 27 January carrying a 4,000lb cookie and incendiaries. Little can be said about this trip, except that we bombed at 20,000ft and had to face the usual defences over the target. The time taken was four hours, and we covered about 1,000 track miles.

As a change from our low-level frolics, the powers that be ordained that we should now practise high-level formation flying, which was the object of our next flip on 29 January. We spent two hours at this, and although the exercise was moderately successful, it was not repeated while I was at Wickenby. At this stage of the war it would have been suicidal to attempt to operate on this basis in daylight, but in later years when France had been liberated and the German airfields overrun, daylight operations of this kind became quite normal. With this trip we had survived another month, and a further forty-two flying hours were signed for by the flight commander.

February opened with an air test on the 1st in ED522, but the real business continued on the 4th when we did our seventh operation. Filing into the briefing room, we found another extended red line on the map, but this time it went south to Turin. Some indication had been given to us that this would be a long trip as a buzz had gone around that all the fuel tanks were being filled to capacity, but our thoughts had all been on Berlin. We did not complain too much, however, as it was known that the Italian defences were relatively light. In fact, our main opposition was likely to be from night fighters, especially as it was a moonlit sky. After a somewhat lengthy briefing we had our meal and were eventually airborne at 17.35 hours, this time in W4836, 'V' Victory being out of action for an unspecified reason. Climbing on course, it was quite an uneventful trip for a change, with no sign of the dreaded fighters. We could not afford to relax our vigil on the long haul over France, though, and I must have spent ninety-nine per cent of my time looking out, with an occasional break to check the gauges and make up my log.

The sky at night had a marvellous beauty at times, and this was no exception, with all the colours of the spectrum appearing in succession. Even the ground had its fascination with the moonlight glinting on it. The Alps were crossed at 21,000ft and even though we were way above Mont Blanc, we appeared to be scraping the top. From above, even the Alps lose, perhaps, some of their dignity. This was marvellous stuff; only a week or so before I had enjoyed flying at ground level, and now here I was enjoying the heights! It was a novelty, of course, but each time I flew in this area I was always enthralled with the view, and I had to concede that operations had their compensations.

As had been anticipated, the defences at Turin were very light and badly coordinated, so we were able to bomb with ease. Over the target the scene was spectacular, with coloured tracer shells bursting at intervals and green and red marker flares being dropped. Fires were now burning on the ground, and all this was being reflected on the snow-covered Alps; on our homeward journey we could see these fires burning seventy-five miles behind us. Some 198 aircraft took part in this raid, and if any had been brought down they had been extremely unlucky. We eventually landed at Wickenby after eight hours and ten minutes.

A few days later, we were off in 'V' Victory for an air test, but it was still several days before we flew again on operations, mainly due to weather conditions. The date of 13 February found us heading for the target of the U-boat pens at Lorient on the French Atlantic coast. Back in 'V' Victory again, we had a straightforward journey and met little resistance over the objective as the defences had been overwhelmed by the weight of the attack. We carried 5 x 1,000lb bombs, plus incendiaries, and altogether over 1,000 tons were dropped. The trip took us five hours, and we were back in bed by midnight.

In addition to the bomb load, we also carried propaganda leaflets on most of our sorties. These were usually stowed in the bomb bay and would be released when the bomb doors were opened prior to bombing. The significance of this will be seen when the story of our next operation is told. The leaflets were usually kept in the briefing room as a security measure, and we were unofficially allowed to take a sample for a souvenir. An illustration of one of these has been appended to this narrative, and it will be understood that they were not the ones that were actually dropped, although we generally took them with us on the raid to give them some sort of authenticity.

To help set the operational scene, one or two other items of interest should be mentioned before I proceed further with the tale of my tour. The briefing hut at Wickenby was a large wooden building, and we sat in rows according to each crew. Around the walls of the building were various posters exhorting us to maintain secrecy between briefing and flying, and how to avoid an enemy fighter attack, etc. It would be pointless for me to describe the actual briefing procedure, as this has been written about many times, but it is appropriate to comment on one or two points of detail. We were told our actual take-off and bombing times, the importance of which was that we went out in two or three waves and had to preserve concentration. In this context the target marking details were also divulged, these usually being green area-marking flares, with red flares showing the point of aim. The Met man was listened to with scepticism, but sometimes he was nearly right! Especially important was to ensure that we understood the position regarding the cloud and icing levels. The final act of the briefing was to synchronise watches. After this (or sometimes beforehand according to the time available), a separate briefing was given to pilots and navigators to finalise the route and timing.

We aircrew were always well favoured with the pre-operational meal, and also with the one when we got back (if we got back). Usually bacon and eggs or liver were served, and in those times they were all regarded as luxuries. On the question of flying kit, this can best be described as a mixture. The gunners, rear and mid-upper, usually wore everything they could as although they had electrically heated suits, these could not be relied upon. The rest of us wore battledress as we were in the generally heated compartment. I normally wore the special silk underclothing and a roll-neck sweater (obtained via the American comforts scheme!), and sometimes some silk gloves. We all wore flying boots. It was imperative for those who wore collars and ties to loosen them as they would have proved troublesome in the event of having to ditch.

There were two inside pockets in the battledress top, and these had been designed to take two packs that we were issued with prior to ops. One was a first-aid kit and the other contained currency of the countries over which we were to fly. Needless to say, these were for use if we had to make an enforced landing, but if we got back in one piece they had to be handed back in. In addition to these very useful articles, we also had various escape aids that were issued by the Intelligence Department. I had a pipe with a carefully concealed compass inside, and also a tobacco pouch to complement it. Inside the lining of the pouch was a silk map of Germany and the Low Countries. This map would have been of great value had I been on the run, but fortunately I did not have to use it. One other very useful gadget was a magnetised button with a faint mark on it; it was actually a primitive compass that would point to north when balanced on a pinhead. To sustain us on our journeys to the enemy lands, we had Horlicks tablets and tins of orange juice and, to keep us awake, flasks of coffee and caffeine tablets. The coffee was usually hoarded until we left the target, whereupon it was consumed with relish.

The weather was the outstanding arbiter of operational progress, and in a county like Lincolnshire with its frequent sea mists and ground fog, it is a wonder that we flew as often as we did. Reconnaissance flights were mounted that gave us information about the weather on the Continent, but with shifting clouds the pattern could change remarkably quickly and operations were on or off at the drop of a hat. Most annoying were the occasions where the trip was scrubbed after we were actually in the aircraft, but they could be cancelled at any time, and frequently were. One amazing statistic is that I was briefed to go to Wilhelmshaven on no fewer than four different nights, but never actually got there at all!

Aircraft serviceability was another bugbear, and many was the time that we found something wrong at the last minute. It could be a gauge, an electrical fault, a magneto drop, or one of plenty of other things; how it could happen to an aircraft that was serviceable in the morning was sometimes hard to understand. On one occasion when we could not get an engine to respond, the oil cooler had to be changed, and I took my coat off to help the ground crew. This was completely in accordance with article four of the 'charter', but I wasn't thinking of rules and regulations – only of the forthcoming trip. In practice, a minor fault was overlooked, but where a spare aircraft was not available, crews were known to take off with more serious things wrong so as not to miss the fun.

The weather also caused us lots of problems; I remember times when we came back from trips when even the birds were walking – we just got diverted to clearer places to land. Once airborne we had to follow our briefed instructions or we were likely to get into serious trouble. The air-craft captain, though, had the prerogative to turn back if the untoward occurred, and this happened to us on more than one occasion. One or two pilots became notorious for aborting operations, and one was charged with LMF (Lack of Moral Fibre). Whatever happened to him I do not know, but he would have received short shift from Hughie Edwards! In my description of the various raids, I have blandly said 'We reached our target', but sometimes it was a navigational nightmare to achieve this. Hardly any track went straight there as it was necessary to avoid pitfalls such as flak concentrations and enemy airfields. The Jerries were very adept in building realistic decoy towns, complete with pyrotechnics to simulate a raid in progress, and many is the bomb load that was dropped on one of these. Last, but not least, was our attempt to fool the enemy by flying in a false direction and only turning towards the real target at the last moment. Timing was not always easy if, for example, we had a following wind after the Met had forecast a headwind, or vice versa. If we were late, we either had to increase the speed or cut a corner, and if we were early it often meant flying dog-legs to use up time.

After this dissertation, I will resume the operational programme and recall that the last sortie carried out was to Lorient on 13 February. On the very next night it was back to the grind again with another long raid, this time to Milan. The bomb load had been restricted to one 2,000lb bomb and incendiaries to allow us to accommodate the fuel load. We taxied out in light snow, a forecast of what was to follow, and took off at 18.45 hours. On the outward journey we flew in and out of cloud, being careful to keep below the icing level, but on approaching the Alps we were forced to climb up through the overcast. We were soon caught in upcurrents and suffered severe buffeting. The engines also started to be troublesome when the carburettor intakes iced up. To avert this problem, a hot-air supply to the carbs was fitted, the control handle being situated on the port side of the cockpit near the pilot. Villiers now went to operate this system, and in doing so managed to open the bomb doors by pulling the wrong lever! In itself, this was of no real consequence as it only required a slight change of trim to compensate, but unfortunately the leaflets that we were carrying were now scattered far and wide. Villiers soon closed the doors again and switched on the hot air. At this, the engines started to behave as we proceeded on our way. It was only afterwards that navigator Bill expressed the view that the leaflet raid had taken place over Switzerland as we had been blown off course.

The weather cleared approaching Milan, and looking down through my window blister I could quite clearly see the town square, which was our point of aim. As before, the defences were sparse, but we had a clear sight of an Italian fighter as it shot past overhead. On the ground many fires had started, to provide us with the same colourful spectacular that we had seen at Turin. The return flight was rather uncomfortable as the weather had deteriorated, but the experience of Villiers brought us safely back to Wickenby again. In the relaxed atmosphere after we had landed, Villiers admitted to being a clot in operating the wrong control, but we magnanimously said that we would overlook it! Nevertheless, we were pleased that he was now even with us, and he was never as pompous again. By this time, the crew was used to each other's ways and were working together as a very good team. Villiers now listened more and more to my opinion and advice, but one could never exactly fathom him out, and it was only years later over a drink in the mess at Scampton that I could talk to him man to man for the first time.

Statistics on the Milan raid show that 142 aircraft took part, of which only 2 were shot down. Our time for the trip was, at eight and a half hours, the longest yet. Our tenth operation was to Lorient again on 16 February, the raid being a carbon copy of the previous one three days earlier, except that we were in a different aircraft, W4855, as 'V' Victory was again out of action. After this, we had a few days 'messing about' in different aircraft, starting with a short air test on the 18th in 'V' Victory. We didn't know it at the time, but the Milan raid was the last one we were to fly in it, and after this air test it went into the hangar for a lengthy over-haul. On the 19th I flew with Wing Commander Wood on a local stooge in yet another Lanc, ED357. I imagine Woody just wanted to keep his hand in but, whatever the reason, it was fortuitous that I was with him, because I am sure that it was on this trip that I was 'noticed' and there-after he always had a word for me when our paths crossed.

On any operational station there were frequent losses of crews and aircraft, and many instances of planes sustaining damage or crashing on return from operational duty. Consequently there was always a constant flow of new machines coming in as replacements. Wickenby was no exception to this sad routine, and when W4794 'V' Victory was taken out of commission, Villiers was very quick to latch on to one of these new kites, ED548, which was subsequently also christened 'V' Victory in his honour! We first had it airborne on 20 February for a lengthy air test lasting one and a half hours, but it needed some adjustments afterwards, so when we were back on operations the following night, it was in ED522, an aircraft that we had flown in once before.

The target in this case was Bremen in northern Germany, and it was one of the most traumatic trips that I flew on. The weather was the first villain of the piece, with thick cloud for most of the way. Navigation was very difficult as our only 'electronic aid', the 'Gee' box, packed up before we had gone very far, and thereafter dead-reckoning was the only method left. Bill did us proud, however, and we reached Bremen spot on time to bomb on the markers, which had been dropped into the clouds as the ground below was not visible. In spite of the conditions we spotted at least three night fighters on the way, which Freddie identified as Junkers Ju 88s. Over the target itself the opposition was deadly, but although the amount of flak was not as great as at Essen, it was extremely accurate and we were hit in one engine, which fortunately was not put out of action. Heartfelt cheers went up when we turned for home, but we still had to battle against the elements for the whole journey. Wickenby, by this time, was closed down and we were diverted to RAF Rufforth near York where we landed at midnight, completely exhausted. As at Waltham, we were received gracefully but had to endure the mess armchairs in lieu of beds. It was late on the following afternoon that we arrived back at Wickenby after what seemed like an eternity.

The MAN engineering works at Nuremberg was the target on the night of 25 February when we took off for our first operation in ED548. This was a very symbolic place to raid in view of the Nazi rallies that had been held there, and we took along a 4,000lb cookie and incendiaries as a calling card. The most memorable incident of this raid took place not at the target, but on the way there, when Mac, the mid-upper gunner, lapsed into unconsciousness due to lack of oxygen. It was routine practice for Villiers to call up the crew members from time to time to check that all was well, and on one of these occasions he was greeted with silence when addressing Mac. Not knowing what was the matter with him, or how long he had been out of action, it became an urgent matter to get him out of the turret, and I immediately clipped on an emergency oxygen bottle and set off down the fuselage to sort him out. The mid-upper turret was bad enough to squeeze in or out of when one was active, but it was ten times worse to drag someone out who could not assist in the process. It was thus some time before I switched on the intercom to tell Villiers that I had managed to extricate him and had got him as far as the rest bed. It was on the way to the rest bed that I discovered what the problem was: condensation had frozen solid in the pipe leading to his mask, cutting off his oxygen supply. It was a simple matter to clear this, and I soon had him coupled up again. After a while he recovered, and was eventually able to retake his place in the turret. The rest of the trip passed off without further incident, except for the usual reception over the target, and we made it back to Wickenby after being airborne for seven hours.

The last raid of the month took place on the 28th, to bomb the U-boat facilities at Saint-Nazaire, not far from Lorient. Here, we had a fairly easy passage with only moderate flak to contend with as we dropped our usual load from the lower height of 10,500ft. We had the chance to return at a very smart pace, and when we arrived at Wickenby in under five hours, we were the first aircraft back out of the whole No. 1 Group. Altogether 437 aircraft took part, so Saint-Nazaire suffered a fair pasting.

It was at this juncture that Squadron Leader Bell was screened after finishing his tour, and Villiers was promoted to squadron leader to take his place as flight commander. At the same time, because our six weeks were up, we all went on leave. As I have mentioned before, these periods were important to our morale and we usually came back raring to go, although I always felt apprehensive when nearing Wickenby! All flying personnel suffered agonies most of the time when contemplating their future prospects, and I was no exception. Each time I went home I was convinced it would be the last, and the best I could do was to adopt a philosophical attitude in hoping that I might be one of the lucky ones. It was very hard to convince myself, however, when I got back to camp to see rows of empty beds, and to hear the always depressing news of happenings in my absence. In this tense situation the atmosphere was very different to a training camp, and the term 'esprit de corps' had a very real meaning. Although there were a few exceptions, one could expect help and comradeship from most quarters, and it was this spirit that made life somewhat more bearable.

There was not much entertainment available on the station apart from the odd concert party, and so we either had to stay in the mess or go outside the camp to amuse ourselves. The nearest pubs were the White Hart at Lissington, a small village about a mile distant, or slightly further away at Wragby where there were also a few shops and a post office.

Lincoln was within striking distance, and a station wagon was laid on each evening to ensure that everyone got back to camp. Most of the amenities appropriate to a small city were available in Lincoln, and they included cinemas, pubs, a theatre, dances and a swimming baths. I attended most of the pubs, including the Saracen's Head (really a hotel), which was the centre for aircrew gatherings, and at which the barmaids knew more statistics about our operations than we knew ourselves. If one wanted to know where the lads had flown off to that night, the Saracen's Head was the place to find out – so much for the secrecy of our briefings! I went to some of the dances, but they weren't very inspiring, the best one being held at the Assembly Rooms on Saturday nights. These were difficult to attend, however, owing to problems with transport.

The average crew at Wickenby was not there for very long, even for the few who completed their tours. During my time this might amount to about six months, and very rarely eight or nine, so that no sooner had one got used to the area, then one was off to pastures new. In the summer months I cycled about in the vicinity of the camp, but as I had left my own bike at home, this was done on a borrowed one. A fair proportion of our spare time was spent in the living quarters as at times we were on call and had to be in the right place in case we were needed. In our hut we had an ancient gramophone and a pile of even more ancient records. To improve the quality of life, some of us occasionally bought new ones, and one of mine, 'The Story of a Starry Night' was judged very appropriate to our nocturnal activities and became a sort of talisman, played just before we sallied forth on operations. We also had a resident artist who painted very pleasing examples of ladies' faces (only the faces!), and he gave all of us copies of these on different coloured pieces of cartridge paper. Again these were regarded as lucky, and were pinned up all around the hut to brighten the drab surroundings.

When Villiers became 'B' Flight commander, his added responsibilities forced a slowing down of our operational progress during the month of March, but we basked in the reflected glory of his new status, and we also benefited from other privileges that went with his rank. He now had his own room into which we had automatic entry, enabling us to avoid hanging around the draughty crew room. Likewise, he was now able to call on personalised transport to ride out to dispersal, and we had the use of this as well, or as many of us who could get aboard! As he was now one of the ruling faction, he had advanced information regarding the operational targets each day, and he usually put us in the know if we were to be involved, although he would never speak except out at dispersal as walls had ears. I remember him once mouthing the words 'ice cream', intimating that we were off to Italy that night. He was responsible for detailing which crews were to fly on operations, and in this capacity he was able to decide when he wanted to fly himself. In fairness to him, it must be stated that he never used his position to dodge the worst targets, as will be evident from a perusal of the ones he did embark on, but he was probably instrumental in ensuring us longer rest periods between them. Signing the logbooks each month was another of his chores, and I collected his signature for the month of February, adding a further forty-nine hours to the total. On every occasion that an aircraft flew, the captain had to sign the authorisation book in the flight office. This book was under the control of the flight commander and had in it brief details of the flights to be undertaken, together with the names of each crew. Villiers now had to maintain this and ensure that the regulation was complied with; probably one of the most niggling tasks he had.

The next operation that I flew on had a most unusual flavour. It was decided, probably in honour of Villiers's promotion, that the aircraft would be manned only by officers instead of the normal crew. He was stymied in my case, though, as there was no such animal as a commissioned flight engineer at Wickenby in those days, so I received an honorary promotion for the night! The bombing leader and the gunnery leader replaced Freddie and George respectively. I recall that there was a preliminary to this flight as well. During our absence on leave, our new aircraft, ED548, had been flown by another crew and the starboard inner engine had developed a vibration. Adjustments had to be made and we had to try it out on an air test, but found that the fault had still not been cured. At this, the ground crew removed the propeller and discovered that one blade had not been meshed properly to the constant speeding mechanism. When this had been put right a further air test was needed and, Villiers not being available, I went up with a spare pilot, Flight Lieutenant Noden, DFM.

All now being well, the super crew took off at 19.45 hours for what was to be the quickest operation that I ever made. The target was Essen and the date 12 March. On arrival we found that the defences had not changed, although in addition to the usual flak there seemed to be more searchlight activity, and we saw one or two poor unfortunates coned in their beams. Experience of this sort of reception did not make us less fearful, and there was nothing we could do other than close our eyes and plunge into it. Having weathered the storm and dropped our bombs accurately, Villiers, determined that his talented crew should not be taken prisoner, literally put his foot down and we were back at Wickenby after only three and a half hours. After leaving at a quarter to eight, we were home before midnight – just like an ordinary night out! My notes on this raid state that Essen was well defended but also left well burning. Unfortunately twenty-three aircraft were lost in the process.

It was at this time that on one of our periodic visits to the White Hart at Lissington, our attention became focused on the piano nameplate. The piano was not a Bechstein or a Blüthner, but it was nevertheless of German origin, and we decided forthwith that we must have this name-plate as a souvenir. It was unscrewed with the permission of the landlord, and ceremoniously borne back to Wickenby. Searching for a resting place for our prize, we hit on the idea of attaching it to ED548 and the ground crew duly obliged. As each operation was completed, a small yellow bomb was painted on the plate, and this carried on until we finished flying in the aircraft during April when it went in for a major inspection. We subsequently flew in various other Lancs until we settled down on a new permanent machine, but we were loath to lose track of our now highly decorated nameplate. It was thus unscrewed from ED548 and ceremoniously borne back to the White Hart, whereupon it was reunited with the piano and became the object of much attention from all who drank there. On our eventual departure from Wickenby, we gave it a final salute and, more in hope than expectation, I asked the landlord whether he would let me have it back as a permanent reminder of our sojourn in the wilds of Wickenby. He refused me on the grounds that it was now his best tourist attraction!

After the Essen raid with a difference, we had a ten-day break from operations but were engaged in some local flying. A fault had occurred on ED548 that necessitated an air test on 14 March. We were then up again in it on the 19th, on another test after a complaint that the plane was flying starboard wing low. This rang a bell in my memory and, bearing in mind our unorthodox methods at Penrhos, I virtually stood over the ground crew to make sure some adjustments were made to the ailerons.

On the 21st we were engaged in some local flying in W4791, an aircraft that we had last flown into Essen two months previously. It was then back to ED548 on the following day on the old theme of formation flying. Why couldn't the authorities make up their minds about operating in this style? After forty-five minutes in the air we were down again in time for lunch, and then off to a briefing as we were journeying to Saint-Nazaire again that night. Take-off was at 19.15 hours, and we had a straightforward run to the target although the weather conditions were again not too brilliant. For this operation we took only 7,000lb of incendiaries and bombed towards the end of the attack to ensure that they would drop on previously damaged buildings. Owing to the cloud-base being very low and the defences light, our bombing height was 8,000ft, which was the lowest we ever attacked at. Worsening weather dogged our return, and once more Wickenby was out of action so we were diverted again, this time to Abingdon near Oxford.

This little episode at Abingdon has remained in my memory, both for the pleasant reception accorded to us and for the difficulties we experienced. A flying training unit equipped with Airspeed Oxfords occupied the airfield which, while being big enough for this type of aircraft, was really much too small for Lancasters, and we had the greatest difficulty in landing. Having achieved the almost impossible we were carted off to be debriefed, and we were treated with the greatest courtesy both here and when we subsequently arrived at the mess to eat. This kind attention continued when we found that we were to sleep in beds! It transpired that they had one or two huts with vacant beds owing to several pupils having left the day before, and we gratefully tumbled in and were asleep by about 1.30am. Our troubles then started at six o'clock when we were awakened by the strident clamour of a bell coming over the tannoy; this clarion call being meant for the pupils and was definitely not appreciated by us operational types! We turned over and attempted to get back to sleep but the damage was done and very few of us got any more rest until our return to Wickenby. The aircraft were refuelled at daybreak, and eventually we arrived to fly them back, but were now faced with our greatest problem of all, getting airborne again. It had been bad enough landing, but taking off was an even greater hazard in view of the extremely small length of run. To solve the problem, a section of fencing was demolished at one side of the field and we taxied on to a nearby road to start taking off. Belting up to almost full power before moving, we hurtled forward over the perimeter track and just scraped over the hedge at the end of the run to become airborne when it had seemed most un-likely. I have it on good authority that only Villiers and I had our eyes open! Anyway, we were up, and lost no time in getting back to base having flown an elapsed time of five hours and ten minutes. I had now defied all the odds and flown on fifteen operations, the halfway mark. All I had to do now was achieve another fifteen but, if anything, they were to be even tougher than the first stint!

The second half started with a vengeance – Berlin again! The nights were now getting gradually shorter, and on 27 March take-off was at 20.30 hours. This turned out to be a normal sortie with the main threat coming from night fighters. We saw quite a number and were fortunate again in not being attacked. Over the target we met moderate flak and plenty of ineffective searchlights, which were a great help on the bombing run and, before we left, numerous large fires were blazing. Fatigue was one of the greatest difficulties on a long run such as this, and when one considers boredom and a feeling of airsickness through the continual motion of the aircraft flying through the corkscrewing pattern, it will be seen that we always arrived back at Wickenby with great relish. We touched down from this trip to the Big City after six hours and ten minutes, a consid-erably shorter time than the eight and a half hours of our previous visit, which I can mainly put down to a following wind on the return leg.

Two nights later, Berlin was again on the menu, but this was to be so utterly different from the previous one that any comparison would be ridiculous. We had been warned at briefing that the weather would be doubtful, with much cumulonimbus cloud likely, and just for once the Met Department was correct as we were into cloud almost from take-off. In this sort of situation one could fly in reasonable safety below the icing level, the main risk then being collision with fellow aircraft. Once above the crucial level, ice would form on the propellers and wings, changing the form of the aerofoil section to the extent that lift could not be maintained. Also affected would be the control surfaces and the control column, which would become impossible to move.

Two courses were open to the pilot. One was to proceed at the lower level in the hope that the cloud would disappear in time; the second was to try to get right above the clouds. Villiers opted for the second course, having tried the first one unsuccessfully, and sure enough we hit trouble when the aircraft started to wallow about. It did not help matters to see the ice forming through the cockpit windows, and things got so bad that he put the nose down to get us into warmer air again. In due course he made another attempt to reach our bombing height, but had to give up the uneven struggle after having to call on me to help move the controls. We were in such a state that we had to jettison the bomb load to give us a measure of safety, and Villiers painfully managed to turn for home, losing height at the same time. Ice from the propellers broke away to hit the fuselage, but eventually the wings cleared to give us intense relief; never were we more thankful to be spared 'the chop'! It was surprising that on this night of all nights, Wickenby should be clear for landing. The statistics for this raid are truly amazing. Out of 481 aircraft dispatched, all of which faced heavy rain, icing and thick cloud, only 3 bombed within three miles of the aiming point! I have no record of our losses that night, but would not be surprised to hear that they were considerable. For our part, we had again flown several hazardous hours that did not count, and we had ironically been on many full raids with much less danger.

Chapter Six

Wickenby – Part Two

At this halfway stage of my tour, the point has been reached where, having read about some of the varying experiences I faced, it will be of interest to hear something of the details and routines of Lancaster flying that lie behind the entries in my logbook. Some of these facts and figures were part of my role as the flight engineer, but the pilot was also inescapably involved in many things as, being the captain of the aircraft, his word was law.

I will start on the ground under the general heading of accidents. During my time at Wickenby very few aircraft actually crashed on the airfield, although there were several landing incidents. The reason for this was in part due to the availability of so many other airfields in the vicinity, so that if an aircraft was short of fuel, a landing could be made elsewhere if necessary. The same situation also applied to aircraft that had been damaged, and in this respect several airfields with long runways were set aside for emergency use (the most notable of these being Manston in Kent). In spite of these facilities, though, numerous crews did try to get their aircraft home, only to crash in the circuit while attempting to land. Wickenby was no exception to this and at least two accidents occurred for this reason. I saw one of these aircraft afterwards and it was completely burned out. Of the landing disasters, the worst one I remember happened to a Halifax that broke up on touchdown, fortunately with no loss of life. A few aircraft force-landed with their wheels up, which often meant ruined engines when the propellers hit the ground. In addition to these unavoidable 'prangs', there were others that could only be put down to pilot error, such as veering off the runway (which often meant the collapse of the undercarriage) or, amazingly, the retraction of the undercarriage while standing in dispersal!

Taxiing mishaps were few, but a heinous crime was to swerve off the perimeter track and get bogged down. This resulted in forced labour for the ground crew, and the pilot was always 'fined' a minimum of ten shillings to compensate them! I cannot remember a take-off accident while I was at Wickenby, apart from one occasion where a pilot swerved but was able to pull up before any harm was done. Another occurrence that merited a fine was to pick up a parachute from the ground by the ripcord instead of the carrying handle if one was not paying attention, and this had the embarrassing result of one having to gather up the opened parachute and take it to be repacked at a cost of at least 2s 6d.

Moving on to deal with the fuel and oil, the fuel used was always 100-octane petrol, which was coloured green for identification purposes and also to prevent theft. The aircraft had six tanks, all in the wings, which contained a total of 2,154 gallons. A cross-feed pipe was fitted that allowed the transfer of fuel from one side to the other if a tank had been damaged. On later aircraft from about 1944, nitrogen was supplied to the tanks as the petrol was used up, minimising the risk of explosion. All the tanks were self-sealing. Some 150 gallons of lubricating oil were carried, 37½ gallons to each engine. The oil consumption was one to two gallons per hour per engine, depending on its condition. An engine exceeding a usage of more than two gallons per hour needed changing.

Now to the actual flying procedure. Having done all the external and internal checks we were ready for take-off. The flaps would be set at twenty-five degrees if the aircraft were laden, or fifteen degrees if light. The engines would be progressively opened up by pushing the throttle levers forward while the pilot held the aircraft against the brakes. At about zero boost, the brakes would be released and the throttles opened fully, with the port side slightly ahead to counteract a tendency for the aircraft to swing. The pilot opened up the throttles, and in case his hand should slip, I had to follow up behind him. The tail would be raised as we charged down the runway with the engines straining away at the maximum power of 3,000rpm and +12lb boost, and making a fearful noise. (Engine development allowed an increase to +14lb boost during

1943 and +18lb in 1945.) Some indication of the power the engines produced can be imagined from the fact that forty gallons of petrol were used up on take-off alone. Take-off speed was 95–105mph and on the runway at Wickenby (other than the short north-east one), the air-craft would lift off without effort. As soon as we were airborne I was instructed to retract the undercarriage, and then to raise the flaps when at about 800ft. At 1,000ft the power was reduced to 2,850rpm and +9lb boost, and shortly after that to 2,650rpm with +4lb boost, staying at that while we were climbing. At 10,000ft it was necessary to put on our oxygen masks. During the climb I would be monitoring the gauges and filling in my log sheet. The rate of climb depended on the air conditions and the engine power, which in turn relied on the engine coolant tem-peratures, so a certain amount of juggling would take place with the con-trols. The normal speed in a climb was between 145 and 175mph. No doubt the word 'boost' is a mystery to most people, but it is quite a simple term that indicates the pressure in the inlet manifold in pounds per square inch above the normal atmospheric pressure. An automatic boost control would advance the throttle levers as we climbed up, but there would come a time at about 13,000ft when the supercharger ratio would have to be changed to a higher one (known as 'S' gear) to maintain the power.

If we were flying on operations we would probably be crossing the English coast by now, and the pilot would normally call out this piece of news, followed by an instruction to the gunners to take the safety catches off their guns. At this point one of them might ask permission to make a test firing of their weapon. Soon after this would come the time-honoured phrase, 'Enemy coast ahead', and we now had to keep a very sharp lookout as trouble could be expected at any time. Having reached our operations height of 20,000ft plus, the engine revs would be reduced to 2,550rpm and the throttles adjusted to give +3lb boost, this being the normal cruising power necessary to maintain altitude. The speed would be about 150mph, but might require some alteration on request from the navigator if his timings were out of step. We were constantly reminded that we flew in the best aircraft of its type in the world, and to reinforce this view we would usually see the other types down below us struggling along! To clarify the word 'see', this would only apply in moonlight, but on dark nights we could spot the pattern of exhaust flames and identify the aircraft by this method. The poor old Stirlings were usually the lowest, but I must admit that we did pass them occasionally at our own height. They had radial engines, and one noticed their exhaust rings glowing in the darkness; often was the time we could observe four red rings flying along and knew that we were actually looking at a Stirling. If we could see them, so could the Jerries, and I wondered why more of them were not shot down.

I have dwelt at length with conditions over the target, so we will now assume that we have closed the bomb doors and are 'getting the hell out of it'! The navigator would have been on the ball and would now be giving us the course to fly on the homeward leg. As I have mentioned before, this was usually flown on a gradual descent accompanied by much twisting and turning. Our speed would have increased to between 180 and 220mph and the engines set to 2,400rpm and +4lb boost. I would have to be alert in order to change the superchargers back to normal ratio at the appropriate time, but there would be no problem in remembering to take our oxygen masks off at 10,000ft. This would be to the accompaniment of three cheers from all and sundry!

Throughout the homeward journey I would be keeping my log and changing the fuel tanks at intervals, and of course not neglecting my other duty as spare lookout. Apart from the unwelcome sight of an occasional night fighter, there was always something of interest to see in the night sky. If there was a touch of moonlight or the glow of the setting sun, there would be scenes of great beauty to behold with the clouds lit up in fantastic patterns; on several occasions I saw the Northern Lights at play. A starlit night was very pleasant to contemplate, and sometimes useful to the navigator too if he required to take an astro-shot. There were other, more sinister things to be seen, an example of which were sudden flashes of fire on the ground, which more often than not signalled shot-down aircraft crashing. Sometimes flares would light up the sky, and as these usually heralded fighter activity, we had to redouble our vigilance to guard against sudden attacks. At times like these I was reminded of the huge notice in the crew room: 'Eternal vigilance is the price of safety'. We couldn't help reading it often enough, and there were a multitude of opportunities to practise it. On some raids marker flares were dropped by our pathfinders to indicate a turning point, but these were usually used on the outward leg only.

Having braved all that the enemy could throw at us (and having faced our own defences more than once!), we would proceed to our bases in a more relaxed frame of mind, helped on our way at intervals over England by radio beacons transmitting a call-sign in Morse code that we could identify. Shortly before reaching home we would don our oxygen masks again, this being the second most dangerous part of the trip as collisions could easily occur, and we had to be completely alert. On landing we were whisked away to be debriefed, via the locker room where our flying kit would be deposited. The aircraft captain did most of the talking on these occasions, but the rest of us had our say if there was anything of note to report. Later on when flight engineer leaders were in existence, the engineer would also report to him briefly and hand his log in. The flight engineer leader would subsequently work out his air miles per gallon ratio, and if it was unsatisfactory a later meeting with the captain would be held to try and improve matters in the future. Normally a figure of one air mile per gallon was acceptable and this rested on the engineer's powers of persuasion over the pilot if it was to be achieved. The crews' lives often depended on it; hundreds of aircraft crashed unnecessarily when a bit more attention might have been paid to fuel conservation.

The final item to mention is that the bombing photographs were displayed in the Intelligence Department on the following day, and were usually perused with great interest. Often they would be incomprehensible or spoilt, but many of them would show a hit near to the target. If a crew had achieved a direct hit it would be an occasion for celebration, and although no prizes were given, it would compensate for the terrible experience one had suffered. During my tour we were fortunate enough to score two bullseyes!

After the Berlin fiasco, Villiers again signed my logbook and this time I had the reduced total of twenty-one hours for the month of March. The first three days of April were taken up with the recurring theme of low-level practice flying, and whether we learned anything from it or not, there was no doubt that we enjoyed the thrills it brought. We were up for one hour on the 1st, and one and a half on the 2nd, all on individual local flying. On the 3rd we flew in formation, this being a short stint of thirty-five minutes.

That same evening we were involved in yet another seemingly endless saga – operations to Essen! There was a slight difference this time as we took with us a second pilot. It was the usual routine for a new squadron pilot to fly as 'second dickey' on their first operation, with the intention of gaining experience while not having to make critical decisions. As I remember it, this was the only time we took a 'spare bod' on operations, and it probably stemmed from Villiers's realisation that he ought to show willing in view of his exalted status. Our novice pilot, Sergeant Lawrence, sat in my seat most of the way, and it was a good job that I normally stood up anyway or else I should have felt a bit frustrated. He mainly acted as an observer, but changed seats with Villiers for a spell to get the feel of the Lanc when it was fully laden.

Of the raid itself, there is not too much to tell as it was practically a repetition of our other visits to this most unfriendly area, and we were there and back in less than four hours, not allowing for the usual life-time over Essen itself! Twenty-one aircraft were lost on this mission. We had apparently picked a winner in Sergeant Lawrence, who went on to complete his tour, during which he had a frightening experience when his aircraft turned completely over due to a flak explosion. Fortunately he managed to get back on an even keel and coaxed the badly damaged kite back to base, for which he was awarded the DFM. There was a sequel to this raid, which took place on the eve of my twenty-first birthday. Some time before taking off I had been issued with a new battledress top, and had not had time to sew on my aircrew brevet. As luck would have it, this omission was spotted at debriefing by none other than the station commander, Hughie Edwards, who proceeded to take me to task. I realised that technically I had committed a serious breach of regulations in flying on operations while being improperly dressed, and there was not a lot I could say in my defence when the CO launched into a diatribe about the Geneva Convention and all that. However, during the conversation it somehow came out that I was standing in front of him on my twenty-first birthday, at which he mellowed his tone and ended up by wishing me good luck! We were stood down from flying that day and had a crew celebration in the hostelry at Wragby, with Villiers manfully paying the largest contribution. That we must have made the most of

Above: 1938 RAF Halton. Ten times around the square.

RAF Halton, 27 January 1938. I am top left.
(All images are from Peter Baxter's collection unless indicated otherwise.)

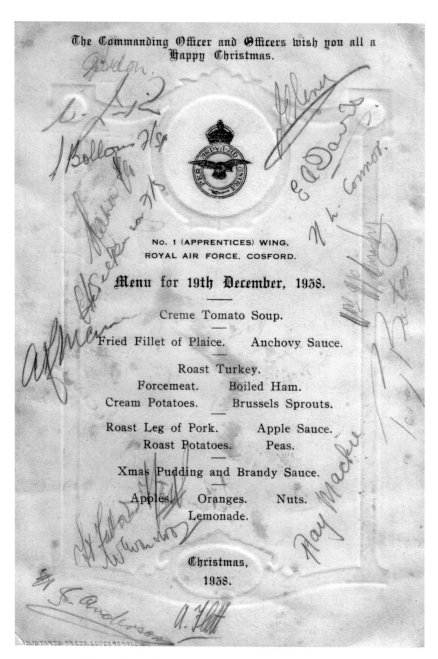

The Commanding Officer and Officers wish you all a Happy Christmas.

No. 1 (APPRENTICES) WING.
ROYAL AIR FORCE. COSFORD.

Menu for 19th December, 1938.

Creme Tomato Soup.

Fried Fillet of Plaice.   Anchovy Sauce.

Roast Turkey.
Forcemeat.   Boiled Ham.
Cream Potatoes.   Brussels Sprouts.

Roast Leg of Pork.   Apple Sauce.
Roast Potatoes.   Peas.

Xmas Pudding and Brandy Sauce.

Apples.   Oranges.   Nuts.
Lemonade.

Christmas,
1938.

Above and opposite page: Menu for my first RAF Christmas dinner.

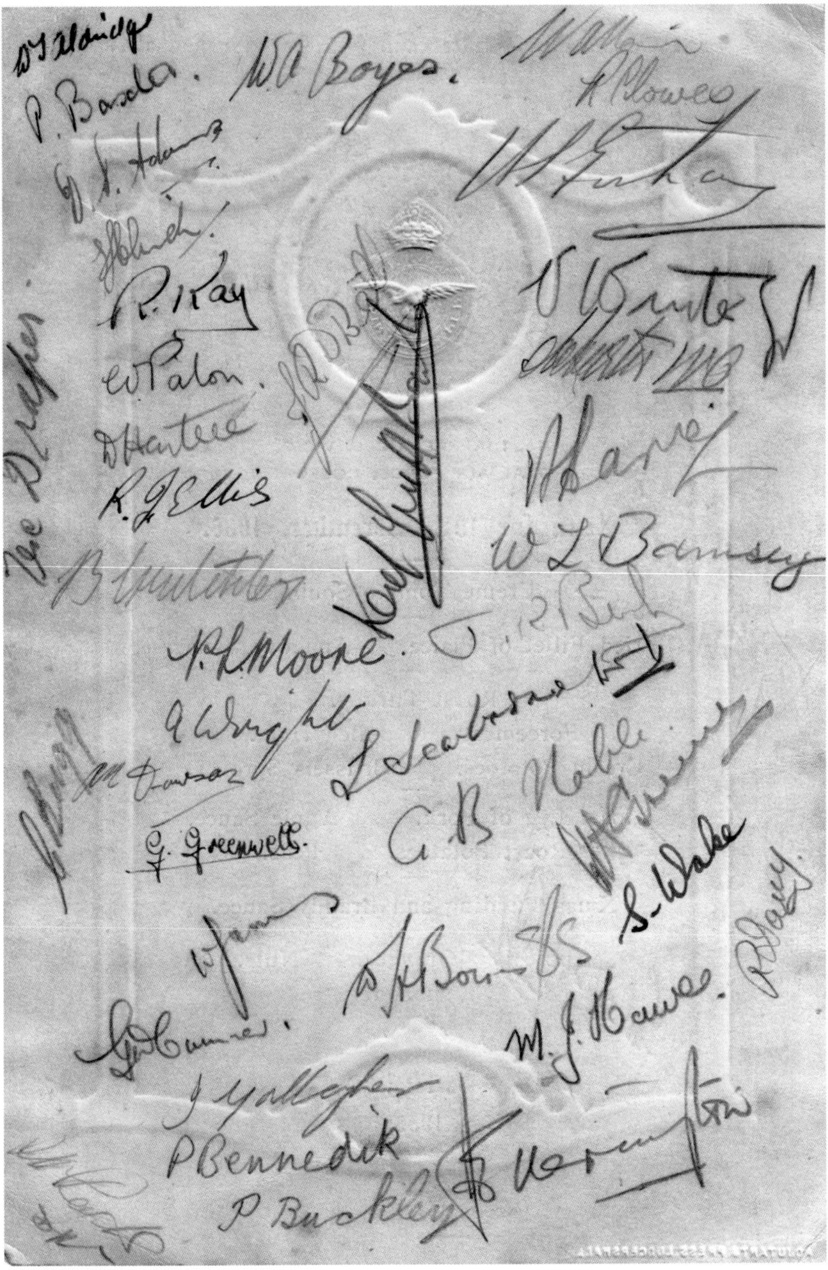

W.A. Boyes.
R. Kay
R. J. Ellis
P.L. Moore
G. Greenwell
C. B. Noble
S. Wake
P Bennedik
P Buckley

Cross country stalwarts at RAF Cosford! 'Tich' Flett, the hero of the 'Halton round the square' marathon, in the centre of the picture. I am to his left.

1939, RAF Cosford. I am second along on the middle row.

ROYAL AIR FORCE.

AIRCRAFT APPRENTICES. ANNUAL REPORT.

Unit... *Nº 1 (App) Wing.* Report for period ending... *Jan 1939.*

No.	Name.	Flight.	Squadron.	Entry.	Trade.
5/3244	Baxter. D		B.	Jan 1938.	Fitter II A.

EDUCATIONAL.

Mathematics ... *Fair. Room for improvement DCB.*

Science ... *Term's work very fair. Exam Result fair. Conduct needs improvement — a.*

Drawing ... *Good. Progress satisfactory DCB.*

General Studies *Excellent worker. Making good progress. OG.*

HR Wight
Education Officer.

TECHNICAL.

Basic Fitting :- above average. Airframe Fitting :- above average. Splicing :- average. Hulls & Floats average.

Very good progress, considering time lost through sickness

JA Brett F/o WSL50
Officer i/c Technical Training.

SQUADRON.

Discipline ... *Very Good.*   *Keen & Capable.*

P. T. and Drill ... *Average.*   *Lacking progress.*

Athletics ... *Plays Football & Rugby.*

Interested in most sport.

L. ___ F.o.
Officer Commanding Squadron.

REMARKS BY OFFICER COMMANDING.

a satisfactory start .   *Alwel 21/6 ch .*

Officer Commanding Unit.

(*2470) Wt. 27908—1700 250 pads 12/36 T.S. 667   *23/12/38 .*

My first report from RAF Cosford.

Our hut at RAF Penrhos, 1940.

Above left: Yours truly at RAF Penrhos in 1940. Above right: 'Passing-out Dinner' menu, RAF Cosford. I can still fit faces to the names!

Möge die deutsche
Nation nie vergessen,
daß die Härte eines Vol-
kes nicht dann erprobt
wird, wenn die Führung
sichtbare Erfolge aufzu-
weisen hat, sondern in
Stunden scheinbaren
Mißerfolge
A D O L F · H I T L E R

WOCHENSPRUCH DER NSDAP. / HERAUSGEBER REICHSPROPAGANDALEITUNG / FOLGE 24,
7.–13. JUNI 1943. ZENTRALVERLAG DER NSDAP. MÜNCHEN   51036

Above: At Criccieth in August, 1942.

Left: Splendid leaflet dropped in 1943 'somewhere in Germany'. A clever piece of propaganda which quotes back Hitler's own words describing the futility of claiming successes amidst obvious failures. It also bears an official imprint at the bottom, making it appear to have emanated in Germany.

The Lancaster. Only the best was good enough! PH-U, No. 12 Squadron from RAF Wickenby.

Date 1943	Hour	Aircraft Type and No.	Pilot	Duty	Remarks (including results of bombing, gunnery, exercises, etc.)	Flying Times Day	Night
					Time carried forward :—	25·30	6·25
Jan 2	11·25	LANCASTER W4794	Flt./Lt. Villiers	Engineer	LOCAL FORMATION FLYING	1·25	
Jan 3	16·35	LANCASTER N4794	Flt./Lt. Villiers	Engineer	OPERATIONS - MINING - LA ROCHELLE (SIX 1,500 LB. MINES)		6·45
Jan 4	14·00	LANCASTER W4794	Flt./Lt. Villiers	Engineer	HEIGHT TEST - (25,000 FT. TEMP - 35°C)	1·30	
Jan 8	18·05	LANCASTER W4794	Flt./Lt. Villiers	Engineer	OPERATIONS - MINING - NORTH OF FRISIAN ISLANDS (SIX 1,500 LB. MINES)		4·30
Jan 9	17·35	LANCASTER N4794	Flt./Lt. Villiers	Engineer	ESSEN OPERATIONS. GOT LOST AND HAD TO RETURN. JETTISONED 4000 LB. BOMB.		3·00
Jan 11	17·10	LANCASTER W4794	Flt/Lt. Villiers	Engineer	OPERATIONS - ESSEN - 1 4000 LB. BOMB P.I. ENGINE WENT U/S OVER TARGET.		4·50
Jan. 13	17·05	LANCASTER W4791	Flt./Lt. Villiers	Engineer	OPERATIONS - ESSEN - 21,000 FT. 1 4,000 LB. BOMB (H.E.) AND INCENDIARIES		4·05
Jan. 15	15·30	LANCASTER W4794	Flt./Lt. Villiers	Engineer	LOCAL LOW LEVEL FLYING	·50	
Jan 17	1640	LANCASTER W4373	Flt./Lt. Villiers	Engineer	OPERATIONS - BERLIN - 21,000 FT. RAN INTO HEAVY FLAK AT KIEL. LANDED AT GRIMSBY. 22 A/C Lost Down — (8) A/C Sent		8·30
Jan 18	15·15	LANCASTER W4373	Flt./Lt. Villiers	Engineer	RETURNED TO BASE FROM GRIMSBY	·35	
Jan 27	17·50	LANCASTER W4794	Flt./Lt. Villiers	Engineer	OPERATIONS - DUSSELDORF - 20,000 1 - 4,000 LB. BOMB. AND INCENDIARIES		4·15
					TOTAL TIME —	29·50	42·20

Logbook, RAF Wickenby, 2 January to 27 January 1943.

'V' Victory, ED584, at RAF Wickenby dispersal. Note flying bomb on side of cockpit, painted by Villiers. March 1943. I am 4th in back row.

Villiers and crew, March 1943. I am at top left. Left to right, top, are Sgt Baxter f/eng, Sgt Prowse r/g, P/O Dear w/op, Sgt Thomas b/aimer. Left to right, bottom, are S/Ldr Villiers pilot, F/O Allinson nav, P/O Saunders m/u/g.

March 1943, RAF Wickenby, Squadron Leader Villiers in ED458 'V'.

March 1943, RAF Wickenby, Squadron Leader Villiers.

FLIGHT ENGINEERS LOG (LANCASTER I)

Captain: S/LDR SLADE   Engineer: SGT BAXTER   30/97

Airframe No. and Letter: ED 993   Total Petrol: 1550 Galls.   Bomb Load: 8,510 lbs.   A.U.W. at T.O. 58,627. lbs.

Pressure Head Cover: OFF   Air Intakes: COLD   Supercharger: M   Auto Controls: OUT   Controls unlocked: YES   D.R. Compass: ON

Target: ESSEN   Track Miles: 932   Squadron No. 12   Date 27.5.43

To be filled in every 20 minutes and whenever flight or engine conditions are changed

Time	Height in Feet	Air Temp. °C	I.A.S.	Attitude C. or D.	R.P.M.	Boost lbs/in.²	Oil Press. lbs/in.² P.O.	P.I.	S.I.	S.O.	Oil Temp. °C P.O.	P.I.	S.I.	S.O.	Coolant Temp. °C P.O.	P.I.	S.I.	S.O.	Supercharger M or S	Air Intake H. or C.	Auto Controls	OXYGEN ON / OFF
2230	Take off	+13	120	C	3000	+12	79	79	81	84	64	63	62	65	120	109	111	115	M	C	OUT	ON 23-03
2231	500	+12	140	C	2850	+9	79	79	81	84	66	65	64	67	119	108	111	114	M	C	OUT	OFF 0215
2233	1,000	+11	160	C	2650	+4	78	78	79	81	67	66	66	68	113	103	106	109	M	C	OUT	
2305	10,500	-2	160	C	2650	+4	77	75	76	81	63	64	68	65	112	105	110	114	M	C	OUT	
2335	17,300	-18	160	C	2660	+4	77	76	77	85	58	64	66	62	117	108	109	114	S	C	IN	
0005	20,100	-23	160	C	2850	+6	77	76	77	83	56	62	64	56	116	107	107	114	S	C	OUT	
0015	21,200	-25	160	L	2550	+3	77	75	77	81	55	60	62	53	110	104	105	113	S	C	OUT	
0035	20,000	-23	160		2550	+3	77	77	77	81	53	58	58	55	113	104	105	110	S	C	OUT	
0105	IN TARGET AREA — BOMBS GONE																					
0105	18,000	-16	180	A	2600	+4	77	80	82	85	50	50	50	50	107	91	95	105	S	C	OUT	
0135	18,000	-15	180	D	2440	+4	80	84	85	87	47	57	46	47	105	95	95	101	S	C	OUT	
0205	11,500	+2	210	D	2200	+4	80	84	85	88	44	58	44	44	96	96	92	98	M	C	IN	
0235	6,100	+1	200	D	2300	+4	81	85	87	89	44	63	44	44	94	85	88	96	M	C	IN	
0315	LANDED BASE — ENGINES OFF																					

PETROL LOG (LANCASTER I)

Tank No.	Tank Capacity	Tank Contents	1	2	3	4	5	6	7	8	9	10	INSTRUCTIONS FOR USE
Time			2230	2331	2335	0035	0135	0235					1. The fuel state is to be recorded in the numbered columns hourly and whenever a tank is turned ON or OFF.
Port 1 (Inner)	580	400	400	320	380								2. A diagonal line is drawn when a tank is turned "ON".
(Centre) 2	383	350	350			170·1	120·1	120·1					3. A reverse diagonal line is added to form a cross when the tank is empty.
(Outer) 3	114	25	25	25	25	25	25	25					4. The calculated tank contents are recorded above the diagonal when each check is made.
St'bd. 1 (Inner)	580	400	400	380	380								
(Centre) 2	383	350	350			170·1	120·1	120·1					
(Outer) 3	114	25	25	25	25	25	25	25					
Bomb Bay Tank(s)	—	—											
Fuselage Tank(s)	—	—											CALCULATIONS
Fuel left	2154	1550		1670	1278		834·2	242					
Fuel used				40	272	—	758	1258					
T.A.S.			TAKE	148		—	257	257					
Galls./Hour			OFF	232	234	—	246	234					
A.M.P.G.				·76		—	1·1	1·2					
Actual fuel used (To be obtained from Form 700 refuelling state.)													
Actual fuel left													
Position of Fuselage Cross Feed Cock			OFF	OFF	OFF	OFF	OFF	OFF					Checked by

Squadron Engineer Officer

G 5,000 D/I 7/00 1/43 P R P

Above: Flight log of my trip to Essen! 27 May 1943.

Right: June, 1943, RAF Wickenby, Squadron Leader Slade and crew. I am front right

Date	Hour	Aircraft Type and No.	Pilot	Duty	Remarks (including results of bombing, gunnery, exercises, etc.)	Flying Times Day	Flying Times Night
					Time carried forward :-	90.00	195.45
28.1.45	1940	LANCASTER PD 378	F/O SEARLE	ENGINEER	OPERATIONS - STUTTGART (ZUFFENHAUSEN) 12 × 1000 LB H.E. 12 × 500 LB H.E. MARSHALLING YARDS BRILLIANT MOONLIGHT. AND THE ENGINE PRODUCTION FACTORY		7.20
19.3.45	1245	LANCASTER ME 544	S/LDR RIPPINGALE	ENGINEER	TO ELSHAM WOLDS AND RETURN	1.00	
23.3.45	1520	LANCASTER RF 205	F/O TOBIN	ENGINEER	ACCEPTANCE TEST	1.00	
27.3.45	1430	LANCASTER LM 754	S/LDR RIPPINGALE	ENGINEER	OPERATIONS - PADERBORN 1 × 4000 LB H.E. 10 × 80 × 4 INCENDIARIES 2 × 60 × 4 INCENDIARIES RETURN ON THREE ENGINES	5.15	
8.4.45	1145	LANCASTER NX 573	S/LDR GEE	ENGINEER	SUPPLY DROPPING PRACTICE	.30	
16.4.45	1340	LANCASTER PA 313	F/O TOBIN	ENGINEER	LOW LEVEL CROSS COUNTRY	1.45	
23.4.45	1625	LANCASTER NG 218	W/CDR RODNEY	ENGINEER	LOCAL FLYING	.45	
24.4.45	1650	LANCASTER NG 500	F/LT LEGG	ENGINEER	SUPPLY CARRYING - 5000 LBS. FOOD	.15	
30.4.45	1525	LANCASTER RA 545	W/CDR RODNEY	ENGINEER	FOOD SUPPLY DROPPING THE HAGUE (HOLLAND)	3.05	
4.5.45	1255	LANCASTER ME 544	F/LT RAMSDEN	ENGINEER	FOOD SUPPLY DROPPING OPERATIONS ROTTERDAM (HOLLAND)	3.05	
					TOTAL TIME ...	106.40	203.05

Logbook, RAF Scampton, 28 January to 4 May 1945.

Before my last operational flight 27th March 1945 to Paderborn. 'Smoky Joe' can just be discerned, painted on the side of the engine. I am in the centre.

BOMBER COMMAND FLIGHT ENGINEER LOG.

'A' TO BE COMPLETED BEFORE FLIGHT :-

CAPTAIN :- W/C VILLIERS	F/ENGINEER :- F/LT BAXTER	BOMB LOAD :- NIL *!!!!* lbs.	TOTAL FUEL :- *1986* gls.	A.U.W. :- *56,700* lbs.
DATE :- 25-5-45	AIRCRAFT TYPE :- LANCASTER	Mk. *1*	AIRCRAFT Nº :- PA 168	LETTER :- G

'B' CHECK BEFORE FLIGHT :-

ITEM	INITIALS	ITEM	INITIALS
PITOT HEAD COVER OFF	OK	ESCAPE HATCHES SECURE	OK
STATIC VENT PLUGS OUT	OK	CONTROLS UNLOCKED	OK
NITROGEN SYSTEM ON	NIL	AUTO-CONTROLS (CLUTCHES IN)	OK
SUPERCHARGER 'M' GEAR	OK	D.R. COMPASS ON	OK
AIR INTAKES (COLD)	OK	GILL OR RAD. POSITION OPEN OR CLOSED	CLOSED
BRAKE PRESSURE BEFORE 'CHOCKS AWAY'	200 Lbs/□"	BRAKE PRESSURE AFTER LANDING	Lbs/□"

'C' TO BE COMPLETED AFTER FLIGHT :-

TIME TO NEAREST MINUTE OF :-

START UP	Hrs.	SWITCH OFF	Hrs.	TOTAL RUNNING TIME	Hrs.
TAKE-OFF 1125	Hrs.	TOUCH DOWN 1814	Hrs.	TIME AIRBORNE 6.49	Hrs.
SET COURSE	Hrs.	OVER BASE	Hrs.	TIME ON COURSE	Hrs.

TARGET :- GERMANY IN GENERAL   SQUADRON :- 153 (SCAMPTON)

'D' FUEL ANALYSIS :-

ITEM	FUEL USED	FUEL LEFT	AIR MILES	TRACK MILES	A.M.P.G.	T.M.P.G.	G.P.H.
F/ENGINEER	Gls.	Gls.					
F/ENGINEER LDR	Gls.	Gls.					

'E' REMARKS :- BY F/ENGINEER.   **REMARKS :- BY F/ENGINEER LDR.**

LOG CHECKED :- _____

_____ F/ENGINEER   F/ENGINEER LDR.

OFFICERS' MESS
ROYAL AIR FORCE, HEMSWELL, LINCS

MAY 1944 .44.

MESS ACCOUNT FOR
NAME F/Lt Baxter P

	£	s.	d.
Balance Brought Forward Last a/c		1	3	
Messing				
Bar Coupons				
No. 480 June 3rd 1944		2	1	
Received from F/Lt Baxter P.				
the sum of three pounds				
four shillings seven pence				
...in full.		6	
£ 3 : 4 : 7		7	
TOTAL	3	4	7
Less Credit ... £ : :			
GRAND TOTAL			

MESS BILLS MUST BE PAID IN FULL
Accounts to be paid by 10th of each month
Cheques to be crossed and made payable to P.M.C. Officers' Mess, R.A.F. Hemswell
MESS SECRETARY.   DATE

RECEIVED

Above: 25 May 1945, flight engineer log for Cooks Tour.

Left: Board, lodgings and laundry for a month –
£3.4.7d! Of course, a pound was worth a
pound then!

Krupps, Essen, photograph taken on 2 June 1945.

AOC's Parade at RAF Scampton, 2 July 1945. I am 4th along back row.

Above: Peter Baxter. Below: The pipe carried on operational flights, containing a compass in the event of coming down in enemy territory.

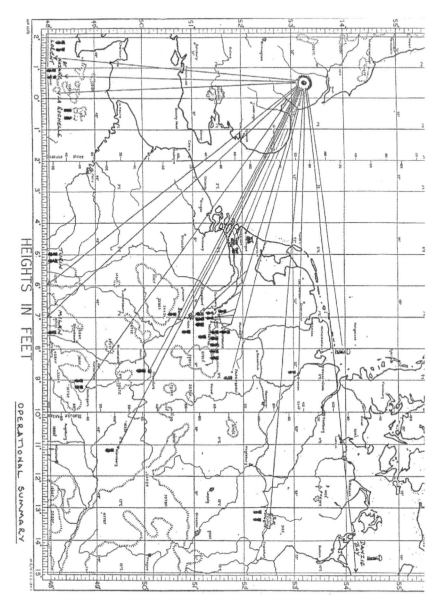

Raids from RAF Wickenby and RAF Scampton.

the birthday occasion is evident from the fact that we were also stood down on the following day, and did not fly again until the 6 April.

On the 6th we took part in a formation cross-country run, when we were joined by all the other squadrons in the group. This was a considerable flight of three hours and twenty minutes, which must have imposed quite a strain on the pilots. I carried my camera with me and took several shots, but the finished product left much to be desired. It was obviously a make or break exercise, and eventually the idea of No. 1 Group operating on this basis was squashed by Bomber Command and No. 5 Group were given the task instead. It needs only to be mentioned that 'Butch' Harris was the previous No. 5 Group Commander for the reason for this decision to be clear. They were given the job of flying all the numerous dare-devil raids that hit the headlines, such as the Dambusters, while we in No. 1 Group were left to soldier on with the bread and butter stuff!

For some time, Villiers had had an idea brewing in his mind that we should find out a bit more about the methods of anti-aircraft gunfire, with a view to employing spoiling tactics during our tours of Germany, and he arranged a visit by our crew to the Bunkers Hill gun site just out-side Lincoln. I enjoyed this visit, and saw the guns and rocket batteries for the first time. We were escorted round by an officer who explained the firing methods and how the aim was predicted, but whether Villiers actually picked up any new ideas is doubtful as we continued on with our normal routine. One feature of this visit that I will never forget was the amazement of the soldiers at our casual relationship. They could not get over seeing a squadron leader talking to a sergeant on a first-name basis, but when it was intimated that we were the elite and that they had missed their vocation, it fell on deaf ears. 'I wouldn't have your bloody job for all the tea in China', I was told!

More tours of Germany now followed, starting with Duisburg on 8 April. Duisburg lies in the Ruhr, some miles west of Essen, and to all intents and purposes it was like going to our favourite haunt. We had the usual bomb load of a 4,000lb cookie and incendiaries, and met the usual reception on arrival. I have a note to say that there was thick cloud en-route, which scattered the raid, and as on the previous trip to Essen there were twenty-one aircraft lost. After a break of a day or two we were then off to visit Frankfurt, right in the heart of Germany, but some distance short of Nuremberg. For the first time, we took off after midnight because of the weather. The raid had been on and off throughout the evening, and when it was cancelled for the umpteenth time we went to bed convinced that it had been scrubbed, but how wrong we were! There was an almighty panic to get us up and away on time when the raid was eventually officially on; this was only one instance of the numerous occasions when we had to fly off bleary-eyed and jittery – it was difficult enough to face the trip itself, without the added drawback of having had inadequate preparation. The weather was still bad and we flew most of the way in cloud or a little above it. Just like the Bremen raid we saw no sign of Frankfurt and had to bomb on the markers above the clouds, and as at Duisburg, the attack was rather scattered. This sortie, on 11 April, took us five and a half hours.

On the 12th we had a short flight to nearby RAF Blyton, the home of No. 1662 Heavy Conversion Unit. I cannot remember the official reason for this visit, but we arrived at lunchtime and had to eat a typical training camp meal! Another frustration awaited us on the 13th when we were briefed to go to the Italian naval base of La Spezia. This sortie was to be the longest one we were to fly, but it turned out to be the shortest as we were back at Wickenby just over an hour after leaving! The reason– was a broken oil pipe that put the rear turret out of action. There was nothing I could do to repair it as it was inside the turret itself and, in any case, within a very few moments too much oil had leaked out for a repair to be practical. Freddie was very upset about this, and so were the rest of us, including Villiers, who had no hesitation in turning back. This was not a case of being too cautious, as the rear turret was of the utmost importance to the defence of the aircraft, and on a lengthy flight such as this no chances could be taken. We were over the Wash at the time, and dropped our bombs therein as soon as we had turned around. Although we did not know it at the time, this was our last flight in faithful ED548 as it went in for major servicing and overhaul, including of course the turret repair, and we went on to fly the next three operations in an older machine, W4861, which had been the squadron spare. We had completed eight full missions and two abortive ones in ED548, and the plane met a spectacular end on 7 July when it suddenly exploded on a training flight and dived into the Firth of Forth.

As we had aborted the La Spezia operation, we were back in action again on the following night, 14 April. This trip was a fairly lengthy one, to blast the railway marshalling yards at Stuttgart, and for this purpose we took the usual 4,000lb high-explosive bomb plus 5 x 1,000lb general-purpose bombs. Taking off in W4861 at 21.50 hours, we flew the whole way in brilliant moonlight with a very clear view of the ground (in direct contrast with the previous raid on Frankfurt), and on arrival at the target we could almost map-read our way to the aiming point. The defences were neither accurate nor intense, and Villiers steadfastly held us straight and level to gain the reward of a bullseye photograph of the main railway station, the first time that we had gained such a success. The homeward journey, again in clear skies, was marked by the continual manoeuvring of the aircraft to afford us a clear lookout for fighters. We did indeed see one at fairly close range, but he was apparently shadowing someone else and did not trouble us. We arrived back at Wickenby after exactly six hours, and apart from being airsick on the way back, I rated this, our twentieth operation, as one of the most satisfying.

Villiers had now completed his second tour at this magical total of twenty. At this point he should have been officially screened, but he went on to fly another two trips with us before eventually calling it a day. Why he carried on is difficult for me to say, but I imagine that he flew on to ensure that Charlie Dear, our wireless operator, completed his quota. Charlie, on his second tour, was on the same basis as Villiers, but it is likely he missed the odd trip through illness or some other cause and could have ended up with the prospect of having to do one last trip with an unknown crew. If this was Villiers's reason for soldiering on I would not be surprised for, as I have stated before, on an operational station such as Wickenby, the esprit de corps was high and people did things like that.

Before we embarked on the final two trips with 'Skipper' Villiers, two other events intervened. On 16 April we had another flight in W4794, our old 'V' Victory. This outing was supposed to be an air test, but when we had climbed to about 10,000ft I smelled something burning, and quickly traced this to a piece of radio equipment that appeared to be smouldering. It was most unfortunate that Charlie Dear was not with us to isolate this, and I could not trace the input leads, so there was no alternative but to land as quickly as possible before fire broke out. This was achieved by means of a dive almost equal to the one at Kiel, and we managed to get down before any harm was done. As things turned out it was the last time we flew in the old 'V' Victory, and the plane's end came some twelve months later when it crashed on landing after a tyre burst.

The other event was a more welcome one to us all – another period of leave. As was usual when one went home on a break, though, it was over almost as soon as it had started, especially with the best part of two days taken up with travelling, and in no time we were back in the briefing room to see Happy Valley beckoning us yet again. This operation, once more to Duisburg on 27 April, can be described in a bit more detail as I still have my log sheet, which is still decipherable even though made out under much less than ideal conditions. Take-off was at a minute or so after midnight and we had reached our operational height of 21,000ft within an hour, indicating an initial climb over base to about 10,000ft and then completing the climb over the course. The French coast was crossed at 01.35 hours, and the target reached at 02.05. After the bomb load of 8,200lb was dropped, it was down and away with our speed increasing from 140 to 220mph. No mention is made of conditions at Duisburg itself, but the reception we met in that area was pretty consistent on each occasion. Landing was made back at Wickenby at 04.35, the distance flown being 900 track miles.

Villiers was in no mood to hang around with just one more trip to complete, and he had us back on the Battle Order on the following day, 28 April. We had seen the fuel tanks being filled right up during our morning inspection of the aircraft, and had had thoughts of some dastardly long flight over enemy territory, probably to Italy again, but we were astonished when entering the briefing room to see the red line pointing not south, but almost due east and, furthermore, practically to the extremities of the map! The grizzly details were unfolded by the intelligence officer when we learned that we were booked to go sea mining in Danzig Bay, which would involve a round trip of about 1,500 miles and take us perilously close to Kiel en-route, where we had had such a rousing reception way back in January.

It might be supposed that a 'gardening' trip (dropping (sowing) mines, referred to as 'vegetables') was an easy option compared with, say, the Ruhr, but as only a few aircraft took part in these sorties, one had a feeling of

being very much alone and far from home, as well as not having any
protection from fellow aircraft in the bombing stream. It meant long
distances over sea, and if detected by enemy radar, several night fighters
could be dispatched to deal with these few bombers. Such was the prospect
when we took off at 21.00 hours in W4861 (for the third successive time),
and set course for points east. Fortunately we had no problems except
for the exhausting eight-hour flight, but one incident on the homeward
leg has always stood out in my memory. A light suddenly appeared to
starboard, and spotting it first I shouted a warning whereupon six pairs
of eyes were craned in that direction. Where was the seventh pair?
Looking the other way in case it was a decoy! The light, however, remained
stationary and intensified as we plodded on. It was the navigator whose
thoughts clicked, and he suddenly announced that we were looking at
the lights of Sweden! Soon more and more lights shone out, and we could
make out several towns illuminating the sky. What a marvellous sight
to see after years of unending blackout in England; they even had a
magnetic power, and we would have loved to stooge around for some
time on a sight-seeing tour!

But down-to-earth Villiers had other ideas and relentlessly pressed
on, anxious to be back on firm ground for the last time, so reluctantly
we watched the lights fade away and returned to the darkness we were
to endure for another two years. On landing back at Wickenby three
cheers were shouted out for Villiers and we all shook hands with him
before being transported back for a very emotional debriefing. The story
of Danzig Bay does not end there, though, for out of twelve aircraft that
set off on this 'easy' mining operation, no fewer than six failed to return
and were never heard of again. That we pulled through was more by luck
than judgement, and we reflected how fortunate we had been throughout our tour to date in having Villiers in charge of affairs. I shudder to
think what might have happened had I opted out of his crew on that first
day, as I might well have done given the chance!

We had a farewell drink with Villiers in the White Hart, after which
he was posted to Group Headquarters to fly his pen in the Operations
Department. That he made a success in his new occupation was evident
when he was subsequently promoted to wing commander. Within a week
or so after departing from Wickenby he was awarded the DFC, and I have

a record of his citation which I quote here in full: 'Acting Squadron Leader D.H. Villiers R.A.F.V.R. No. 12 Squadron. The numerous operational sorties completed by this officer include attacks on Berlin, Turin, Milan and Essen. On all of these, intense anti-aircraft and fighter opposition was encountered.'

Although this might be a slight exaggeration, it is likely that he had a rough time on his first tour, and all in all we thought he thoroughly deserved the honour. As far as I was concerned, this was not the end of my association with Villiers, for I met him on several other occasions and even flew with him again, as will be related in due course.

We now had an interregnum of about a fortnight while wondering who our new pilot would be. As might be imagined, we were very apprehensive over who would turn up, and couldn't really contemplate getting anybody who was even a patch on Villiers – a very worrying time was had by all. During this waiting period we were left to kick our heels about, but we spent a fair amount of time in the Intelligence Department where there was an interesting library of books, reports and magazines appertaining to operational matters. I also remember attending an escape lecture given by a staff officer from Group HQ, who had some hair-raising experiences while on the run in Germany. These lectures, several of which I heard at Wickenby, were not only very instructive, but also at times very amusing, and they were an excellent morale booster. We lost a great many aircrews during the time I was operating at Wickenby, but naturally a good number of them were taken prisoner or managed to escape back to England, and I recall one of them in particular. This crew had ditched in the North Sea and fortunately had been picked up within twenty-four hours. When they returned to Wickenby they couldn't help looking conspicuous, hanging around the mess in battledress stained bright yellow from the dinghy! We were not completely let off the hook while we awaited news of our next pilot, but had to report to the crew room each morning as usual, and had to be available to fly as a spare crew member if necessary. In my case, I did not have a call for my services, but I believe that several of my other colleagues had to stand in.

Towards the middle of May our suspense was ended with the arrival of our new skipper who, much to our relief, turned out to be another experienced senior pilot. Squadron Leader Slade had already completed one tour of operations and had recently converted to Lancasters at a Heavy Conversion Unit as a single pilot without a crew, so we were very happy to join up with him when he came to replace Villiers as 'B' Flight commander. We soon found out that Slade was a splendid chap and very easy to get on with; in fact he had all the attributes of a gentleman. He had the same confidence as Villiers in the air, but there were some differences in his life-style on the ground as he brought three things with him to Wickenby – a wife, a dog and a car! We saw very little of the dog as it was usually left in the officers' mess during working hours, but we had many a lift in his car, and when one remembers that he had an entitlement to service transport also, it will be seen that our internal travelling needs were well catered for! I cannot recall ever having met his wife, though strangely enough she had an influence on our initial flying programme. When Slade arrived at Wickenby he came complete with dog and car, but owing to accommodation difficulties had left his wife behind at his previous unit, Whitchurch Heath in Shropshire, although he contrived to pay her several visits while being engaged with his familiarisation practice.

As a new boy to Lancasters, he had to have a period of training before becoming operational so, commencing on 14 May, we flew a number of local trips during the following seven days in a variety of aircraft. Three of these flights were worthy of mention. The very first one was predictably to Sleap (a satellite of Whitchurch) to see his wife. This was repeated a few days later when we actually landed at Whitchurch itself. Apart from the obvious reason, these were genuine practice flights as each one was over an hour's duration, but just to make sure that Slade had got everything right, we also did a daylight cross-country, Oxford–Land's End–Oxford–Base, which took three hours.

We flew every day that week and were even briefed for an operation on the 19th although it was scrubbed just before take-off. The big day came at last on the 20th, when we were detailed to go on a 'gardening' trip to the Gironde River in the Bay of Biscay to drop 6 x 1,500lb mines full of deadly ingenuity. It will be recalled that Charlie Dear had left us at the end of April, and we now welcomed Flight Sergeant McIntyre as our new wireless operator on his first flight with us. We took off in 'K' King, ED629, at 21.55 hours and landed back at 03.40 after a fairly routine trip apart from a skirmish with some flak ships near our dropping point. As usual with a mining operation, we had no direct evidence that the 'vegetables' had been dropped in the correct area, unlike a bombing sortie when a photograph was obtained, but true professionals that we were we always did our utmost to ascertain the correct position using dead-reckoning navigation and radio fixes; we were thus able to gain some satisfaction even from a mundane trip such as this.

Two days later we were back at Whitchurch Heath again – for the last time as it turned out – but there was a variation to the theme as on this occasion we stayed overnight. Slade had arranged accommodation for us at the camp, and after landing he made off and we didn't see him again until it was time to depart on the following morning. Having had tea, we decided to sample the delights of Whitchurch town, which was two or three miles distant, and we started to walk there as there was no service transport available. Suddenly, however, after we had completed the first mile a bus materialised and stopped to pick us up, much to our relief. It is a safe bet that there would be no such obliging gesture in these days, but such was the power of a uniform in wartime! There was very little to do when we arrived in Whitchurch, and after having had a drink and paid a visit to the local hop, it was back to camp in a taxi to find a mix-up over our billeting arrangements. Amazingly, we ended up sleeping in the mess just as though we had been diverted from operations!

After this visit Slade brought his wife to Wickenby, and they found accommodation at Snelland vicarage not far from the station, a very pleasant spot now that the nice summery days had returned after a miserable winter. On a point of interest, the airfield at Whitchurch, later renamed Tilstock, was disbanded at the end of the war, and the main A41 road to Chester now follows the line of the main runway on which we landed during Slade's periodic visits to see his wife. The control tower still stands as silent testimony to this once busy RAF station.

Operations loomed once again on 25 May, with another visit to Düsseldorf, my second visit to this industrial city in the Ruhr. We had flown in 'J' Jig, ED993, on several local trips, but this was the first time we took her on operations. In all we flew three sorties in this aircraft, all of them to Happy Valley. Of this particular raid I have very little to say as it was essentially a run-of-the-mill job. Some 750 aircraft took part, but the fires were rather scattered.

Our second trip in ED993 on 27 May was – surprise, surprise – back to Essen again. It was the fifth time we had been to this most inhospitable place, and although it turned out to be for the last time as a target, we saw it at close quarters on several other occasions, much to our disgust. I can report the figures of this raid in some detail. The fuel load was 1,550 gallons, of which we used about 1,100 – enough to motor around the world in a modern car! We took the usual 4,000lb cookie and incendiaries, giving us an all-up weight of 58,627lb (about 26 tons), this being slightly below the maximum of 60,000lb allowable. Take-off was at 22.30 hours, and two hours later we were over the target at 20,000ft, but unfortunately owing to thick cloud (10/10ths in RAF parlance), we could not see the aiming point and had to bomb on the pathfinders' sky markers. We had plenty of directional guidance from the Ruhr defences, and really only had to penetrate to the heart of the barrage to know where we were. No exceptional problems developed on the return journey and we landed at 03.15 after an elapsed time of four hours and forty-five minutes. So ended my twenty-fifth operation – only five to go if I was lucky!

Before the final phase there was a break of about a fortnight while we were engaged in some local flying, and no doubt during this period Slade managed to catch up with his paperwork. On 1 June we went practice bombing to Market Rasen. (This does not mean that we actually bombed Market Rasen, but more that there was a small ground target laid out nearby!) Next came a night-flying test on the 2nd that took over an hour, and then on the 6th a mini cross-country, Base–Mablethorpe–Base, which was probably to keep our eye in ready for the trials and tribulations to follow. After a short local flight on the 9th we were involved in a very different exercise during the following day – flying round the sky trying to dodge a Spitfire for the best part of an hour. This fighter affiliation exercise certainly showed up the degree of manoeuvrability of the Lancaster as we twisted and turned, dived and climbed, and virtually stood up on our tail on one occasion. It was of course, a beneficial ex-perience for us all, and should have been repeated more often, but Spitfires were very valuable fighting aircraft and could only be used sparingly in this way. Whether ourselves or the Spitfire were deemed to have been shot down I was past caring about, as I was feeling decidedly queasy after it was all over!

We now came to 11 June and our third and last trip in ED993, which also turned out to be our third and last trip to Düsseldorf. I have the details of this trip from the third and last log sheet that I retained from those days. Had I realised the need for detail some decades later I would have endeavoured to have kept more of them. Take-off was at 22.40 hours, with a fuel load of 1,650 gallons and a bomb load of 9,060lb (the cookie plus incendiaries), giving an all-up weight of 59,890lb. I can remember this raid very clearly, and one of the outstanding features was the difficulty in climbing owing to the very warm outside temperature, which impinged on the efficiency of the engines. We managed to struggle to 20,000ft by the time we were over Düsseldorf, and dropped our bombs successfully although visibility was affected by layer cloud. On the journey back the cloud thickened and we met icing conditions that necessitated the use of the hot-air intake (manipulated correctly by Slade, unlike Villiers's epic mistake!). Slade also tried to get out of the poor conditions by climbing higher, which he was now able to do without the weight of the bombs, but eventually decided that there was no future in this and had to resort to a descent through the cloud at a far greater rate than normal, bringing us into clear air at about 5,000ft. In all we had lost 19,000ft in forty minutes, one of the advantages of which was to be able to turn off the oxygen sooner than we had expected, but a sharp look-out for enemy fighters had to be kept as we were now flying in isolation. Fortunately all went well, and we landed back at Wickenby at 03.25 hours after a very memorable flight of four and a half hours' duration and having covered 1,080 track miles. Some 783 aircraft were sent on this raid and 38 failed to return, one being ED357 in which I had flown four months earlier, and after the war a propeller salvaged from it by the Dutch was mounted on a memorial to Allied pilots who had lost their lives in the Netherlands.

A period of leave now interrupted our progress, but it was not long after our return that we were back in action. On 22 June we took possession of a brand new Lancaster, 'F' Freddie, DV168, which was to remain in our area for the rest of our time with Slade. We were due to fly the aircraft on operations that night, so we went up in it for a trial spin of forty-five minutes to iron out any snags, after which it was heigh-ho to

the ops room to face the cold chill of another Ruhr briefing. Our destination this time was Mulheim, a big steel-making centre in common
with most of the towns in Happy Valley. Apart from its industrial
capacity, it also had important railway yards, so it is rather surprising that
this was the only main attack ever mounted directly against it. Although
owing to its geographical position, no doubt it came in for more than
its fair share of punishment from incorrect bombing of adjacent targets.
At any rate, we found the defences every bit as fierce as those at Essen,
including myriads of searchlights.

While checking the aircraft over in the early evening before the raid,
I spotted several civilians strolling along a nearby path, savouring the
country air. It was a lovely day and I was somewhat irked that these people
should be able to enjoy themselves in peace and safety whereas I was
about to embark on a mission through most unfriendly skies. Take-off
was at 23.15 hours, and these thoughts lingered on the outward journey,
particularly over the target area, and my mind cast back to the wonderful
summer days I had spent at Penrhos, now light years away; what a mad-
ness it had been to leave there! This reverie did not affect the performance
of my duties, and in any case things seemed a little bit better when we
were haring home. I contented myself with the thought that by not still
being at Penrhos I had at least avoided that terrible rail journey!

The statistics of the Mulheim raid were that 35 out of 557 aircraft failed
to return, and we took a different type of bomb load; this time it included
3 x 500lb general-purpose bombs as well as the 4,000-pounder, and all
in all 1,848 tons were dropped in a very concentrated attack. This pattern
was repeated two nights later on 24 June with a raid to Wuppertal, also
in the Ruhr about forty miles east of Düsseldorf. Wuppertal had been
created in 1929 by the amalgamation of Elberfeld and Barmen, and as
with Mulheim, this was the only main force attack made against it.
Crew member Bill Allinson had missed several raids through sickness,
but by now had completed nineteen of his second tour and arrived at
the last one, so we just had to keep out of trouble on this trip. I have
obtained a copy of the squadron raid report, which gives a little more
detail than my own notes, and also helps to sharpen my memory after
so many years. The bomb load was 9,100lb, consisting again of the cookie,
general-purpose bombs and incendiaries. After take-off at 23.16 hours,

height was gained to 5,000ft over base before setting course to rendezvous at Southwold, by which time we had achieved 15,000ft. Visibility was reasonably good but there were patches of cumulus cloud up to 19,000ft that persisted most of the way to the target. After leaving Southwold, we steadily reached the bombing height of 18,500ft and were guided along the route by yellow track indicating markers dropped by the pathfinders at various intervals. The aiming point, marked by red flares, was the centre of Elberfeld, and with the visibility being clear we had no difficulty lining up the aircraft to bomb spot on time at 01.07 hours.

What the raid report does not mention, but which I remember vividly, was that after leaving the target we were caught in the searchlight belt that encircles Happy Valley, and we were in trouble for some time when we were pinpointed by some thirty or forty lights that held us in a cone. The glare of these lights had to be experienced to be believed; it was no good looking outside or we would have been blinded, and the instruments inside could not be seen either, so Slade could only put the nose down to gain speed and twist from side to side in an effort to shake them off. We were aware of the dangers; apart from the flak, night fighters could be stalking us, and as the pilots wore dark glasses we could easily be picked off in the confusion. Our luck was in, though, and after several minutes of flying by guess and by God, we were suddenly swallowed up in the darkness again, badly shaken but intact, and after an interval while we found our bearings, we managed to get back on course for home, where we eventually landed at 03.31 after four and a half hours of action-packed flying.

This mission was a great success, with the target glowing brightly by the time we had bombed, and when our photograph was developed it turned out to be a bullseye, which I was rather glad about for the sake of Slade who was a very good captain and deserved some success. (It will be remembered that our crew had had a similar achievement at Stuttgart back in April with Villiers at the helm.) Altogether, 1,879 tons of bombs were dropped on Wuppertal or in the immediate vicinity on this single raid, so perhaps enough damage was done to avoid the necessity of visiting there again.

After our hectic experience, Bill Allinson was very pleased to be back on terra firma again and must have thanked his lucky stars; what a terrible blow it would have been to be downed on his fiftieth and last operation! Anyway, we bade him farewell and in his place welcomed Pilot Officer Ralph Carpenter, who had flown with Slade previously and who had been earmarked to join us at the first opportunity. I struck up an immediate rapport with Ralph for various reasons, paramount of which was that he lived in Moseley, and I once went on leave with him to visit his wife and baby son at their home in Springfield Road. He was an accomplished navigator, very much in the mould of Bill Allinson, and once again we were fortunate to click for a first-class replacement to the crew. His first flight with us was on 27 June when we had a little stooge to Skegness and back, which took all of thirty minutes. I don't think he was overtaxed in navigating us in the right direction, especially as George was up in the nose map-reading at the same time! Slade had signed my logbook at the end of May, and he now endorsed it once more to verify a further forty-four hours to my flying total. I had now completed twenty-eight operations and could see the light at the end of the tunnel with just two more to do, but knowing that many aircrews were shot down at this stage, and indeed even on their last trip, I could not afford to be complacent and had to keep my fingers crossed. Before the last lap a couple more local flights followed, the first one to Binbrook and back, the second a night-flying test on 7 July as a prelude to our operating the same night.

Although I did not really want to visit either place, I had always had a hankering throughout my tour to go to Hamburg and Cologne; Hamburg because it was the second city of Germany and equivalent to Birmingham in England, and Cologne because it was so well known, unlike a lot of other names in my logbook. I narrowly missed the battle of Hamburg, but my penultimate raid satisfied part of my ambition, and I was almost pleased to see Cologne on the board when entering the briefing room. After having been granted the chance to pay Cologne a visit, there was rather an anti-climax when we found the place covered with 8/10ths cloud at the commencement of the bombing run. The target-indicating markers gave us the aiming point, of course, and the intensity of the flak confirmed that we were pretty well spot on when the bombs dropped, but the absence of a ground photograph was most disappointing. Subsequent aerial photography confirmed that Cologne had been well hit, however, and the raid was deemed to be quite a success.

Thankful to escape the flak barrage, we came in for more of it on the way home, when of all things we were nearly downed by our own anti-aircraft fire while crossing over Southend Pier. It is a great mystery why we were not actually hit considering our low height and straight and level course, but we got away with it as we had done previously near Portsmouth – perhaps they had painted the wrong number on the shells! After this episode we arrived back at Wickenby without further ado to land after being airborne for five and a half hours.

Our return to Wickenby heralded the departure of two further stalwarts from the crew: George Thomas and 'Mac' Saunders. I had flown practically all my trips with these two old faithfuls, and was very sorry to see them go, even though I only had one more op to complete. To be perfectly honest I was never really on the same wavelength as either of them as they were both on the quiet side, besides which Mac had been rather remote, having spent most of his time in the officers' mess. I had no complaints with their performance in the air, though. George was very meticulous with his bomb aiming and map-reading, and if he thought he was right and others wrong he would not hesitate to say so. Mac, likewise, was very vocal if there was a chance of a night fighter near us, and, just as important, we never caught him asleep! In their place we had Flight Sergeant Manning to drop the bombs and Flight Sergeant Milton in the mid-upper turret.

There was a nerve-wracking delay of several days before I was able to climb aboard for my last operation, and it was not until the night of 12 July that the suspense was ended. Again we had had early predictions that it was to be a long run as the fuel tanks had been topped right up, and this was confirmed when on entering the briefing room it was seen that the route marker stretched further than it had done before on any of our previous trips. The target was Turin, and although we were to approach this city by the orthodox route, there was a drastic alteration to the return journey where, after crossing the Alps, we were to descend right down to 1,000ft and do a cross-country leg over France to cross the Atlantic coast north of Bordeaux. From this point the idea was to follow the coastline right round the Bay of Biscay, flying at about 100ft above the waves to avoid radar detection. As it would now be approaching daylight, we were to fly in loose formation over this leg as a further security measure. After rounding the tip of France, the last stage took us over the Channel to make landfall at Land's End, from where we were told to proceed to Wickenby if we had sufficient fuel, or to land at Chivenor (near Barnstaple) if reserves had been used up.

What an exciting prospect for my last operation! It was deemed very necessary to organise this raid as the forerunner to a series of attacks on Italy with the intention of hastening its surrender now that the Allied forces were advancing up from the south, and it came immediately after Mussolini was deposed. Although the weather was very difficult – to the point where the operation would have been cancelled under normal circumstances – it had to go on in this case for the aforementioned reasons, and these conditions were the probable explanation for the complicated 2,000-mile route.

It was the heaviest raid yet made on Turin, and No. 12 Squadron turned out a full complement of twenty aircraft. The bomb load was about 7,000lb, including the ubiquitous cookie, this somewhat lighter load reflecting the greater need for a full load of petrol. Taking off at 22.15 hours and climbing on course, we immediately met the force of the weather and were soon flying blind. Every thirty minutes a regular wind forecast was broadcast from England, and with corrections made from this the navigator managed to keep us pointing in the right direction. Even though thick cloud dogged us most of the way to the Alps, we were found to be almost spot on course when at last a welcome break in the conditions enabled us to see the mountains approaching. From here the weather cleared and Turin was outlined below us as plainly as in daylight and we were able to bomb at will, helped by the very poor defences. As in our previous journeys to Italy, the colours were the outstanding feature with the fires and flares and light flak combining to make it look like fairyland. A description of the attack is given in the No. 1 Group Operational Summary, and it can be seen that the defences were described as puerile, but nevertheless it was no place to hang around over, so we made our exit as soon as possible and started on the long journey home.

As can be imagined, this trip has stayed in my memory, and if the leg over France was thrilling, with many twinkling lights below, the run over the sea can only be described as exhilarating. We flew with two other aircraft, rising over slight fog banks and falling back to sea level again, our only hint of trouble coming from flak defences at Belle Isle, which we approached a bit nearer than we should have done, but with a sharp turn we were away and out of danger. Flying as low as this enhanced one's sense of speed, but although we hurtled along, much time passed before Land's End hove into view.

It was just seven o'clock on a summer's morning when we swept over the English coastline, rising to 1,000ft from which vantage point we could see Cornwall laid out beneath us as we set course for Chivenor. Earlier calculations had convinced me that it would be very touch and go to try to reach Wickenby without refuelling, and I was in no mood to take chances at this stage, so Chivenor it was, and this was the consensus of all of us. It was the fourth diversionary landing of my tour, and when we arrived the traffic was quite brisk with many aircraft anxious to get down quickly, but all was well with flying control staff, well aware of the situation and landing us as quickly as possible. Our time of touchdown was 07.40, so we had been airborne for nine and a half hours, the longest trip that I had flown both in terms of distance and time, and by far the most important – and the last one! As was customary on such an occasion, I bent down to kiss the ground with heartfelt thanks to my lucky stars that I had been spared the 'chop'.

The stop at Chivenor was just for refuelling, but they provided us with breakfast before we were off again at 09.40 hours on the last leg home, and Slade joined in the spirit of the occasion by declaring that we could smoke a cigarette if we wished. This was such a surprise announcement that most of us were caught without any and Slade had to pass his packet round so that we might indulge! I do not recall any other instance of smoking while we were in the air, although I heard of other crews doing so, and cannot imagine why there wasn't a total embargo against it considering the amount of petrol and other explosives there were on board an operational aircraft. Perhaps there was a rule about it, and if so it was the only one I ever knew Slade to break.

Wickenby was reached after an hour and a half, making a total of eleven hours' flying for the whole trip, and this was the point where I parted from skipper Slade who I never flew with again. What good fortune I had had drawing Villiers and Slade out of the pack, both of whom had great expertise and were remarkable chaps into the bargain!

I also said farewell to 'F' Freddie, DV168, which had seen me safely through my last few ops; although I did not fly in her after the Turin raid, I often saw her at dispersal and waved her off on other operations, sometimes with the strange feeling that I would have liked to fly another one in her. I could not have done so, though, even if I had tried, for I was now officially screened from operations for a minimum period of six months. I am slightly uncertain as to when my erstwhile companion in the rear turret, Freddie Prowse, ended his tour. He was certainly with us at Turin, and may have done a further trip to finish, but finish he certainly did, and he was with me at Wickenby for some time afterwards. Good old Freddie, who was so utterly dependable, both in the air and on the ground. We sat down one day and worked out how far we had flown on all our missions, and reckoned that we had covered a distance equivalent to going around the world, but the last laugh went to Freddie, always the humorist, when he said that his was the greater distinction because although I might have flown it standing up, he had flown it backwards! After landing from our marathon effort we were whisked off to debriefing and then tumbled into bed to catch up on some much needed sleep. Immediate leave was granted to all those who had completed their tour, and the following morning I was up bright and breezy to collect my travel warrant for the journey to Birmingham and I was soon off to enjoy a long rest. To my recollection, the only non-restful activity at home was a small party organised for the occasion of my safe return, and a day's round of visits to neighbours and near relatives who were all anxious to hear the tale. I then subsided into doing small household chores until Wickenby beckoned once more.

On return from leave I was interviewed by Wing Commander Wood, the squadron CO. He informed me that he had been watching my progress for some time, and requested me to stay awhile on the squadron to take over the running of flight engineer affairs from Sidney Chapman, the engineer from Squadron Leader Bell's crew who had now joined up with Slade to replace me. For this purpose I was ensconced in a small office that had just enough room for a desk, a filing cabinet and a couple of chairs, but the meanness of the establishment was of little consequence to me then as I had at least aspired to an office of my own after nearly six years' service. More importantly, perhaps, I was now also in charge of a department for the first time, even though it was only an acting temporary job and I was virtually unpaid! My duties were not particularly onerous, and were mainly concerned with collecting logs, checking that they had been filled in correctly, and ascertaining that attempts had been made to fly economically etc. I also spent a lot of time with the new engineers on the squadron and often went out to dispersal with them, making sure that they used the correct procedures to check the serviceability of the aircraft. Liaison with the ground crews, and with the engineering officers now that I had my new status, was also an important function that I had to perform. There was no necessity for me to fly during this period, and it was indeed nearly two months later that I became airborne again, and this was only on a familiarisation flight for the new squadron CO, as I will mention in due course.

About a week after I had started in my new occupation, I was hauled up in front of Woody again and wondered where I had gone wrong, but I need not have worried as he appeared to be pleased with my progress and casually asked me if I had ever thought of applying for a commission. Apparently word had circulated that flight engineers were now eligible to be promoted to officer rank; Woody had considered this and decided that I was a suitable candidate. Thoughts had crossed my mind on this subject, but not realising that commissions were available to engineers, I hadn't applied. Now that the opportunity presented itself, I seized it with both hands, and after Woody had confirmed that he would put forward a strong recommendation on my behalf, I left his office in somewhat of a daze! Things move quickly in wartime, and a week later I went in front of a visiting selection board to answer a barrage of questions, none of which mentioned golf or newspapers, to be finally informed that I had satisfied the board of my suitability for promotion, and that confirmation would filter through in the fullness of time. I was hardly prepared for the news that came through after merely a few days of waiting: I had been elevated to the giddy heights of pilot officer with effect from 3 July. From that moment it was all go and I had to change my accommodation and messing arrangements, but the first priority concerned the uniform, and to enable the new officer to acquire the necessary articles of clothing, commissioning leave was usually granted. So once again, I was off home, this time with a warrant for £100 in my pocket, which was the uniform allowance at that time.

Owing to the suddenness of this great event, I had decided not to tell the folks at home until definite confirmation had been received, and now I thought I would surprise them by appearing on unexpected leave bearing the good news. So I set off the same day, being assisted on my way by a lift to Lincoln from Slade's driver. As I was late starting, and because of some inordinate delay on the line, I finally arrived home some time after midnight and had to knock everybody up to get in, but peace was restored after I had related my story! Another round of the neighbours had to be survived on the following day, after which it was off to Austin Reed in New Street to kit myself out.

It was necessary to acquire the whole range of clothing for me to appear as an officer and a gentleman, and this included a greatcoat, a raincoat, two tunics with trousers, two shirts, socks, a tie and two hats – one a side cap and the other a ceremonial flat cap, commonly known as a cheese-cutter. Most of these items were a standard quality and price, but as my hands were perpetually cold in wintertime, I also bought the best pair of gloves that I could find. As to the tunics, I had one off the peg that fitted me nicely, but as it was the only one they had in my size, the other one had to be made to measure, and sad to say that although it was well made it never really fitted me properly, even after being altered, and I can recall wearing it just once or twice. The only article that I can remember the price of after such a long time, was the hat band and badge, which had to be bought separately and cost £1. The allowance had been well calculated, though, for after the purchase of a pair of shoes from the shop next door, I had about £5 left. This I kept very carefully, for from now on, I had to replace any worn-out items at my own expense.

I went back to Austin Reed a couple of days later to check the fitting of my tunic, and bumped into an old colleague who was there for the same purpose as myself. He was Vincent Knight, a flight engineer from No. 101 Squadron at Ludford Magna whom I had known well at St Athan. Vin, as he was known, had also survived his tour and was commissioned at the same time as myself. He was also retained on his squadron as acting flight engineer leader, and was confirmed in this appointment on being promoted. He lived at Walsall, and although I met him once later at a group conference, I lost touch with him afterwards, and can only hope that he saw the rest of the war out in one piece.

Soon it was time to return to Wickenby (travelling first class of course!), and my initial act on arrival was to move into my new living quarters, which were in one of a block of huts some distance away from hut 13. It was a bit of a wrench doing this; the hut, although a bit primitive, had served me well and kept me in luck, and also having to leave Freddie behind was regrettable. But there was no alternative but to abide by regulations and so out I went. The new accommodation was no palace either, but was much less crowded and at least we had supplies of hot water brought to us each morning by a batman, which meant that our standards of personal hygiene moved up a peg or two! Unlike the pre-war service when there were almost as many batmen as officers, by the time I was commissioned the ratio had dwindled to a proportion of about one to six officers, and from my albeit faulty memory, at Wickenby only one per hut. Apart from the water carrying, their duties involved making the beds and cleaning out the hut, polishing shoes and buttons and pressing clothes, and with six to eight of us per room, I suppose this would constitute a fair day's work.

On the following morning, after the novelty of having had a decent wash, I put on my cheese-cutter and strolled down to my office, soon being back to the old routine. After this initial try-out, I took a dislike to the flat hat and thereafter wore my side cap on all occasions, except when I had official duties to perform. In the course of time, the cap got dirtier and greasier but I would not part with it and it became the most comfortable one that I ever wore. In any case, as I did a fair amount of cycling it was the only practical one to use.

During my absence from the operational scene, the squadron had still managed to keep going. I had just missed the Battle of Hamburg, which began at the end of July and consisted of three or four very heavy raids on Germany's second city, leaving it in ruins and almost completely burned out. Slade had taken part in several of these ops, and the first one (on 24 July) had been the venue for the initial dropping of 'Window' – small strips of silvered paper that confused the German radar operators into believing that each one was another aircraft and completely jammed up their system. On the night of 17/18 August the target was

Peenemünde, the German experimental rocket base on the Baltic Sea coast. No. 12 Squadron supplied twenty-five crews to this raid, which had been meticulously planned with a diversionary attack by Mosquitoes on Berlin to fool the German radar. In spite of the importance of the occasion I did not attend debriefing as I had been on duty several nights previously, and I was approached while having breakfast on the following morning by one of the WAAF intelligence officers, who informed me that Slade and his crew were missing. This was a blow that jolted me greatly as I had considered Slade to be invincible and had never entertained the idea of him being in trouble. Some hours had already passed since his expected return time was up, but there was a chance that he might have landed elsewhere, or even have ditched in the sea and was waiting to be rescued. Sadly, all these possibilities ran out of time and I had to come to terms with the realisation that they had flown their last flight. It was idle to speculate how they met their end as so many factors were involved, but I have often thought about them over the years and have imagined all sorts of reasons why they didn't return. Together with so many other of my contemporaries, their names are inscribed on a tablet at the RAF Memorial at Runnymede.

Particularly poignant for me was the loss of Sydney Chapman, whom I had been in constant contact with during all my time at Wickenby, and I was left to reflect that it would have been my neck had our roles been reversed. There was also the case of Ralph Carpenter, who I had been very friendly with in spite of not knowing him for long, and I knew that the next time I was at home I would have to visit his wife to offer my condolences. This meeting duly took place a few weeks later, by which time some of the shock had been absorbed, but Mrs Carpenter was naturally very upset and it was a very difficult time for me. She had moved across the road to live with her mother-in-law, so at least she had some companionship. I did not see her again after this because when I called some months later she had moved away. A bevy of the top brass went to visit Slade's wife, but I didn't go as I hadn't met her before, and in any case I assumed that she wouldn't want to see all and sundry. It was some consolation for Mrs Slade when her husband was posthumously awarded the Distinguished Service Order a short time later, and in my humble opinion there could be no finer recipient than this splendid man.

Freddie was posted away shortly afterwards, and ended up in Brussels with the Second Tactical Air Force. I was therefore the last member of our former crew to remain at Wickenby, and I had some consolation in being left by myself in enjoying the relative comforts of the officers' mess. The mess was a wooden building that comprised an ante-room complete with bar, a dining room, kitchen, cloakroom and a few smaller rooms used for special purposes. I was only in residence for a matter of weeks, but I have a few odd memories of the place that mostly concern the main meeting lounge, known on all RAF stations as the ante-room. On entering the room one immediately noticed two large oil paintings hanging one either side of the fireplace; these were portraits of the squadron's two VC recipients Garland and Gray, who were the heroes of the attack on the Veldwezelt bridge over the Albert Canal in the Belgian town of Maastricht in 1940. Next, one saw a replica of a fox's head (after the squadron crest), which was over the fireplace itself; this head was the subject of a humorous ritual, for each time that operations were on, a cigarette was placed in its mouth, only to be taken out when the raid was finished or was cancelled. In a corner of the room was an old piano (British this time) that was normally played by the 'resident' pianist, an equipment officer. His best piece was a rendition of 'Rustle of Spring', and it was on his repertoire each time he sat down to perform. There were always groans when he played it, but it made no difference; we heard it whether we liked it or not!

Standards of dress were kept up in the mess, and although it was normal to wear battledress in the daytime, one had to put on service dress for dinner in the evening. This was a good thing for various reasons, including the fact that it was a discipline to be obeyed (and there weren't too many of them on an operational station), and also a change into more formal clothes acted as a psychological relaxation from the daily duties one had to execute. Other forms of relaxation also took place, paramount of which was the mess party. I was present at only one official party at Wickenby, and it was held in style with printed invitations being circulated; mine bore the legend 'Pilot Officer Baxter and Lady', but not having a lady I went by myself! Glasses of punch were served on entry, and the bar was well stocked. A buffet meal was laid on and the station orchestra played background music. This later changed to ballroom music and the officers and ladies tripped the light fantastic while the officers without ladies frequented the bar. High spirits abounded and various stunts were attempted, but things were kept within bounds and all were ushered out fairly peacefully in the early hours. It was customary at these parties to invite higher-ups from Group HQ and neighbouring stations, and in the group party I was very pleased to see my old 'boss', Villiers. On this his return to Wickenby I met him on slightly more equal terms than before, and he was pleased to hear that I had gone up in the world. He enquired about the rest of our crew and was very sorry that Slade had come a cropper. I had a very pleasant chat with him, during which I gathered that he was quite happy at Group HQ. After doing two tours he could not be hauled back on operations and was pleased to remain chairbound for the time being.

From time to time there were numerous impromptu parties in the ante-room, all stemming from the natural exuberance of young people who, although fit as they were then, fully expected to die on the morrow. There were also the quiet types who just brooded on the issue, and I classed myself as somewhere in between – have a drink with the crowd and enjoy a bit of fun without letting it go to excess. The unofficial parties all centred around the drinking of beer; I did not think the beer at Wickenby was all that good, and although the saying is that there is no such thing as bad beer, the Wickenby variety was very near the mark! The best drinking game that I remember was the beer relay where two lines of chaps faced each other, each with a half-pint of beer in his hand, each person having to empty their glass before the next one could start. Bearing in mind that the person opposite was always in view and he could be seen trying to drink his beer at a double quick pace, the outcome was hilarious. The prize for the winners was that the losers paid for the beer. After two of these relays and we were all staggering about! During my short stay in the mess at Wickenby, I enjoyed myself to the full, and when I was posted away it seemed as though I had been there for years.

Apart from my role as overseer of the flight engineers, which included debriefing, I was nabbed for various other duties, one of which was as a member of the 'Committee of Adjustment', an odd-sounding title to cover up the very unpleasant job of dealing with missing persons' kit. Whenever a crew did not return from operations or was killed in training, the personal kit of the various members had to be collected without delay. It was then sent to central stores where it remained for a short time before being transferred to a depot and kept until it was claimed by relatives of the missing person. Very often the belongings of a friend had to be dealt with, and it was a macabre duty sorting out the clothes and dealing with any valuables. Sometimes a letter may have been left for posting, and occasionally the note came with instructions as to the disposal of certain items. Perishables such as eggs were handed out to the room-mates to eat, but nothing else was dispersed by us, and any instructions were passed on to stores, together with the effects. Two of these duties were reckoned to be a 'tour', and then the job was handed over to some-one else with alacrity.

I also acted as observing officer on one or two pay parades (having been on the other side of the table on innumerable occasions!), and did a stint as duty officer when I had to be present in the control tower during take-off on operations, and also during the landings afterwards. Being duty officer also involved the receiving of messages, either by telephone or telex, and making decisions as to their urgency or otherwise, or managing disturbances and a host of other matters. The job was not always a sinecure because things did actually happen; the runway lights petered out one night, but fortunately not while I was on duty, and some time after I left Wickenby the bomb dump caught fire – what a blessing I was not involved with that!

At the end of August 1943, Wing Commander Wood followed Villiers to Group HQ (although he was to serve there in a different capacity), and he was replaced by Wing Commander Craven, ex-Training Command. By all accounts Craven was not very popular on the squadron, but as I left shortly after he was appointed, his presence did not affect me one way or the other. I was involved with him in the first instance, however, as he was not familiar with the then modern operational aircraft, and so he had never flown in a Lancaster before arriving at Wickenby. I spent several sessions lecturing him about the layout of the aircraft and engine handling etc., before he went airborne for the first time. I did not accompany him as he was partnered by Flight Lieutenant Noden, with whom I had flown back in March. Noden had been posted to Lindholme on completing his tour, and he came over to Wickenby specially to get Craven converted to Lancs. It was on 4 September that I ventured up with Craven and it was the first time I had flown since the Turin raid. The occasion was for night circuits and landings, or in the RAF vernacular 'circuits and bumps'. Noden was with us for the first part of the exercise, but then he stepped out and left me to carry on the good work, and off we were again round and round, up and down. I have no record of how many circuits were completed, but we were up for two and a half hours and I must have been pretty well exhausted after this marathon session in the darkness! I was airborne with Craven again on the night of 16 September, this time for just under two hours. He must have been a bit more competent by this time as he flew solo and trusted himself to use a brand new aircraft, LM362.

The date of 24 September was a notable day for me as it heralded my last flight from Wickenby. The exercise was an hour's circuits and bumps, again with Craven, but this time accompanied by Wing Commander Roberts, who had come over from the conversion unit at Lindholme in place of Noden. It was fitting that Craven should sign my logbook after this rather tame ending to my career with No. 12 Squadron; in all I had flown 254 hours since arriving there some ten months earlier.

The simple reason why I did not fly at Wickenby again was that a surprise posting came through for me – I was to go to 1667 Heavy Conversion Unit at Faldingworth as an instructor. It appeared that there was a grave shortage of experienced flight engineers on the training units, so an SOS was sent round the group to identify any eligible persons, such as myself, and shunt us off to impart as much knowledge as we could to the new crews coming through the system. So on 26 September, my kit and I were put on board a tender and I went through the camp gates for the last time on my way to Faldingworth. Weatherwise I had arrived at Wickenby at the wrong time as it was in the rainy season, and my first impression had been very gloomy, but as winter passed and the mud dried I became quite attached to the place, and I left with the same bittersweet feelings that I had when leaving Penrhos. The parting was very gentle, however, as Faldingworth was literally just up the road and the airfield circuit overlapped that of Wickenby; but best of all I was still in No. 1 Group with the same attachments as before.

Chapter Seven

Faldingworth

RAF Faldingworth, like Wickenby, was another wartime camp that had been built in a hurry at a cost of about £800,000, and it had just been opened although still incomplete. I also arrived there at the wrong time of year, for it was raining hard and most of the camp site was churned up into a thick glutinous mud, which persisted throughout my stay there. The only hard surfaces were the runways and dispersals, with the addition of a few roads leading to the living quarters. Even these roads did not go directly to the huts, and we had to walk the last ten to fifteen yards either on planks or by struggling along wearing gumboots. Indeed, the standard practice when going to the mess was to don gumboots and change into shoes on arrival, but if one was merely going to work or to fly, the gumboots remained on until the last minute! Officers and men lived in the same type of Nissen huts, usually remote from the water supply, and about the only advantage gained by the officers was to have some of that water delivered to the hut. Apart from that, we had to fend for ourselves as the batting services were almost non-existent.

The only flying unit at Faldingworth during my time there was No. 1667 Heavy Conversion Unit (HCU) operating Halifaxes and Lancasters, all of them of ancient vintage, being cast-offs from the operational stations. The role of the HCU was to receive crews from the initial Operational Training Units (OTUs) and, together with the addition of a flight engineer and an additional gunner, to weld them into a fully competent team ready to sally forth on operations. Because there was a shortage of Lancasters due to the priority of the operational squadrons, most of the training was done on Halifaxes, of which there were two flights, A and B, but the final phase of the course took place on the Lancaster flight. There was also a static Lanc, unfit for flying, which was used for ground training.

My brief was mainly to lecture and demonstrate, and although I only flew on three occasions during the three months that I was there, I was quite busy most of the time. Owing to the remoteness of the station there was very little outside life to explore and, apart from a couple of visits to Lincoln and Market Rasen, the local pub was the main port of call. For this reason we had to fall back on the officers' mess, which was in fact one of the bright spots of the camp. Once one had changed into shoes and entered the ante-room, one was conscious of a dramatic change of environment from the mud that characterised the rest of the station. Even though the mess was only a wooden building, great efforts had been made to make it cheerful and comfortable, with tasteful furniture including plenty of relaxing chairs, but the main feature was a magnificently built stone fireplace that dominated the centre of the room. This great edifice was constructed on the directions of the commanding officer, which led to an inquiry as the Messing Committee had refused to authorise the expenditure. We did not know the full story, but word went round that he had been reprimanded by Group HQ and had only escaped more serious consequences on the grounds that he had done his best to enliven an otherwise dreadful existence for his fellow officers. It is hardly surprising to hear that the fireplace became known as the CO's Folly!

While I was at Faldingworth I attended another official mess party, which went off in similar fashion to the one at Wickenby, and I also attended several unofficial parties that sprang up, notably when crews 'graduated' from the training course. These all followed the same rowdy pattern as before. On the same theme, a dance was held in the airmen's mess to which, in accordance with protocol, the officers were invited. To make the event successful, as much of the local talent as possible was rounded up, but this had the effect of crowding the place out and dancing became somewhat difficult. I did not meet anyone of interest and in common with a lot of others, drifted away before the end.

A notable event took place just after my arrival at Faldingworth – I was awarded my first campaign medal! The decoration itself was the 1939–45 Star, which had a three-coloured ribbon: dark blue representing the Royal Navy, red for the Army, and light blue for the RAF. Supplies of the ribbon were available on the camp, and it was a very proud moment when we sewed a piece on to our tunics. Those eligible for the Star were flying personnel on aircrew duties who had been on an operational squadron for sixty days and had flown on one sortie. The medal itself was issued after the end of the war, for naturally nobody knew in 1943 when it would end! I well remember making my first appearance in the mess after sewing on the ribbon, and the few of us who were there, although feeling very self-conscious, had a definite air of superiority over the rest who had not qualified. Little were we to know that as more and more people became eligible for this award it would become very common, to the extent of hardly being worth bothering about. It was known as the Spam medal, after the processed meat of the time, presumably because the ribbon colours, with red in the middle, represented a sandwich.

There was a small band of flight engineer instructors, about six or seven in our department, and we were under the control of one Harold Kershaw, who had recently been promoted to flying officer. Harold had good engineering qualities for the post, but his capability as a comedian came a very close second. One only had to look at his face with its mischievous grin to start laughing, and his lectures were a scream. He would develop the theme in all seriousness, but at the vital point would say something amusing and in no time would have everyone in stitches. It was really an ideal way to instruct as it laid emphasis on the important detail, which one would then remember when other things were forgotten. I sat in on a number of Harold's lectures and it was he who really taught me the art of instruction, even if my version was a little more mundane!

One of his episodes was concerned with survival in a dinghy after ditching. He had experienced this traumatic situation himself so he was able to speak with authority, and he gave his talk in a serious vein until he came to the pigeons. For the previous two or three years it had been customary to take pigeons on bomber operations to enable word to be sent back to base in the event of ditching in the sea, but Harold's pigeons were not very reliable. 'We released them after putting a message and location on their legs, and off they went, but within a few minutes they were back again and perched on the side of the dinghy, where they stayed. Time and again we picked them up and launched them off, but back they came, and in the end we had to give it up. They were still there the following day and, being soft-hearted and not quite hungry enough, we decided not to kill them and so had to feed them. The only thing we could spare was some chocolate, which they ate with gusto, and this went on for another day, by which time we were getting really hungry and the chocolate had all gone. We were just about to do the dark deed when we were sighted by a British ship, which picked us up, and the pigeons left with us perched on the rigging. They remained that way until we reached England – having travelled the easy way!' I can vouch for the story, having heard it at first hand, but cannot confirm the truth of it, and am not so sure that pigeons eat chocolate either, but it was Harold's way of telling the tale and this sort of nonsense enlivened many a dull lecture.

The talks that we gave were aimed more at the pilots than the engineers. Most of the training they had undergone at the OTUs was on ancient Wellington bombers that had radial engines with only one throttle control, whereas now they were required to operate the Merlin engine, which had a lever governing the revolutions as well as a throttle lever controlling the boost. The engineers had come straight from St Athan and were well up on the theory of this type of engine, so some of the information we imparted was wasted on them. It was a battle royal with some of the pilots to make them see how essential it was to save fuel by using the throttle control and leaving the revs at the lowest possible speed, but we managed to convert them in the main, although how they acted when on operations depended to a large extent on the engineer's powers of persuasion. After an initial contretemps with Villiers he had seen reason and usually left the engine controls to me, except in an emergency, and we tried to instil this idea into our pupil pilots in the presence of the engineer, giving the latter a few more strings to his bow! The syllabus included rescue and escape (from the aircraft) procedures in addition to covering the layout of the aircraft, fuel systems, pre-flight checking, hydraulics and electrics – quite a packed programme. The flying course covered about twenty to thirty hours, and in the initial stages the pilot was accompanied by either a second pilot or an engineer instructor. I did three such duties, the first of which was the most interesting.

The Mk I Halifax had attained a great notoriety for being accident prone due to the small fins and rudders, and many of them had spun into the ground while being flown by pilots of little experience. They were present on all the group conversion units as at that stage in the war there was nothing else available to replace them with, and of course we had our share of them at Faldingworth. With this history in mind, it will be readily understood that I had a certain reluctance to chance my arm in one of them, but I was eventually persuaded to do so by a good friend of mine, Pilot Officer Lawrence, DFM, who had flown second dickey with us to Essen back in April and was now on the Faldingworth staff.

I have only a hazy recollection of the Halifax crew layout, but it was much different from the Lancaster in the cockpit area, with the engineer being somewhat further back from the pilot and the instrument panel being halfway across the fuselage behind the pilot's seat. I had a short conversion course from Lawrence before going on board, mainly concerning the fuel cocks and hydraulic controls, but the engines were Merlins and I knew how to handle those!

The exercise was a two-hour stint of circuits and bumps with a pupil pilot, Sergeant Berry. We took off at 09.40 hours on 9 October, and although the cockpit was a little crowded with Lawrence in the second dickey seat, I soon got used to my routine, which in the event turned out to be only a gauge-watching exercise. I had plenty of confidence in Lawrence, especially when I saw how well he handled the aircraft and heard his words of wisdom to his pupil, and apart from the fact that we were continually circling the airfield, I quite enjoyed the experience. My second flight was a short trip with the chief flying instructor, Wing Commander Donaldson, DSO, DFC, which took place on 18 October in Lancaster R5692 – a proper museum piece! This was a test flight to check the engine feathering, following adjustments made to the electrical circuits after a crew was unable to feather a faulty engine. It was a disturbing flight in some respects as Donaldson instructed me to feather each engine in turn until we were flying on only one, the port outer, and this in turn was stopped as soon as we had restarted the starboard outer. This drastic exercise was not really necessary, and I suspect it was done only because Donaldson wanted to show off his flying skills. My last flight from Faldingworth was a short period of circuits and bumps in Lancaster W4248 on 13 November, just to keep my hand in.

The next step in the flying course was that after being passed out from solo circuits, the pilot then flew with his own crew, mainly on cross-countries. These trips were treated as though they were operations, with the crew having to navigate to a specific landmark on dead-reckoning timing, and to prove their success at locating the target a photograph was taken that also indicated the time. Many of these flights were at night, when infra-red photography was used. To enhance the operational atmosphere a full briefing was given to the crews, and I had to attend a lot of these to give last-minute instructions to the pilots and engineers, with particular regard to correct engine handling, which was especially important if there was any bad weather about. Afterwards I had to check the logs and use praise or reprimand, whichever was due! Unfortunately, there was a high incidence of crashes on these exercises for various reasons – the aircraft were all old, and many had been repaired after flak damage; there was still a stability problem with the Mk I Halifax; crews lost their way and got disoriented at night; and sudden bad weather caused difficulties. These were some of the dangers facing the airmen; I used to think it a wonder that even more accidents didn't happen.

I have already mentioned that the life of a junior officer was bedevilled with various duties, and now I was saddled with one of the most thankless tasks of all. I was required to travel to Sunderland to represent the station at the funeral of the victim of one of these tragic flying accidents. The lad in question was just nineteen years old and had been recently married, so I had a young wife to contend with as well as the rest of the family. I travelled a day early, and I well remember the train journey from Lincoln to York, where I had to change, and on to Durham where I changed again. On arrival in Sunderland on a bleak November day I booked into a hotel and then set off to contact the family.

Fortunately for me another RAF officer, a relative who had obtained special leave, was also there, and together we managed to calm the distressed family. I arrived early the next morning to check that all the arrangements were in order, and shortly before the funeral I was surprised by the appearance of almost the entire Sunderland football team. It transpired that the lad had been a member of the colts side and the team had turned up to pay their last respects. After the funeral the family insisted that I stayed for the traditional meal, and it was late by the time I made it back to the hotel. For once I was not sorry to return to camp, and it took a long time to get the episode out of my mind.

Shortly before I left Faldingworth I was roped in for another duty. A petrol bowser had caught fire – although fortunately the fire had been put out with a hand extinguisher before any damage was done – and I was asked to conduct an inquiry into the incident. In true detective fashion I visited the scene of the 'crime' and also interviewed the driver, who proclaimed his innocence and made out that it was a great mystery. In the absence of witnesses I had to decide the cause for myself, and ended up with the verdict that it was indeed the driver's fault in being negligent. Apparently, when trying to start the pump motor, which was located in a compartment at the back of the bowser, he had managed to flood the cylinder with petrol and had removed the spark plug and lead to blow it out again, turning the flywheel by hand. I did not need to be an engineering genius to fathom this out, as it was the correct procedure and I had seen it done several times – in fact I had even done it myself on a cement mixer! However, the driver had left the lead in contact with the floor of the compartment and a spark had occurred when the flywheel was turned. Fortunately the driver did have the presence of mind to grab the extinguisher and quench the resulting fire. I took no further part in the case after I had finished the inquiry, so all I had to do was write my report and hand it to the commanding officer, but there was a sequel to this that I shall mention later.

During the latter part of 1943, the supply of Lancasters from the manufacturers was keeping up with demand, and it was considered that one or two more could be spared for the HCUs, although a decision was made afterwards that all the training Lancasters should be regrouped together into one unit. Consequently, the Lancaster elements in the group were detached to RAF Hemswell, and so No. 1 Lancaster Finishing School (LFS) was born (a similar arrangement was made in the other groups so that there were also Nos 3, 5, and later a No. 6, LFS).

About the middle of December I was told to report to Group HQ and was interviewed there by my old chief Wing Commander Wood. Without beating about the bush he dropped the bombshell of asking me if I would be interested in taking up the post of flight engineer leader on the new LFS now being formed. Obviously I wasted no time in accepting, and was overjoyed to hear him say that it would also mean an immediate promotion to flight lieutenant as soon as the unit opened on 1 January 1944. Naturally I carried on in my lowly position at Faldingworth, but did go to Hemswell on a couple of occasions to establish an office and meet my future colleagues, but I couldn't really wait to get away from the muddy morass of such a terrible camp and the end of the month seemed remote!

A word must be said to explain the vagaries of officer promotion, to put my new rank into context. Starting off as a pilot officer, there was an automatic advancement to flying officer after six months. There was also automatic promotion to flight lieutenant afterwards, but in this case the qualifying period was two years. An acting rank could be granted at any time during this period, and this was the arrangement that I was under at Hemswell. In the event, my new acting rank was not confirmed until sometime during April when I had been a flying officer for a couple of months, but it was backdated to 1 January and the extra money I received came in very handy. It is of interest to note that official confirmation of these ranks was very sluggish, and one invariably had the first indication from the bank when the additional payment was made; in fact, it became standard procedure to adopt the new rank when notified by the bank!

At the end of 1942 I had been very doubtful of surviving much longer, but my gloomy outlook had turned out to be at variance with reality, for here I was a year later not only alive and kicking but actually looking forward to the next one! Not only had I been through a tour of operations – which was the ultimate in an airman's career – but I had advanced from corporal to flight lieutenant in thirteen months; not bad going by any standards. Naturally, I was greatly indebted to Woody who, both at Wickenby and Group HQ, had followed my progress with interest, the culmination of which was his landing for me the plum job at Hemswell.

There was one complication with my establishment at Hemswell, and that was it was necessary for me to take a flight engineer leader's course beforehand. This meant that although I arrived at the station on 1 January, I left again three days later to spend a further month at St Athan!

Chapter Eight

St Athan Revisited

I had to endure another dreary cross-country journey on my way to South Wales, changing trains at Gloucester as usual. On leaving this city I fell asleep and woke up to a deathly silence. The train had stopped and the carriage door was open, which resulted in my having a momentary panic wondering where I was. Tumbling out on to the platform I was most relieved to see a name board, 'Cardiff General', and then realised this was as far as the train was booked to go. On enquiry I found that it had been in the station for nearly two hours, which had not mattered as far as the journey was concerned but it meant that I had missed my connection and had to sit about until 05.00 when I caught the milk train to St Athan.

Little had really changed since my last visit there, but one noticeable difference this time was that I was now enjoying the relative comforts of the officers' mess. As before, the course was conducted entirely on the ground and we did not even have to board an aircraft. The course members were drawn from all types of squadrons, including Coastal Command, and the lectures were mainly on general subjects, common to all, but the emphasis was aimed at leadership and the art of instruction. Technical matters were also covered and these were mainly concerned with updating us on the modifications and improvements that had been made to engines and electrical equipment. Much stress was also placed on an effective liaison with the squadron engineering staff. We were required to give lectures ourselves to our fellow sufferers, to give mock briefings and debriefings, and to exercise plenty of thought on methods of assessment and judgement. A new type of inflatable dinghy was being introduced at that time, and we had an enjoyable period getting acquainted with it at the baths. With all the concentration we had to apply, the time passed quickly and suddenly the month was up. We were now being assessed ourselves to see if we had made the grade. It had been a case of practically all work and no play, but I had managed to visit Cardiff once or twice to break the monotony.

About a week before the course ended, I became the victim of a monumental entanglement with red tape. I was called before the station CO and informed that an error had been made with regard to the inquiry I had conducted into the fire at Faldingworth. Unfortunately, I had forgotten to append a copy of the fire regulations to the report, and I was required to return there immediately to do so. The CO himself was amazed at this when I explained what it was all about, and to say that I was flabbergasted was to put it mildly. Why couldn't someone else attach the offending document to the report? After all, it didn't affect the material evidence or the conclusion. Apparently this couldn't be done as I had to sign it first. Why couldn't it be posted to me for signature and then returned? No, because I had to attach it personally. Why couldn't some lowly erk who could travel third class bring the whole lot down to me and witness me attaching it? No, for some other reason.

By now it will be obvious that I had no alternative but to go and do it the hard way, and plans were made to get me on the way. As this interview took place on a Saturday, it was decided that I should travel on the Sunday because it was the only free day we had each week, and so at a very early hour on the following day I was picked up by a car and transported to Cardiff station ready to commence what was to be a marathon journey. Anyone who has had experience of travelling by train from Wales on a Sunday, especially with the wartime dislocation of traffic, will sympathise with me when I say that it took me over twelve hours to reach Lincoln, having been routed via Manchester of all places! I ended up at Faldingworth in the early hours of Monday and (shades of Wickenby) had to kip in the mess until the working day started. It took about twelve minutes to deal with the paperwork, and after obtaining a packed lunch I was on my way back south again. Travelling on the Monday was much more straightforward, but it still took me most of the day to get back to

St Athan, when, to the best of my recollection, I retired to bed early to recover! I had lost a whole day of the course in addition to suffering frayed nerves. The main subject I had missed out on was the calculation of centres of gravity, and I had to have special tuition on the subject one evening to catch up.

The assessment at the end of the course was made partly on our past work and partly by oral examinations, and with a mark of seventy-three per cent I thought I had made a reasonable showing. On 2 February, a week after my never-to-be-forgotten journey, I left St Athan for the last time and once more headed north.

Chapter Nine

Hemswell

From the old Roman city of Lincoln, Ermine Street (A15) runs almost due north in a dead straight line. About eleven miles from Lincoln the A631 road to Gainsborough crosses Ermine Street at right angles. This crossing is known as Caenby Corner and is easily distinguishable by a large public house, known as the Moncks Arms, which is situated there. This was our local pub. RAF Hemswell was sited on the A631 four miles west of Caenby Corner and nine miles from Gainsborough. To say that the camp lay on this road is no exaggeration because the road actually bisected it, with the airfield and administrative buildings on one side, and the officers' mess and some married quarters on the opposite one. The station was constructed in the 1930s, being equipped with substantial brick-built accommodation, and apart from Halton, it was the first permanent camp that I was stationed at. The officers' mess was a dream, and compared to conditions at Faldingworth it was like staying at the Ritz! The building was not unique, but was in the same style as those at most of the other pre-war stations and comprised a large ante-room, a sizeable dining room, a billiard room, entrance hall and various other smaller public rooms, one of which was used as a bar. There was a corridor running the length of the building with bedrooms leading off, and with doorways giving outside access. At the ends of the corridor were two large staircases to the upper storey where more bedrooms were situated. These rooms were big enough for two single beds, a small table and a wardrobe, and had a washbasin built into an alcove. The bathrooms were spaced at intervals along the corridors; the hot taps actually dispensed hot water and the whole building was centrally heated – luxury indeed!

As we were an entirely new unit, a lot of the personnel were unknown to each other. I had a staff of between eight and ten as time went along. Two of them were officers and the others were sergeants, one of whom had come with me from Faldingworth. My immediate superior was Wing Commander Powley, DFC, AFC (Air Force Cross), a Canadian who was the chief flying instructor (the equivalent of squadron commander). I hit it off with Powley right from the start and was to serve under him for a much longer period of time than anyone else, but strangely enough I never flew with him, although during my career I did take to the air with no less than nine other wing commanders!

The instructional team was completed with the navigation, bombing, gunnery and signals leaders and their staffs, each lecturing on their own subjects as applied to the Lancaster aircraft. There was a set curriculum of lectures, and each course had a week of ground training followed by approximately twelve hours' flying, which meant that trainees were at Hemswell for about three weeks. The courses started on Sunday and my department dealt with pilots and engineers, who we had for about six periods during the week when we lectured to them on such diverse subjects as engine handling (they must have been fed up with this by the time they reached the squadrons), carburetion, dinghy drill, hydraulics and, of course, all matters relating specially to the Lancaster. My forte was engine handling and the Stromberg carburettor, my diagrammatic version of which was a veritable work of art on the blackboard! I had specialist lecturers among my staff who dealt with electrics and hydraulics etc., and although I say it myself, I think we did a competent job and worked together as a very happy band. At the end of the course I had to assess each engineer and the results of this assessment were recorded on a special form, which was then attached to their records.

I used to start each course off, and it was usual for the pilots and engineers to give me custody of their logbooks so that I could check on their depth of experience, types of aircraft flown in and so on. Looking through these one day, a familiar name hit me, one Flying Officer Jones. I was aware that there were many men named Flying Officer Jones in the service, but something made me examine his logbook more closely and, sure enough, it was the same pilot that I had so many difficulties

with at Penrhos when he was never satisfied with the aircraft serviceability! In a flash I realised that I was now above him in rank, and pondered what revenge I might take. After giving the matter a little thought,
though, I concluded that there wasn't a lot I could do even if I had wanted
to. However, I could not resist asking him to come and see me, whereupon I identified myself to his amazement. I told him that his attitude
had rankled a bit, but that naturally the previous episode wouldn't affect
things while he was at Hemswell, and we ended up having a laugh over
the irony of it all. It really was a great coincidence with the odds against
a meeting like that being enormous. I do not know how he ended up after
he left us, but if he always insisted on flying perfect aircraft he wouldn't
have done many operations!

As in civilian life, there had to be a continuous updating of information
in the RAF and other Services, and for this reason I was sent to Rolls-
Royce Engines Ltd, at Derby for a week's course sometime in April. I
was billeted in a private house not far from the works, and staying with
me were several other people who were attending the same course, one
or two from the Army and one from the Navy (Rolls-Royce were everywhere!). Engine handling and fuel conservation were top of the agenda,
but we were also shown many of the stages of manufacture of the Merlin
engine, including the milling of the engine blocks and grinding of the
crankshafts. A visit was made to the drop-forging department to see the
valves being made, but the highlight of the week was seeing (and hearing)
the engine test-beds. Each engine made had to undergo rigorous tests,
and for these to be carried out they were bolted to a framework with
the exhaust manifolds being coupled to a pipeline leading the gases away
from the area. We were allowed to run one up and a thrilling experience
it was, although the noise was deafening – but great stuff! While we
were in Derby we also took the opportunity to go out on the town once
or twice, and on one occasion ended up at an old-time dance.

   All too soon I was back at Hemswell to learn that my rank had at last
been confirmed. I had promoted myself to flying officer in February on
receiving the notification from the bank, and had had a thicker ring sewn
on my uniform. Now I could have another one added, but when it came
back from the tailors it was noticeable that the older ring had weathered

slightly and they were now two different colours. I meant to have them altered but never got round to it. Ironically, the rings on my spare tunic were a perfect match but I hardly ever wore it.

The flying instruction we gave at Hemswell was similar to that at Faldingworth, so there was always a constant juggling around with the staff to fit in lectures, and while I was personally not obliged to do much regular flying I did carry out a number of training flights when I could get away from my administrative routine. Most of these flights were the same as ones that I had undertaken at Wickenby or Faldingworth, and as such it would be boring to describe them in detail. I will merely mention them in passing, then, except to describe the first time I flew, as it was so significant and there is quite a story to tell about the pilot.

The details concerning the arrival of both pilot and aircraft cannot be remembered, but at the beginning of April a Wing Commander Campling, DSO, DFC, appeared at Hemswell in a Halifax, presumably to undertake a conversion course to Lancasters. Campling had acquired the reputation of being mad-headed during his operational career and nobody was really keen to fly with him. So my consternation can be imagined when he approached me in the mess and asked me to go up with him in the Halifax on an air test! It was bad enough dicing with death with Campling at the controls, but added to that the aircraft was a Halifax III with Hercules XIV radial engines, different as chalk and cheese from the Merlins I was used to. Although I demurred diplomatically, with the latter reason for my dissent, he was adamant that I should accompany him. Thus it was that on 5 April I became airborne again after the shortest conversion course ever. 'We shan't be up long enough to change the tanks, just watch those cylinder head temperature gauges and tell me if they go above 60 degrees', was all he had to say, and then we were off on one of the most awful flights I ever made. A new engine had been fitted, which was the reason for the test, but he flung us around the sky as though the aircraft itself was on trial. We were only up for 15 minutes, and it was just as well that Campling never asked me to go with him again, for if he had I would have refused point-blank.

His lady friend, an ATA (Air Transport Auxiliary) pilot who was staying in Lincoln, came to visit him at Hemswell a short time afterwards; she was quite good-looking and he flaunted her round the mess to the distraction of most of the inmates! There were one or two repeat visits, and we had just about got used to seeing her about when he decided to take her flying. Quite a number of people turned out to see them take off, just as though they were going on operations, but this was the one Campling did not return from, for within half an hour he was dead. He crashed near Caister and eyewitnesses said that he was showing off by beating the place up when a wingtip caught a tree, causing the aircraft to dive into the ground, killing all on board. He had not only wrecked a valuable aircraft and caused the deaths of himself and his girlfriend, but he had also taken one of my engineers with him, and to me that was the unkindest cut of all. It took a long time for the department to settle down after that, for while we could have accepted the loss of one of our number in a genuine accident, it was hard to come to terms with losing a young lad in such a senseless incident as that. As far as I was concerned it was a clear case of 'there for the grace of God go I'.

The next time I flew was on 13 April, on dual circuits for half an hour; the senior pilot on this trip was Flying Officer Lighton, an ex-No. 12 Squadron chap whom I had flown with on one occasion at Wickenby. This was followed by a three-hour stint of circuits, exactly one month later on 13 May, this time with Flight Lieutenant Gersekowski in charge. It will not be apparent from his name, but Andy Gersekowski was actually an Australian, probably of Polish descent, and I chummed up with him during my stay at Hemswell. He was mad keen on photography and developed all his own films. I well remember going to Lincoln with him on the bus and helping him carry back a load of equipment that he bought from the photography shop there. Where he got his films from is a bit of a mystery, for they were one of the items that were very much 'under the counter' during wartime, and I could only get one very occasionally from a friendly chemist when I was home on leave.

Back to the circuits and landings, during this particular session we touched down at Sturgate, a local RAF station, to give the pupil pilot practice at landing at an unfamiliar airfield. It was business as usual with further training flights, clocking up a total of nine hours over the next couple of months (many were the circuits in nine hours!). During these sessions I flew with Lighton and Gersekowski again, but on one of the others was a pupil pilot flying solo for the express purpose of checking his engineer, who was of doubtful calibre. Another unusual trip was made on 20 September when we landed at Bottesford and stayed overnight, returning the next day. The aircraft was piloted by Flight Lieutenants Lighton and Wishart who were both instructors. I cannot remember the stated reason for the trip, but when I mention that the station was sited not far from Nottingham, anyone with a slight imagination can conjure up the real reason! My last flight from Hemswell was made on 28 September on the same familiar merry-go-round of familiarisation and dual circuits, which took my total hours flown at No. 1 LFS to sixteen, and Wing Commander Powley signed my logbook in confirmation.

With a complement of ancient aircraft that were unfamiliar to the crews who flew them, it was inevitable that accidents would happen to mar the smooth running of the conversion course, and I have records of at least seven Lancasters that crashed while I was at Hemswell. These were W4132 on 3 February, R5851 on 14 March, R5672 on 9 April, W4793 on 6 May, W4965 on 16 May, W4790 on 28 August and R5866 on 25 September. Five of these aircraft were littered around the countryside, but W4790 came to grief at Hemswell when it overshot the runway, and W4965 crashed while taking off from Sturgate. The end of W4965 was a spectacular affair, and the following details are taken from *Lincolnshire Air War* by S. Finn, published by Aero Litho Co. of Lincoln:

The aircraft was taking off from Sturgate from a runway covered with wood shavings. A tyre burst causing it to swerve off the runway, across the grass and through a hedge, colliding with and snapping off three trees which changed its direction and it crashed into some farm buildings. The crash crew soon arrived, driving their vehicle over one of the mainplanes which had broken off. The aircrew got out of the aircraft and water and foam were pumped into the burning plane. The crew went into the house and the farmer's wife made them a cup of tea which she had difficulty in providing because the electric cable had been broken, but she got her old oil stove going to a background noise of exploding ammunition. Gainsborough Fire Brigade now arrived, which threw a great strain on the water resources, but eventually the fire was put out. The farmer counted his losses – a new Dutch barn, two pigs, chicken and chicken huts, a garage with a damaged car, a shed full of farming equipment, roofing, slates, brickwork etc. Water was everywhere as 20,000 gallons were used to dowse the fire, and lastly they lost their dog, which had to be put down. In claiming damages, which took a very long time, they were confronted with the fact that the aircraft was not taking off on operations, and this raised many difficulties. Their claims were finally settled.

This sort of thing was happening with monotonous regularity all over Lincolnshire and the expenditure must have been enormous, apart from the deaths of many aircrew members. I had a young engineer on the course who by coincidence lived in Warwick Road, Acocks Green, about 400yds from my home, and I promised to look him up when I was on leave. When I eventually knocked the door I was faced with his mother who told me that he had been killed on his second flight after joining his squadron, and it was only a training exercise at that.

At the beginning of June I was sent on another special course. This time it was on Stromberg carburettors (which I already thought I knew backwards!) and I had to journey to London. The firm I was to visit was Zenith Carburettors Ltd, who made the Strombergs under licence from America, and they were situated in Honeypot Lane, Stanmore in Middlesex. I arrived at Queensbury (the nearest tube station) on the Bakerloo Line from King's Cross station and walked a few hundred yards to the house I was to stay at, and was given a very warm welcome by the retired couple who owned it. The date was 5 June. After having tea and chatting to them for some time, I retired to bed ready for an early start in the morning, but was rudely woken in the early hours by a colossal force of aircraft passing overhead. More and more aircraft appeared, a veritable armada, and soon the whole household was up and wondering what it was all about. No more sleep was possible that night, and in the morning all was made clear – we had witnessed the beginning of the second front in Europe, 6 June of course being D-Day. This onslaught had been widely advocated for some time and much speculation had been given to its timing, but I never dreamed that I would be in London to see the start of it; an unforgettable moment!

My hosts were such good company that I did not go out at night during the week I was there, with the exception of Sunday when I was taken to the local pub, the Queen of Hearts, to see a cabaret show, and as a member of the armed forces I was highly honoured with a seat at the front. As to the course, well, the carburettors were getting bigger and bigger (they already weighed more than 28lb!) and we had to know more about the new modifications because they gave a better performance. In a way I did think it a bit of a waste of time, but it was very interesting to see them being made.

Back at Hemswell again, I was 'collared' by the station commander to give him several talks about Lancaster procedures, as I had with Craven at Wickenby. His bosom friend was an Army major who was stationed at Hemswell to deal with airfield defence and anything pertaining to the military. He once gave us a lecture about air-raid precautions but otherwise did not worry us. One abiding memory I have of him concerned his obsession to keep up with the war situation, and to this end one would always see him seated next to the wireless set in the mess ready for the nine o'clock news. To get in this prime position he had to 'bag' the seat early, and I often saw him dash to it straight after dinner even though he was an hour or so too soon.

There was an occasion when the CO invited the officers to his house (within the station perimeter) for drinks. Naturally we all turned up, but how we all got in goodness knows. I have a recollection of perching on the arm of a settee with about six others on the seat proper, and many others sitting on the floor. We were met at the door by the CO and his wife, and I must say that off-duty he was the life and soul of the party – after all, he had been young once himself! Mess orderlies had been recruited to deal with the drinks, and I don't think there was much left by the time we finished. The CO was very approachable and this sort of get-together at the right time and place not only boosted morale, but made cooperation with him and his policies much more palatable.

The same sort of thing applied to the mess parties, of which there were two or three while I was there. The routine and atmosphere at these gatherings was about the same as I have described elsewhere, but a new item was introduced at Hemswell – the Derby races. The horses were officers who had had a minimum of two pints to drink beforehand, and they had to race on all fours in lanes that had been roped off. The race was run in heats and the winner was completely exhausted at the finish – and fairly drunk as well. The spectators had only to guarantee fair play and bet on the contestants. A hand bell was used to start each race, and the cheering was ear-splitting; I wouldn't have been surprised if they had heard us in Lincoln!

The mess at Hemswell was set back slightly from the road and had a concrete forecourt in front of it, behind which was a row of garages. Several officers had cars, and they could often be seen tinkering with them on the forecourt, including Flight Lieutenant Eric Weaver, the gunnery leader, who had the oldest of all bangers it was possible to own. His vintage Morris Eight was always breaking down, but as I was a good friend of his and had no other form of transport except for my bicycle, I deigned to accompany him on several runs, always being ready to get out and push.

Two of these excursions were to Nottingham, and both were memorable. On the first one we arrived without any problems, except for a bit of rough running, which was normal, and after a 'do' round the town we ended up dancing at the Nottingham Palais. The drama happened on the way back. First of all the engine wouldn't start as the battery was flat, and no amount of cranking and pushing had any effect, so Eric decided to give the contact points a clean-up with the sandpaper on his matchbox. By this time a resident had ventured out of a nearby house to see what all the fuss was about, and we recruited him to give us a push, with Eric at the controls. Fortunately the engine kicked and he managed to catch it; we were then able to proceed back to base, providing he did not stall the engine or take his foot off the accelerator. However, about half way back he wanted to spend a penny rather urgently, and his contortions with one foot on the pedal and the other on the road were amusing in the extreme! After all that he did let the engine die out when he had to stop at a crossroads, but by then there was a bit of charge in the battery, and a few cranks started it again and enabled us to roll up at Hemswell in the early hours.

I swore I would not tempt fate again in that old car, but changed my mind when the second trip came up. One of our colleagues invited us to a party in Nottingham on the occasion of his girlfriend's twenty-first birthday. The event was a posh one and was held at the George Hotel, Eric and I booking into the same hotel to stay the night. The meal was very ordinary owing to wartime rationing, but the drinks were there in abundance and soon the festivities were going with a swing. It was rather sedate in comparison with the mess parties, but with the dancing and various games we thoroughly enjoyed it, and it was very late when we eventually rolled into bed. Amazingly, we had a trouble-free journey back to camp on the following morning, and although I did not go on any more long trips with Eric, it was not the last time that I was to push his car, for we even once ground to a halt on the way to the Moncks Arms, and eventually had to abandon it and walk back!

Apart from these car trips I got about by bus and bike. It was nine miles to Gainsborough, which I could cycle comfortably, especially as I was almost always accompanied by one or more other excursionists. We used to visit the local hostelry as there was not much else to do, and it was a very drab place even when the sun shone. There was one establishment of interest that provided a highlight on the odd Saturday that we were able to get off. The State was basically a cinema that had a performance starting at about two o'clock, and after this we went on to the State cafe upstairs for tea, followed by a local hop in the State ballroom adjoining. In this case, as the hop went on until quite late, it was usual to travel to Gainsborough by bus and come back by taxi. Lincoln was too far away for me to reach by cycle, and apart from some official visits when I travelled by station transport, I saw very little of it. On the other hand I explored several places in the opposite direction where I had never ventured before, principally the old coaching towns of East Retford and Worksop, which were reached by bus with a change at Gainsborough. I learned to play bridge at Hemswell, where we had sessions in one of the smaller mess rooms. Sadly I never really advanced past the mediocre stage, but as most of my contemporaries were of a similar ilk, my shortcomings did not show up and some very exciting games developed. I was slightly better at the snooker table and I did once win a competition, but I must admit that it was more through luck than judgement!

On 9 August I was sent on yet another course, this time to RAF North

Luffenham, near Oakham in Rutland. I travelled by train from Lincoln and had to change at Grantham and Peterborough before arriving at Grantham in good order. I then became a victim of a piece of 'duff gen' from a porter, which completely transformed the journey. He directed me to the correct platform and told me not to catch the next train to arrive as it did not stop at Peterborough, but to get on the following one. Obeying his instructions to the letter I boarded the said train but was dismayed when it ran straight through Peterborough North, and also Central, and I pinned my hopes on Peterborough South only to find that no such station existed. I then realised that the blighter at Grantham had mixed up the trains and I was unavoidably heading for King's Cross, where we pulled in an hour or so later. My first instinct was to change platforms and go straight back, but then I mused that I was a day early and by coincidence it was also a bank holiday, so I decided to stay in London overnight and journey back the following day. I managed to talk my way past the ticket collector who accepted my reason for travelling to London on an Oakham ticket, and caught the tube train to South Kensington to book in at the Wings Club.

My impromptu holiday was marred, however, by the presence of German flying bombs, which were now falling on the capital at regular intervals. These unpleasant objects were pilotless aircraft about 22ft long with a warhead not far short of a ton in weight. They were set on a course with a timing device calculated to stop the engine when over the target. From the ground they made a horribly distinctive noise, but at least people were safe while they could be heard; the danger point came when the engine cut out. There was suddenly a very pregnant silence and one could only dash for cover in the way that I did that evening while eating in a restaurant in Piccadilly. The only cover available was underneath the table, which is where I ended up, and when the bomb exploded it was near enough to shake everyone up and to break a window. After this I was rather pleased to wave London goodbye, especially as I was woken up the following morning by the sound of more bombs going over, and after a lengthy explanation regarding my irregular ticket, I was off again on a train that actually stopped at Peterborough.

The course I was about to embark upon was administrative rather than technical and lasted a fortnight, during which time I had lectures on many subjects including law (and an appraisal of King's Regulations), methods of instruction and administration. Of particular interest was a mock trial where I was supposed to have been the villain of the piece (I got acquitted though!), and a court of inquiry where I acted as a witness. We were in a permanent mess similar to Hemswell, and in view of the fact that we had a lot of homework to do, I went out only once, for a Saturday night in Oakham. Like most courses of this nature it was considered to be a 'bind', but I reckoned that as I was there I might as well make the most of it, so I approached it conscientiously and certainly left North Luffenham wiser than I had arrived.

Two other small items are of interest in connection with Hemswell. I have already mentioned that I had a very happy relationship with my staff and although we may have had minor disagreements, I cannot recall any incidents of consequence. To illustrate the harmonious atmosphere that prevailed, my minions cajoled one of their number (an artist in civilian life) to paint me an attractive door sign, which was presented to me on my birthday in April when my promotion had been confirmed. I always thought highly of that sign and took it with me wherever I was posted afterwards, and still have it to this day. The other interesting matter was my meeting with a familiar face one day, towards the end of September. I was walking down the road to station headquarters when this fellow hove into view, and after a moment I recognised him as Tommy Thompson, ex-Hut 13 at Wickenby, and by now a flying officer. We stopped to have a good natter, but he was rather cagey and wouldn't tell me the reason for his being there, so we shook hands and went our different ways. I pondered for some time over this reluctance to put me in the picture, but I supposed that he had good reasons for not doing so, and as events turned out I was soon to find out what they were.

When, at the latter end of 1944, the supply of Lancaster aircraft became more satisfactory, there was a reversal of policy concerning the training programme, and it was now decided to supply all Heavy Conversion Units (HCUs) entirely with this aircraft, in consequence of which the Lancaster Finishing Schools were disbanded. This was my first experience of redundancy, but it only lasted a day or so before Wing Commander Powley asked me to go with him to a new squadron now being formed at RAF Kirmington. I had enjoyed a very close association with Powley, and besides which the idea of going back to a squadron appealed to me, so the answer was yes. I had to say goodbye to my staff, who were to be posted in all directions, and take down my noticeboards and other paraphernalia, which I took with me to my new domain. Altogether I had been at Hemswell for nine months, but with time taken out for the various courses and periods of leave, it amounted to about six months of active service. It had been quite a hard slog, boring at times, but also quite rewarding as a succession of crews passed out. I was sorry to leave the camp too, and in particular the comforts of the officers' mess, for Kirmington was one of those wartime stations that I had come up against before!

The date of my posting was 7 October 1944, and I had to travel a distance of about twenty miles as Kirmington was situated in north Lincolnshire within easy reach of Grimsby. I was to join No. 153 Squadron, which had been disbanded after previous service as a night-fighter squadron in the Middle East and was now being re-formed from a nucleus of twenty-seven aircrews from No. 166 Squadron, the home unit of Kirmington. On the arrival of the full complement of personnel and other preliminaries, the squadron was then to transfer to a permanent base at Scampton near Lincoln. This was great news! I had envisaged another dreary winter in the mud, but now we were told that we would be moving in about a week's time to a pre-war station with all the advantages that that entailed!

Chapter Ten

Kirmington

One of the first people I met on arrival was Tommy Thompson, and now all was revealed! He had been invited to take over as bombing leader, and had been to Hemswell for an interview with Powley. As the whole operation of re-forming a squadron was done under a cloud of secrecy he had not been able to 'spill the beans' as it were. Naturally, I now understood the situation and applauded him for his discretion. I was very pleased he was joining us in view of our old association, and I was to work very amicably with him during the period at Scampton. Apart from Tommy, I met the other section leaders: Flight Lieutenant Jehan – gunnery; Flight Lieutenant Wheelwright – navigation; and Flight Lieutenant Stewart – signals. I got along very well with Ron Stewart, a New Zealander who came from Wanganui on the North Island, and it was an amazing coincidence that the system of flare marking by the Pathfinders was code-named after this very place. Ron had a small car that was in much better shape than the one previously mentioned, but I didn't travel with him very often. When I did it was only to nearby places such as Lincoln, and it was very handy to call on him to drop me at the station with my case when I went home on leave!

Powley introduced all the new officer members to each other and we gradually sorted ourselves out, but with so many crews it was some time before we could name each other with certainty. I held a meeting with the flight engineers, partly to get to know them, and so that they would know me. I made clear the standards that I expected of them and warned them that I would not accept slipshod methods. All this was done in a very friendly manner, but I think they got the message. The aircraft arrived, some old and some new, and the squadron identification letters P4 were painted on. Owing to the weather situation only one operation was flown from Kirmington, when eleven Lancasters bombed Emmerich, but a few cross-countries took place to keep the crews on their mettle. For the move to Scampton elaborate details were issued. All the maintenance personnel and clerical staff were involved, and they were transported by road together with their belongings, tool kits, record files, etc. Even the bicycles had to be taken; the whole operation must have been a real headache for the MT (Motor Transport) officer! Most of the aircrew flew across to the new base, except for those with private vehicles. I was honoured by being taken by Powley in his official car. The station commander at Kirmington, Group Captain Carter, followed us a short time later when he was promoted to air commodore and made base commander at Scampton.

Chapter Eleven

Scampton

RAF Scampton is situated on the A15 Ermine Street almost exactly five miles from Lincoln, and I had passed the camp several times on my travels from Hemswell. It was a peacetime station in the same mould as many others, with a few Nissen huts added that were used by the ancillary services arising from the wartime situation. To me it was a fine camp, undoubtedly the best one that I was stationed at, and had the glamour of a long operational tradition that was further enhanced by it being the home of the Dambusters, who had made their epic raid on the Ruhr dams eighteen months previously. Furthermore I was now back with an operational squadron where the morale and general attitudes to life were vastly different to those pertaining to the training units. The atmosphere was such that I felt very proud to be there, and when I arrived on 14 October 1944, I was very much looking forward to my period of residence.

Apart from the flying aspect, the focal point of life on such a station was the mess and one's living quarters, and I was not disappointed here for Scampton was well endowed in this respect. The mess was very similar to the one at Hemswell, but the internal appointments were somewhat better, the ante-room looking very impressive with the walls covered by a sizeable mural. There was an imposing fireplace at one end of the room, flanked by bookcases that constituted the officers' library, run by a member of the Messing Committee and open during lunchtimes. The large central entrance doors opened into a spacious lobby that was frequented as much as the ante-room, mainly because of the inevitable piano situated there. I have always been fascinated by someone playing a piano, probably making up for not being able to perform myself, and I was found on numerous occasions sitting next to this one, lapping up the music played by our resident pianists, be it good or (more usually) bad!

Around the walls were oil paintings of men who had won the Victoria Cross while being stationed at Scampton – these were Sergeant Hannah, Flight Lieutenant Learoyd and Wing Commander Gibson (of Dambusters fame); as I said, a place of tradition! Also in the lobby was a large wall map showing the war situation, which was continuously updated each day, and also a book wherein officers were required to record their movements if they were away from camp for more than twenty-four hours. This book was mainly for the use of the catering staff in regard to meals, and for the mess orderlies, in order to save them searching around for an officer who was away on leave. Mention of the orderlies reminds me of their role as 'wakers up' of officers due to fly on operations, and their unfortunate duty of having to do the rounds when operations were cancelled. This happened to me at least once when I was woken up to hear that I need not get up after all! We appreciated that the reason for this was to avoid us waking up later and thinking that we had missed our date with destiny, but it was not accepted very well at the time.

The bedrooms were of the standard pattern and I always occupied one in the upper storey, but owing to the continual comings and goings on the station I had a succession of room-mates, starting off with Flying Officer Coxon, the 'A' Flight commander's navigator, with whom I also later flew on my last bombing operation. The batting services were some-what better than those described at Wickenby, but of course as there was no need to cart water all over the place, they had more time to clean buttons and press clothes. Batwomen had been introduced by this time, and they were present in about equal proportion with the men.

Living in an officers' mess where one was at the centre of things gave a great advantage in building up contacts with fellow officers. High and low rubbed shoulders together, and it was very useful to meet squadron executives on almost level terms. The only officer who kept to himself, living in his own house, was the station commander, Group Captain Lloyd – more of him anon.

My terms of reference on No. 153 Squadron, apart from acting as flight engineer leader, were to proceed with my second tour of operations. This

I could only do at a rather leisurely pace as I had no fixed crew and was only able to fly in a spare capacity. In practice, this was no bad thing as it was much more preferable to the concentrated effort that characterised my first tour at Wickenby, but it did not mean that I could pick and choose which operations I flew on, for I could not suddenly displace a crew member when the occasion suited me. The usual arrangement when an engineer was unable to fly, mostly due to sickness, was for the 'official' spare engineer from another crew to take his place, which was normally a satisfactory move as the spare man was not averse to getting 'one more in' to hasten the end of his tour. The onus was on me, of course, and if there was no spare available, I had to be prepared to step into the breach. In view of this, the fact that I only flew on four more bombing missions points to the extraordinarily good health of my gallant band of engineers!

My department was housed in the first of a row of large Nissen huts behind one of the hangars, and my lads worked with a will to erect a partition across the hut to provide me with an office. Tables and chairs had to be scrounged, and in no time at all these appeared as from nowhere. Up went the noticeboard and the Lancaster fuel and hydraulic diagrams I had brought from Hemswell, and with the installation of a telephone we were ready for business.

To provide some exercise and to try to avoid boredom during non-flying periods, we dug up a patch of land next to the hut and in the spring planted flowers in it. It became quite a showpiece, admired by all. We could not practice dinghy drill as there were no baths at Scampton, but there was plenty of air there and we indulged in a fair amount of kite flying. Part of the survival kit for use in the case of ditching was a radio transmitter, which was positioned near to the top escape hatch, and it was the engineer's responsibility to collect this on his way out, together with the ration pack. The transmitter was shaped so that it could be held between the knees, and had a handle that was turned to produce the power required to send a simple signal giving the approximate position of the dinghy. Also necessary to the sending of this message was an aerial, and this is where the kite was required. A box kite was provided that could hoist the aerial up to a height of about 50ft, but it needed a bit of experience to keep it up consistently, hence the reason for our practice sessions. It was the first time that I had handled a box kite and I was amazed at the ease with which it flew, although it was a bit tricky in a high wind. There were no complaints about the kite-flying exercises, and if we practised a bit longer than was necessary, at least it kept a lot of minds off more foreboding matters.

Another function that took up some time was the reading of the station flying orders, which were amended from time to time and had to be read and signed by all crew personnel. These included the safe height to fly in the vicinity, knowledge of various landmarks, taxiing speeds and so on. In addition to these matters there was always the ubiquitous Link trainer to fly (I considered the use of the Link trainer of great importance to engineers who might at any time be called upon to fly their aircraft, and kept a roster to ensure that everyone had their turn). I also encouraged my people to use the intelligence library, which I had always thought to be most interesting and instructive to all would-be escapers!

The normal routine for new crew on the squadron was also adopted at Scampton. They flew at first on cross-country runs, and then the pilot flew his first operation as second dickey with an experienced crew. I normally attended the briefing for these trips, as well as operational ones, although I was only at debriefings for the latter. I bought a slide rule that I used for working out the air miles per gallon ratio, thereby making the calculation less laborious and also enabling me to make an immediate assessment in the briefing room, so that I could strike while the iron was hot if necessary.

Five days after arriving at Scampton, on 19 October, the squadron flew on its second operation when fifteen aircraft went to Bremen, and to show that nothing much had changed in the way of targets, the next two raids were both to Essen on 23 and 25 October. My first flight from Scampton was on operations, when, after having been briefed for two trips that had been cancelled, I finally took off on a sortie to Wanne-Eickel, an industrial town three miles north-north-west of Bochum in Happy Valley. I joined Flying Officer White's crew for this trip on 18 November, displacing Sergeant Thompson who was on the sick list, and we flew in Lancaster 'W' William, appropriately numbered with my initials, PB642. I noticed several differences in comparison with my earlier operational experience, the first of which was the increased bomb load, made possible by a big improvement in the engine performance. Our load in this instance was 12,000lb (nearly 5½ tons), made up of 1 x 4,000lb and 16 x 500lb high-explosive (HE) bombs. There was a difference too in the navigation equipment carried, for we now had H2S, an airborne radar set that showed a good outline of the territory flown over.

On the outward leg, I had to release bundles of 'Window' through a small chute in the side of the aircraft; these were small strips of silvered paper that were dropped to confuse the enemy radar, as described when Slade had flown on the Hamburg raids from Wickenby. Over the months since this procedure had been started, the Germans had been forced to alter their tactics to counteract it, and had come up with two main methods. One of these was to concentrate the fighters over the target and silhouette the bombers by playing numerous searchlights on the cloud layer, and by dropping flares from high-altitude aircraft above. This practice was known as Wilde Sau (wild boar). The other method, known as Zahme Sau (tame boar), was for fighters to infiltrate the bomber stream (easy to locate by the Window being discharged), and use their airborne radar to strike down individual bombers. On the outward journey, we had plenty of evidence to substantiate the use of these different tactics, particularly in respect of the flares dropped from on high that turned night-time into day, and in consequence we had to redouble our eternal vigilance. Luck was with us, though, for apart from the usual flak reception from nearby Essen, we had an untroubled bombing run followed by a patch of bad weather on the way back that helped to keep the fighters at bay. Approaching the English coast we flew through blinding rainstorms, and once again the message came through for us to land at a diversionary aerodrome, but this time the situation was very different!

We were diverted to RAF Horham in East Anglia, about halfway between Ipswich and Norwich, and landed there at 21.55 after being up for six hours. Although for official reasons Horham was an RAF station, it was actually operated by our American allies, and a squadron of Flying Fortresses was based there. About six Lancasters landed along with us, and our first priority was to ensure that the aircraft were safely housed for the night, but in reality there was little we could do except park on the tarmac with noses into the wind and batten all the hatches.

Met by our American hosts with a fully upholstered coach, we were conveyed in comfort to the administrative block where debriefing took place, and then taken to the mess kitchen for a meal. All ceremony was brushed to one side (I do not think there was much there anyway), and we queued up by the stove upon which bacon and eggs were sizzling away; there was no restriction on quantity – we who were conditioned to a shortage of eggs now saw them in volume, and the same applied to the bacon. Naturally we took advantage of this and fed our faces to the full, but more was to come. Fruit salad, again a scarce commodity, was the next luxury to appear, in huge canteens complete with ladle. 'Help yourself bud' was the only instruction given, and of course we forced down a fair helping. The next course was biscuits and cheese, which hardly anyone could manage, and the whole feast was rounded up by a large box of cigars that were free to all!

It so happened that an officers' mess dance had been arranged at Horham for that very same evening, and a coach had been sent to Norwich to collect some nurses and other female personnel to make up the party. We were invited to join in and so we did, with the CO granting an hour's extension in honour of the gallant British airmen (his words, not mine). I personally found it very difficult to dance in flying boots, and so did many others, with the result that most of us sat it out, not wishing to upset our hosts by leaving too early. It ended eventually, and we were honoured once more with a rendering of the National Anthem before gratefully retiring to our very comfortable beds.

I will make no comment on seeing the next morning that a fair proportion of the female contingent had somehow missed the bus back and were having breakfast with their escorts in the mess, but for our part we were once more regaled with bacon and eggs, and toast and coffee – almost three-star treatment! An officer was assigned to escort us around the camp, which included a call at the PX (American equivalent of the NAAFI), where we stocked up with cigarettes, orange juice, soap and a host of other items that were virtually unobtainable elsewhere. We then headed for the airfield. After storing the purchases in our own aircraft, we were shown around the Fortresses, which were examined with great interest, and I am bound to say that I was not overly impressed with what I saw. The bomb holds were pathetically small, and the aircraft itself looked like a great lumbering beast; in fact it all looked a bit futile. I have great admiration for the airmen who flew these aircraft in daylight over Germany, but although great improvements were made later on in the weight of bombs each aircraft could carry, especially with the advent of the SuperFortress, they never came within a whisker of our own splendid Lancasters.

After another first-class meal it was time for us to make our way back to Scampton. The Lancs had been refuelled and it only remained for us to do our pre-flight checks, start up and taxi out. But we met a snag right at the beginning when an engine proved troublesome to start. The normal method of engine starting at our home base was to use an out-side trolley accumulator to save the aircraft batteries. These trollies were available at this American station, but the connecting plugs were incompatible with the Lancaster sockets. So there was no alternative but to use the internal power. This procedure was a trial for me, because when the aircraft battery power was used the engines had to be well primed with fuel, and the priming pumps were situated in each inboard engine nacelle. This required me to clamber on to the top of the wheel amid all the dripping oil and glycol and pump away without having any direct contact with the cockpit. I also had the fear that someone would inadvertently operate the undercarriage retraction lever, in which case my future prospects would not be very bright!

We got the starboard outer engine started all right, but the inner one proved very stubborn, and by the time we managed to get it going, the other one had overheated and had to be shut off. Eventually the other three were ticking over and the starboard outer restarted, and we were ready to go. Our route to the runway took us past the control tower and someone had the bright idea that we might open the bomb doors in pass-ing, hoping that the Yanks inside the tower would be very impressed with the large bomb-carrying capacity thus revealed. The doors were duly opened and we spoke to the tower on the intercom to draw their attention, but unfortunately our scheme backfired on us when, for the only time ever, the doors refused to close again! After passing by, there happened to be a convenient bend on the perimeter track out of sight of the tower, where we stopped and several of us ran out to shoulder the doors closed. How are the mighty fallen! All this delay caused the engines to overheat, and the outboard ones started to stream out glycol vapour. The correct procedure at this point would have been to shut them off to allow them to cool down, but we had had enough embarrassment by this time and so, tempting fate, took off with them likely to pack up at any moment. It was the first and only time I flew without doing the all-important runway checks, but under the circumstances who would blame us for this lapse in routine? Scampton was reached without further ado, and our total flying time was just over six hours.

A little background information on the development of the Merlin engine would probably be of interest here. The Lancaster started life in 1941 when the Mk I was developed from the ill-fated Manchester, and was fitted with four Merlin XX engines of 1,280 horsepower (hp). By the middle of 1942, Rolls-Royce could not supply sufficient engines to meet the demand, bearing in mind that the Merlin was used in many types of aircraft including Spitfires; even the 18,000 per year rate by 1943 was not enough. So attention was focused on the possibility of producing them in America as well. The Ford company was approached, but they could not agree to help, and eventually Packard stepped in. The drawings were already in America, having been sent there at the fall of France, but much work remained to be done before production could commence, and the drawing staff had to work night and day to prepare working diagrams from the master copies.

Packards went into production in a big way, clearing their car-production lines (for three-quarters of a mile!) and then installing completely new tools. When they started to make the engines they found some difficulty in working to Rolls-Royce tolerances, but still managed to produce their first engine within a year. The American Merlins developed 1,460hp, and were designated the Merlin XXVIII; at first they were fitted with a Bendix carburettor because the British SU could not be produced in time, but eventually the Stromberg carburettor became standard.

Another important difference with the introduction of the Packard engine was the use of rounded-end propellers, known as paddle blades. These props improved performance, particularly in the climb, and they were later adopted on all Lancasters. With the Merlin XXVIII came magnificent tool sets, which were much appreciated by the ground crews.

The Lancaster manufacturers were allotted specific quantities of British and American engines, so that in general, the serial numbers of the aircraft were a guide to the initial engine installation, although in service, when an engine was changed, it could have been replaced by either type. The aircraft was originally designated a Mk I or Mk III respectively. A Lancaster Mk II was also introduced during 1942, this version being fitted with Bristol Hercules radial engines (as an insurance against delay in supplies of Merlins from America), but as I did not fly in this type I am not qualified to pass comment on it.

Continuous improvement was made to the Merlin engine as time passed, and it eventually produced over 2,000hp; each succeeding modification allowed us to go faster or higher or carry a heavier bomb load, but never was it more apparent than on take-off when the boost pressure was increased from +12lb in 1942 to +18lb in 1945 (a fifty per cent advance). I honestly expected the engines to blow apart at this extreme power, which was coupled with excruciating noise, and never was I more thankful to throttle back than when we had attained sufficient height!

After a time, the navigator with whom I shared my bedroom moved out as he had an opportunity to join up with one of his crew members, and in his place I had the dubious pleasure of welcoming a young flying officer who had been posted into a staff job. This chap had been a fighter pilot in the Middle East, but had been disabled when he was shot through one of his knees, and had to have an operation to remove the knee-cap entirely. With his stiff leg he could no longer fly so had been given a desk job, and was also allowed to use a specially adapted car to enable him to get round the camp. We were all very sympathetic towards this fellow, which was a bit disconcerting for me as he had the loudest snore that I have ever heard! I put up with it for a couple of nights, but then I had to broach the subject with him; he was very apologetic and suggested that I wake him up on occasion to see if that did the trick. Unfortunately, I could hardly wake him by pushing and had to resort to throwing things at him (for this purpose he even supplied me with his own gym shoes!), but it was all to no avail, and after I had had a quiet word with the medical officer, he was found a small room on his own.

For me, it was almost a case of out of the frying pan into the fire, as he was replaced by another troublesome ex-overseas officer. This time it was a flight lieutenant who had arrived to take over as station adjutant. He had been out in India for a good number of years, having actually been born there, and his posting back to the UK was nothing short of a disaster as he was completely disorientated. He was a nice enough fellow who just could not adapt to the new routine, and he earned me a black mark that I did not deserve.

I went out one evening straight after tea and everything seemed normal when I returned, but on the following day I received a shirty letter from Group Captain Lloyd, slating me for not observing the blackout regulations! It transpired that while I was away my new companion had entered our room and left it again, leaving the lights on without having drawn the curtains. This was a bad enough thing to do in civilian life, but at a military unit of operational status it was a crime of huge proportion that could not be overlooked and, as sometimes happens on such occasions, the CO had been out and about and had witnessed the incident personally. Of course the new chap, having recently arrived from India where blackout conditions did not exist, had absent-mindedly omitted to pull the curtains, thereby landing us both in the soup. The CO, typically of him, had not bothered to investigate the circumstances but had, unfairly in my case, apportioned blame to both of us equally, sending us the aforementioned letters. I sent a submission up to him but did not get very far as, according to him, I should have closed the curtains before leaving the camp. One can imagine my thoughts on this verdict in consideration of the fact that on the day in question I had actually reached Lincoln in broad daylight! Our friend the adjutant must have made a few office blunders as well, for he did not last very long at Scampton, and was very soon replaced by another officer who also took his place in my room.

Flight Lieutenant Jerry Brill was an entirely different person to my previous companions; he was an older man approaching his fifties, who had been called up to the Services to do his wartime stint. As he was a completely sensible person, and did not snore, we weren't involved in any incidents or escapades, so I have no dramatic stories to relate, but I do particularly remember him from one or two items that cropped up. Jerry was a successful businessman who owned several gents' outfitting shops in his native Leeds, and always wore silk shirts with his monogram on the pocket. He also owned property in Leeds, and while

on leave would spend a lot of his time collecting rent money. For some
reason he preferred to bank this in Lincoln (for tax purposes?) and would
appear back in our room with hundreds of pounds in paper money. Until
he was able to bank it he hid the money in rolls among his clothes, with
only myself being in the know, and he was quite oblivious to the possibility of some of it being stolen. His wallet was always bulging with money,
and once when I had a cash flow problem and asked him for a temporary
loan, I was offered anything up to hundreds of pounds!

In similar vein, he had a highly sophisticated camera that he offered
to me on loan at any time; I did borrow it once to take some photographs
of Lincoln and it took him ages to explain the modus operandi. It was
loaded up with a new film, for which no payment was expected, and I was
able to snap away with gay abandon. Jerry Brill remained at Scampton until
after I had left, so I was spared any more traumas with new room-mates.
Several years later, when he was back in civilian life, he took over Thrussells,
a well-known Birmingham outfitting shop in the City Arcade, and his
brother came down from Leeds to be the manager. I did see his brother
once and asked him to convey my regards to Jerry, but it is doubtful whether
he actually came to Birmingham again, and so I lost touch with him.

Owing to our close proximity to Lincoln (for the first time we were
not out in the wilds), it was natural that we should visit there fairly
frequently, and in the course of time I got to know it quite well. The
cathedral was the star attraction, and as it is situated on the highest part
of the city, it is an outstanding landmark; during the war the red light
on top of the tower could be seen for miles in clear weather and was a very
welcome sight when we returned from operations, quite apart from its
navigational value. Lincoln was reached easily by cycle or bus and was well
frequented by the RAF; indeed, it was always thronged by Service personnel, whom I am sure at times outnumbered the civilian population.

Because of the wartime ration restrictions, the public houses could
not rely on supplies of beer being delivered on a regular basis, so it was
not unusual to see us going round on a pub crawl. This situation was forced
upon us and did not mean that we were hardened topers, but rather
that we were chasing the meagre supplies of beer that were available. In
any case, I only joined in this drinking activity for something to while
away the time, and never drunk more than two or three half-pints.

As in my days at Wickenby, I went to some of the dances held on Saturday nights at the City Assembly Rooms, a rather 'posh' place where one could meet anybody who was anybody, so to speak. Although I mixed with the local girls at these dances, I did not form any lasting friendships, with the exception of Rita Moss whom I met at the Assembly Rooms. Rita was a very nice girl of about my own age, and worked at the Lincoln Food Office dealing with ration cards. I went to the cinema with her once or twice in addition to several dances, and after a short time she invited me to her home in Prior Street to meet her parents. I received a warm welcome from her mother and father and her sister Jean, but I was surprised to find that I was one of a great number of airmen who had been introduced by the sisters to the home comforts of Prior Street! Most of the previous acquaintances had been posted away as time went by, but they had kept in touch with the Moss family, and mother and father helped with the letter writing. I took to visiting the house frequently when duties at camp permitted, even having my tea there; we played all sorts of card games and sometimes went to the nearby cinema, returning for a meal before I set off back to camp. The house was only a short distance from the Lincoln City Football Club at Sincil Bank, and on occasional Saturday afternoons I was to be seen on the terraces with the family, especially after the end of the war when I had more time on my hands. This pleasant arrangement lasted until I was posted away from Scampton, but when I later came back into the Lincoln area, Prior Street was a port of call I often made. My association with Rita was always platonic, and we finally parted as good friends; she now lives in a different part of Lincoln with her husband and son, and we still exchange cards at Christmas.

Since I had flown to Wanne-Eickel, the squadron had been pressing on with operations to such places as Freiburg, Aschaffenburg, Dortmund, Karlsruhe, Merseburg and Koblenz, and on 28 December I had the opportunity to fly on another raid when Flying Officer Bolton's engineer was not available. The target on this occasion was Bonn, a town situated south of Cologne and the Ruhr Valley, and now the capital of West Germany. We flew in NG201, an aircraft delivered to the squadron a few days after we had arrived at Scampton, and the bomb load was another heavy one consisting of 1 x 4,000lb cookie, 15 x 500lb incendiary clusters and 120 loose 4lb incendiaries. Little can be said about the actual operation as it was a straightforward in and out job, but the dangers were there as we were within range of enemy night fighters for about four hours. The trip itself lasted for five hours, and we were tucked up fast asleep before midnight. This raid was mounted at the time that the Germans had counter-attacked in the Ardennes, when all the forces that we had were really needed to repulse them. For the best part of a week, though, the weather had been atrocious, and although briefings had been held on each day except Christmas Day, the operations had had to be cancelled. Indeed, on one occasion the crews were actually on board the aircraft when the fog came down and they had no alternative but to abandon the raid. We had envisaged that we might be sent to attack the German front line when the weather cleared sufficiently on the 28th, but unfortunately this was not to be and it was left to other units to perform this task while we were involved with this routine strategic bombing operation instead.

As it was the end of the year, I had to have my logbook signed for the two raids that I had been on, and Wing Commander Powley who had signed the previous page as chief instructor of No. 1 LFS, now did the honours again as officer commanding No. 153 Squadron. The year 1944 had now passed by, another one of death and destruction. For me it had been a year of interest and variety, my seventh in the RAF. We were now on the way to winning the war after the doubt and uncertainty of the past, and I looked forward to 1945 with relish.

There were a few events at Scampton that I cannot date with any certainty, and so at this juncture, between the old year and the new, it may be the best time to recall them. Firstly, it appeared that my prowess at lecturing had been heard about in distant quarters, as for the third time I was called to give Lancaster tuition to the CO. This time it was the dour Group Captain Lloyd that I had to face and try to educate in the ways of handling Merlin engines, fuel systems and hydraulics etc. I had about half a dozen sessions with him in the mornings, and as with the CO at Hemswell it was purely ground instruction without even venturing out to an aircraft. Presumably he wanted to know something about the subject just in case it cropped up, for I am pretty certain that he did not fly in a Lancaster or any other aircraft while I was there.

Secondly, we had a visit from broadcaster Richard Dimbleby when he came to fly on a raid and make a recording in one of our aircraft. I was assigned to look after him, and in particular to advise him of the best place to put his equipment inside the Lanc so that it would not interfere with the workings of the crew. I found him to be very genial with a good sense of humour, which he needed to have in his dealings with hard-bitten aircrews! I did not fly with him in a Lancaster, but my abiding memory of him was being airborne in his specially constructed jeep that had four-wheel drive and five-speed gears. Roads did not matter to him, and we headed for the dispersal point in a direct line across the grass, which had a surface much removed from that at Wimbledon, and we were up in the air as much as on the ground! We all survived the journey and, much to my amazement, so did the equipment. Richard Dimbleby was the first celebrity that I met during my Service career.

The third item of interest was the changeover in airspeed measure-ment from miles per hour to knots. This did not affect me to any extent apart from noting it down hourly in my flying log, for all my calculations were based on distances flown rather than airspeed. The speed of flight was largely dictated by the navigator, and my job was to manipulate the engine controls to maintain that speed in the most economical fashion. I am not certain as to the reason for this change, but it was very likely made to standardise with naval practice, i.e. the Fleet Air Arm, and after all there were a few heavy bombers in Coastal Command.

The last episode to relate took place towards the end of 1944, and as I was in the control tower at the time, I actually saw it happening. Aircraft 'A' Apple, NG185, captained by Flying Officer Holland, was taxiing along the perimeter track to take part in a daylight raid to Dortmund, when the wireless operator attempted to load a Very pistol which, as it happened, was already loaded. The cartridge went off inside the aircraft. Seeing a blinding flash followed by smoke, the pilot, imagining the fuel tanks to be on fire, ordered the crew to get out, and in the panic he him-self fell out of the forward escape hatch and had to be carried away. Meanwhile, the navigator had stamped on the cartridge and put out the fire. Most unfortunately, Holland broke his back in the fall and had to be invalided out of the Service. Years later I had this incident related to me in Birmingham by a person who then informed me that he was the uncle of the injured pilot – indeed truth is much stranger than fiction!

During January 1945 the squadron mounted a succession of operations that included Nuremberg, Merseburg (again), Munich, Zeitz and Duisburg. Most of the aircraft came back safely during this period, but there were more to be lost in the coming months, and by the end of the war in Europe more than twenty had failed to return, a greater number than the whole complement of the squadron when it moved to Scampton.

On a personal note, owing to the weather conditions, my journeys outside the camp became rather infrequent and I joined in with a number of bridge parties held in the mess, playing with fellows of about the same standard, although there was one whiz-bang among us who adjudicated on the finer points of play! Like most officers' messes we had a snooker room, which I also frequented at regular intervals, and I remember play-ing a game there at three o'clock in the morning when we were in the middle of a long succession of postponements for an operation that was finally cancelled. Other activities in which I was involved included table tennis – where I found a worthy opponent in the WAAF squadron officer (colloquially known as the Queen Bee!) whom I could just match on level terms – and also the sedentary occupation of listening to the piano in the lobby. Scampton was no exception when it came to mess parties; formal or informal, they were a regular event. I have no need to describe them as they conformed to the universal pattern and we had the usual visitations of VIPs from Group HQ and the surrounding stations. I had hoped that Villiers might turn up at one of these parties, but he never came, and when later on I did see him at Scampton it was much more in the line of duty rather than socially.

I flew on my thirty-third operation on 28 January with a trip to the Zuffenhausen district of Stuttgart with Flying Officer Searle. We flew in 'X' X-ray, PD378, and had a bomb load of 10,000lb: 1 x 4,000lb and 12 x 500lb HE bombs. As the engines were now rated at 18lb boost pressure for take-off, the din that they produced further enhanced the dangers of getting airborne, but we made it safely and throttled back with alacrity when enough height had been gained. Although the take-off power had been increased (primarily to allow a heavier load to be carried), the other engine settings had not been altered, so that 2,850rpm, +9lb boost, and then 2,650rpm, +4lb, still pertained. Familiar too, was the bomb aimer's cry, 'Crossing English coast', followed by 'Crossing enemy coast', but these pinpoints, which were mainly made for the benefit of the navigator, were not appreciated by the rest of us, as in the clear moonlight they were obvious to all. In my case it was a curious coincidence that on my previous visit to Stuttgart nearly two years earlier, I had also flown in brilliant moonlight, and on this occasion we were to attack the same marshalling yards and engine production factories. It was necessary for me to keep a very sharp lookout for fighters and I only broke off at intervals to change the petrol tanks and make up my log, a job that normally would have been done with the aid of a torch dimmed down with paper, but which could now be done quite clearly with the naked eye.

On approaching Stuttgart we were given aiming instructions by the Master Bomber, a Pathfinder pilot who circled the target to ensure that the bombing was concentrated in the right area. (One of the problems that developed during a raid was for the fires to obliterate the marker flares, and the bombing line thereby had a tendency to creep back further and further. The Master Bomber had to correct this by ordering new markers to be dropped, and by broadcasting to the main force, giving precise details of the new aiming points.)

Fighters were seen over the target, but with good luck we were not singled out. When the bombs were released, it was the wireless operator's duty to ensure that the camera flare had dropped correctly out of the chute, and having had his assurance that this was so, the customary eleven seconds was endured in straight and level flight, and then it was all systems go to get back home in one piece! This was accomplished after much weaving about and changes of course, and Scampton was reached at precisely three o'clock on the following morning after a longish flight of seven and a half hours. I have a clear recollection of walking back to the mess from the briefing room after this trip. It was still a bright moonlit night, and as I breathed in the cold night air I experienced the usual feeling of elation at having returned safely. I was not to know it at the time, but the Stuttgart operation was the last one I would fly on at night. A sobering thought – the aircraft in which we flew, PD378, was shot down by a Junkers Ju 88 night fighter only six nights later on 3 February. One of the crew was killed, but the other six managed to bale out successfully.

Although I had been a section leader for over a year, it was only at Scampton that I was given the authority to make recommendations for promotion within my department. At Hemswell this procedure had been carried out by my immediate superior, Wing Commander Powley, but in any case, I cannot remember whether there had been any promotions or not apart from my own! During the previous two or three years there had been slow advancements of rank among NCO aircrew members, but by this time, at the beginning of 1945, the policy was biased more towards commissioning, and I was allowed to put forward the names of two of my lads to be elevated to this status. I gave the matter a lot of thought, but I could not get past the fact that there were only two sergeants worthy of this promotion, and they were the ones who got the nod. It was fortunate for me that I didn't have only one person to recommend, as that would have made it a very difficult decision. These two, Sergeant Sadler and Sergeant Taylor, were both live wires, and their promotion was very helpful to me during the rest of my time on the squadron when they stood in for me at various times, in particular when I was away on leave.

The one who I remember most was Roy Taylor, a Scotsman, who with Flying Officer Coxon (with whom I had originally shared my room), was a member of the 'A' Flight commander's crew. He approached me one day in the mess and asked me whether I would miss him if he had a weekend off so that he could visit his lady friend who was a nurse at Lichfield. He explained that although she was at the hospital at Lichfield, she actually lived in Birmingham, and when I questioned him further it transpired that her home was in Shirley Road, Acocks Green! Naturally I gave him my approval to be absent. The irony of this decision was that a 'maximum effort' operation cropped up while he was away and so I had to fly in his place – but more of this presently. Some time later we travelled to Birmingham together on leave, and left Pilot Officer Sadler to hold the fort for us. While at home I visited Roy at Shirley Road and had tea with his lady friend's family. In due course he became engaged to her, and I officiated as best man when they were married at Hall Green church in 1947.

At Scampton I was also involved in recommending one of my charges for a Distinguished Flying Medal. Honours were awarded to aircrew who had performed heroic deeds or had had a very tough time during a tour of operations, but nothing had come the way of our flight engineers, so an allocation of one DFM was made to the department to 'even things up'. I was asked for my opinion, and although I had someone in mind I thought it best to confer with Wing Commander Powley as I was very anxious to avoid the stigma of favouritism. My choice was Sergeant Jenkinson of Flying Officer Jones's crew. They had been through the mill on a number of operations and Powley had no hesitation in agreeing with me. Approval of the award came through in a very short time, but Jenkinson did not have much time to enjoy it as the crew went missing soon afterwards.

February came in like a lion and went out like a lamb, and during the early part of the month we were heavily engaged in snow clearance. On such occasions the whole station would turn out to man brooms and shovels, working around the clock in order to clear runways, dispersals and roads – an arduous and back-breaking task. For our Australians, many of whom had never seen snow, it was an ideal opportunity to let off steam and indulge in snow fights, which always seemed to end up as Australia vs Great Britain! Naturally I had to do my stint with the shovel alongside the other squadron officers, but the people who were worse off were the ground crews, who had to clear the aircraft of snow and then continue to service them out in the bitter weather. By joining the aircrew ranks I had at least been spared from working in these bleak conditions, even if I had more than made up for it in other ways!

Towards the end of February I went north for a few days when I was sent to join a seminar to discuss fuel conservation and methods of refuelling. The interesting point of this visit was that it was held at RAF Rufforth near York, the very station that I was diverted to after the Bremen raid exactly two years previously, which meant that it was another station like St Athan and Wickenby where I had used both the sergeants' and officers' messes! Rufforth was in No. 4 Group, Bomber Command, and housed a squadron flying Halifaxes. We did not fly while we were there, but I remember a demonstration when an aircraft had its tanks drained and was then refuelled again to test the accuracy of the gauges.

The bad weather experienced in February did not have much effect on the operational progress of the squadron at Scampton (after we had cleared the runways!), and raids were made on Mannheim, Bottrop, Cleves,

Politz, Dresden and Pforzheim among others. I was at the debriefing after
the Dresden operation during which fifteen No. 153 Squadron aircraft took
part, and this raid (which in later years became the subject of much debate)
has remained in my mind especially because of the long distance flown.
Certainly I was more interested at the time in the amount of fuel my
engineers had managed to conserve rather than any other considerations.
During March the squadron flew on fifteen operations, most of which
were in daylight, and these included attacks on Gelsenkirchen, Misburg,
Nuremberg, Hildesheim, Langendreer, Paderborn and Essen again. The
last-ditch efforts of the enemy's defences cost Scampton seven aircraft in
this period, and several more crashed on landing owing to battle damage.

     March was also the month when I started to get airborne once more,
commencing on the 19th when I flew with Squadron Leader Rippingale,
DSO, DFC, the 'A' Flight commander, on a local flight to Elsham Wolds,
the home of No. 103 Squadron. The trip took an hour there and back, and
served to give me a proper introduction to 'Rip' as he was affectionately
known. Rip was a very likeable person, cast in the same mould as our
late-lamented skipper, Slade. He had been awarded the DFC after his
first tour and the DSO at the start of his second one when he was badly
shot up over Germany, fortunately managing to steer his aircraft back
to England. As previously mentioned, Roy Taylor his engineer had joined
his crew when they came to Scampton. His bomb aimer, now tour
expired, was Harry Howling, and I will mention him later in my story.

     A few days afterwards, on the 23rd, I flew in Lancaster RF205 on an
aircraft acceptance test that again took one hour. My pilot this time was
Flying Officer Tom Tobin, an Australian from Adelaide who became a
good friend of mine. Tom was one of our drinking party at Lincoln, but
unlike most Australians he drank in moderation, so we made a good
pair! A month or so after the end of the war he went back home and we
promised to write to one another, but inevitably we did not, and so
sadly I lost touch with him. The flight itself was memorable for one
reason: it was a dull, misty day with very low cloud, and shortly after
becoming airborne the ground was completely obscured. We were not
too concerned about losing our bearings for on board we had Gee, H2S
and other navigational aids, but just to make sure of our position we
suddenly saw Lincoln cathedral poking out above the cloud level. Nothing

else in all directions as far as the eye could see, just the cathedral above the clouds. It was a wonderful sight, never to be forgotten, and I was only too sorry that I didn't have my camera with me. Fortunately the weather cleared in time for us to land.

Squadron Leader Rippingale, like most of the other pilots, had his own dedicated aircraft that he flew at all times unless it was unserviceable. Unfortunately his plane, 'E' Edward, LM754, had a long record of unserviceability, mainly on account of the port inner engine having a bad habit of misfiring and throwing out clouds of smoke. It was a fairly new aircraft, and the senior engineering officer refused to change the engine, preferring to have it serviced instead. It would appear that it had some sort of valve trouble, but ran reasonably well on all important flights, although it often misbehaved on the local ones. It became so notorious that it was christened 'Smoky Joe', and had the name painted on the side!

The reason for my relating this story is that I became involved with Smoky Joe when I next flew with Rip at the end of the month on a daylight operation to Paderborn. The first time that Lancasters had operated in strength during daylight was in June 1944 after the opening of the Second Front, and daylight raids had been mounted ever since, usually with fighter escorts. No. 153 Squadron had operated on a large proportion of these 'daylights', but this was the first one that I had flown on and I was quite looking forward to it. In the event, it was a bit of an anti-climax because most of the target was obscured by cloud and we had to bomb with the aid of the H2S equipment.

It was at 14.30 hours on 27 March that we took off for Paderborn, loaded with a 4,000lb cookie and nearly three tons of incendiaries. Strict radio silence was observed as usual even though it was a daylight sortie, and we were signalled away with a green Aldis lamp. On most night take-offs for operations, a fair number of well-wishers were present to wave us off providing the hour of day was not too unearthly, but in the darkness it was impossible to tell how many were there. On the daylight raids, however, it seemed as though half the camp usually turned out. These send-offs were very emotional and the atmosphere was electric, part of the pageant of an operational station against which nothing could compare. As soon as we started moving, though, it was eyes front with no more in mind than the job in hand, and we ran most of the runway

length before becoming unstuck (a normal RAF expression), and then
it was undercarriage up (with the brakes being put on to stop the wheels
rotating) and we were away. We went into orbit round the airfield for a time,
waiting for the rest of the squadron to take off, and then set course flying
in loose formation. For identification purposes, our aircraft were covered
with white stripes and other markings, and we were to keep in formation
the whole time, closing ranks slightly when nearing the target area.

The cloud thickened appreciably right from the start, but we quickly
climbed above it, even though by doing so we made ourselves a fine target
from above. Yet it turned out to be our lucky day, because for some reason
no enemy fighters were seen; perhaps they were grounded because of the
low cloud, or they may have been dispersed by our fighter cover. Maybe
they had even been given the day off! It is certain that at this stage of the
war the Germans were very short of fuel. Be that as it may, we achieved
the journey unmolested until we neared our destination, when we were
met by quite a barrage of flak. This was something that one couldn't
dodge in such a situation, so we had to press on regardless and drop our
bombs, even though we couldn't see any results.

No sooner had we turned for home, though, when trouble struck us
as Smoky Joe started to live up to its name! I tried all manner of possible
remedies, including switching the engine on and off and alternating the
power, but it was no good, and when it started to belch out clouds of
smoke, it had to be feathered. There was no great problem in returning
on three engines, even though the power of the other three had to be
increased a bit, and we reached base together with the other aircraft after
being airborne for over five hours. On approaching Scampton we sent
a radio message informing them that we were returning on three engines,
and on arrival we were given a priority landing. Imagine our surprise
when all the emergency services turned out to meet us on the perimeter track, the cavalcade headed by the CO in his car – they were a bit
disappointed when they reached us, however, as our message had been
misheard as 'returning with three injured'! So ended the operation that
I had taken part in because Roy Taylor was away for the weekend and,
as things turned out, it was the last one I flew on. The occasion was marked
by a crew photograph that was taken before we set off, although this
was a pure coincidence as I had no way of knowing that I had finished

with bombs and targets!

A short time later, I came across an article about this raid that included photographs of Paderborn before and afterwards, and these showed that the place had been practically devastated. This was a good example of the efficiency of our navigational aids and target-marking techniques; at the beginning of the war it was an achievement to bomb within a few miles of the target, whereas towards the end the margin of error came to be counted in yards. I must not forget to mention Smoky Joe – this trip turned out to be its swansong, for it was finally wrecked beyond repair and had to be replaced.

The squadron had a shock at the beginning of April, when on the night of the fourth our commanding officer, Wing Commander Powley, went missing on an operation; I am sure about the date because it happened on my birthday. Powley was an immensely popular figure and had been my commanding officer for longer than anyone else. He was one of the few Canadians with whom I had much contact, and after news came through that he and his crew had been killed, I, together with the rest of the squadron, were stunned. It was all the more galling to reflect that he had been flying throughout most of the war, only to fall victim within a month of the end of it. He was replaced after a week or so by Wing Commander Rodney, DFC, a veteran of many operations, who was to remain in command of the squadron until it was finally disbanded.

Other operations flown from Scampton during April were to Nordheim, Kiel, Plauen, Potsdam, Heligoland and Bremen, with the final raid of the war to Hitlers hideout at Berchtesgaden on the 25th. Several of these operations were of note. Squadron Leader Rippingale finished his second tour on one of them, and Tom Tobin completed his tour on the one to Heligoland, giving him the immense satisfaction of returning home to Australia with a full tour under his belt. The raid on Kiel was a curious one as it was undertaken on 9 April, the anniversary of the German occupation of Denmark in 1940. This leads me to believe that Kiel was attacked on each anniversary of the occupation, as I know that No. 12 Squadron took part in one raid on 9 April 1943. I have one of the leaflets dropped on that occasion, which is written in Danish. The intention was obviously to release them as near as possible to the border of Denmark as a gesture of support to the Danish population.

The war in Europe was now obviously drawing to a close, and consideration was given to relieving the food situation in Holland, where people were approaching starvation. The Germans had been systematically plundering food from the Netherlands, and now with communications in Europe at a standstill, coupled with a mass withdrawal of labour by railway workers due to continuing German demands, all food distribution was paralysed. In desperation, a truce was arranged with the Germans to allow food to be dropped by the RAF, and the Dutch government in exile in England approached Winston Churchill with an appeal to relieve the sufferings of their country. The upshot of this was Operation Manna, the dropping of food by Lancasters over Holland.

The supplies were packed in sacks and released at a pre-determined height over appointed places in The Hague, Leyden and Rotterdam, but first of all the aircraft had to be modified to carry the sacks, and experiments had to be carried out to find the optimum height for dropping, all of which took time. One of the places chosen to carry out these tests was Scampton, and throughout April several aircraft were engaged in practice. I took part in one of these flights on 8 April when I went up with the 'B' flight commander, Squadron Leader Gee, for a few runs over the airfield in NK573, which had been fitted with hooks in the bomb compartment. The tests were not successful, though, for a number of sacks did not release, and some of those that did burst open on impact with the ground. Undeterred, the squadron kept up the search for an answer to the problem, and eventually a solution was found – the sacks were to be stowed in special slung panniers, five to an aircraft, with some seventy sacks in each one, and they were to be released at 200ft. The weight of each load was approximately two tons.

During the trial period I flew on a further three occasions, which were all associated with Operation Manna: on 16 April with Tom Tobin in PA313 on a low-level cross-country flight that simulated the proper operation to come; on the 23rd with Wing Commander Rodney, the new squadron CO, in NG218 for a spot of local flying so that he could familiarise himself with the Lancaster again, ready to take part in the Manna flights; and lastly on the 24th for a short flight with South African Flight Lieutenant Legg in NG500, when we carried 5,000lb of food at low level, making practice passes over Scampton. The armourers, who were more used to handling weapons of war, were the people instrumental in devising the suitable method of dropping the food, and when the panniers had been made and fitted (literally in days), they were congratulated by no less a person than the ex-Chief of Air Staff, Marshal of the Royal Air Force Lord Trenchard, who paid a visit to us on 21 April together with the No. 1 Group commander, Air Vice Marshal Blucke. I recall this visit very well, for Trenchard made time to address most of the camp personnel, who were assembled in the airmen's mess, operations having been cancelled for the day. It was nice to hear the old boy speak, but the pep talk he delivered was largely ignored as it was obvious that the end of the war was very near – as it turned out, it was only about three weeks away!

As soon as the squadron was 'operational', it was all hands to the pump in the race against time to feed the starving Dutch people. Scratch crews were made up to fly all the available aircraft, and the first consignment of food was dispatched from Scampton on 29 April. I did not take part in the opening round, but I helped to make up a crew, captained by Wing Commander Rodney, on the following day when we flew to The Hague in RA545. Our load of food was estimated to be capable of providing a balanced ration for over 3,000 people for a day, and included flour, yeast, powdered egg, dried milk, peas, beans, tins of meat and bacon, sugar, pepper, vegetables, margarine, cheese and special vitamin chocolate.

Orders to each squadron were to drop the panniers in their allotted area, which they would find marked out with white crosses from having liaisoned with the various Dutch municipal authorities, and in our case the dropping point was The Hague racecourse. It was an afternoon run, and take-off was at 15.25 hours. No sooner had we crossed the Dutch coast than we were greeted by the sight of many flags fluttering, and this wonderful welcome continued throughout the whole journey. Over The Hague itself there was a sea of hands waving handkerchiefs and flags, and it appeared that only the bedridden had not turned out!

Dropping the goods was very simple, with no Master Bombers or target indicators necessary, just a large white cross! The only problem was to avoid the other aircraft, but this was accomplished satisfactorily and no collisions took place out of all the 3,300 sorties flown during the eight days of the operation. Although, as has been stated, a truce had been arranged with the Germans to allow the food drop to take place, several

Lancasters were actually fired upon, and each aircraft flew fully crewed and armed 'just in case'. One of the planes was hit in the bomb bay by small arms fire and was unable to get all its sacks away. Back at base it found difficulty in lowering the undercarriage, and while 'jinking' the aircraft to jolt the wheels down, a package fell, strewing tea, sugar and tins all over the countryside, which caused somewhat of a race between villagers and the official recovery party!

On 4 May I went on another of these Manna flights, this time with Flight Lieutenant Ramsden in ME544. On this occasion our 'target' was an airfield at Rotterdam, and the journey and reception were the same as at The Hague, with much flag waving and wild cheering. I particularly saw a group of people flapping what looked like an orange-coloured table cloth. They were standing on the top of a hut, and in their enthusiasm lost their balance and went over backwards! Likewise I saw a person who was waving while riding a bicycle lose his balance and fall off. On the way back, we spotted some German gunners as we crossed the coastline, but fortunately they were leaning on their guns and seemed to be enjoying the spectacle. We were back at Scampton after three hours, exactly the same time as the previous trip to The Hague.

The last day of this mercy mission was 7 May, and once again I flew to Rotterdam. I was with another pilot, Flying Officer Freeborn, and also in a different aircraft, ME485, just one of the fifty-five Lancasters that I flew in during my career! Basically, of course, this run was similar to the others, but on each journey I noticed some other aspect of the Dutch appreciation of our efforts, and this time there were numerous houses with whitewashed messages on the walls and roofs, 'Thanks RAF' and 'You have saved us' being typical. Again, as on the other flights, I was struck by the enormous number of greenhouses we flew over. I was well aware that Holland was a large grower of flower bulbs, but the amount of glass we saw seemed ridiculous, almost as though the whole country was covered by it. Our time for this trip was three hours and twenty minutes, somewhat longer than the other ones I flew on; perhaps we spent more time sightseeing on this occasion!

Altogether 6,684 tons of food were dropped in Operation Manna, all of which was gathered in by the municipal officers and distributed correctly to ensure that everyone had a fair ration. Because the Germans were still in occupation of the Netherlands, and with the possibility that their gunners might open up on us (which as mentioned did happen in a few instances), each of these flights was counted as an operation. At the time I was happy enough to add these to my total and this is why, in the official records, I was credited with having flown thirty-seven operations. On reflection, however, I do not see how I could claim that Operation Manna was a military one (this was a universal feeling), and so morally I am sticking to the total of thirty-four. Perhaps if the authorities had counted each of these trips as one-half or one-third of an operation, it would have had wider acceptance.

This same day, Monday 7 May, was the last day of the European war, with the German High Command signing the surrender terms in Berlin. The following day, Tuesday the 8th, was designated VE Day (Victory in Europe), and was treated as a public holiday, as was also Wednesday the 9th. Most Service personnel were given immediate leave, with the promise that those on essential duties would have at least two days off at the earliest opportunity. As far as we were concerned at Scampton, our essential duties had ceased, and there was a mass exodus, resulting in my travelling to Birmingham following my visit to Rotterdam the day before!

There was naturally great elation that the European war was over, not least among the aircrew ranks, and VE Day was marked with many celebrations. There were bonfires, parties were hastily assembled, people danced in the streets and the public houses were well patronised! The festivities went on until well into the small hours, but the mood was joyous rather than riotous. For many people, including myself, the occasion was tinged with sadness over the thoughts of the constant loss of young lives that had taken place to bring us eventual victory. I had known literally hundreds of such people on active service – including most of my own crew who had not returned from operations – or those who had been killed in training, and I was very thankful that I had survived to see this day.

The trains to Birmingham, or to anywhere else, were very crowded, but I managed to reach home by late afternoon, in good time to join in the local activities. There was very little happening in Arden Road where I lived, as most of the people were elderly and staid in their habits, and so I wandered into Alexander Road nearby where a gigantic bonfire had been built, completely stopping all the traffic. Here I met up with several of my old school chums, and we celebrated in good style, in due course paying a visit to the Great Western Hotel in Yardley Road, the first and last time that I did so! What happened to the rest of my family on this night of nights I cannot say, but I have a good idea that there was a quiet gathering of the clans with a broadcast speech by Winston Churchill being the top attraction. Certainly my mother, who was not very well at the time, would not have relished charging around the streets!

I spent the rest of my leave on visits around the neighbourhood, and had to parry numerous questions as to what the future would hold; my answer to this was that I hadn't a clue, and that I was content to stay put as I was for the time being. I also visited my old school, Yardley Grammar, and met quite a number of my old teachers who were still there, most of whom were very surprised to see that I had survived in one piece. In the early part of the war the school had received a direct hit from a German bomb, which had demolished a corner of the building including my first classroom, and although the rubble had been cleared away, no rebuilding had taken place because it wasn't classed as a priority job. I was taken to inspect this damage, and was able to reflect that I had just missed being killed at school instead of during my safe occupation in the armed forces! Some time later I was sent a copy of the school roll of honour, and was saddened to see that there were over forty names on it, including seven of my contemporaries.

In next to no time my leave was up, and back to Scampton I went to find that it was business as usual, except for the operations of course. Although our sphere of combat had now fallen silent, the war in the Far East was still in full spate, and there was a grave possibility that some Lancaster squadrons would be sent out there to attack mainland Japan. It was necessary, therefore, to keep both aircraft and men in good working order. The main way in which this was achieved was by carrying out the normal training programme of cross-country flights and bombing and gunnery practice, but there were also a few special tasks to perform, two of which were the dropping of surplus bombs in the North Sea, and the repatriation of ex-prisoners of war from Germany (Operation Exodus). No. 153 Squadron was not involved in either of these projects, but was allotted other duties instead, primarily the repatriation of Eighth Army personnel from Italy (Operation Dodge); the assessment of damage caused by bombing to the Ruhr and on Berlin (Operation Post Mortem); and also mock raids conducted to assess the efficiency of German radar (Operation Spasm). Before this, however, we were all given a treat with the staging of Operation Cook's Tour, which, as the name implies, was a flight over mainland Europe viewing a number of our ex-targets and other war areas. Determined not to be left out of this, I approached Wing Commander Rodney and enquired as to the possibility of being included with one of the crews, and he promised to make arrangements for me to go, possibly with Flying Officer Freeborn, with whom I had flown to Rotterdam.

A day or so before we were due to go, I was called to see Rodney who had had a call from an old friend of mine who also wished to take part, and imagine my surprise when the friend turned out to be my former skipper, Villiers, by now a wing commander! Villiers had approached No. 153 Squadron because I was there, and he was hopeful of being able to form a scratch crew to enable him to fly just once more in a Lancaster. I have an entry in my logbook as follows: '24.5.45 Lancaster LM754, Circuits and local flying, 1 hour 5 minutes, Pilot Wing Commander Villiers under instruction from Flight Lieutenant Langford!' This entry tells it all; Villiers got his wish and I flew with him once again, more than two years after he retired from operations. I do not think that he had flown at all since the Wickenby days as he had been incarcerated at Group HQ, hence the reason for his training session. If only my old crew had been present, to see him being shown how to fly a Lanc!

The momentous flight took place on the following day, 25 May, and was preceded by a briefing. The route was outlined with a familiar length of red ribbon, which just happened to lead to Essen of all places! The main idea was for us to fly as individuals at 2,000ft, and to enjoy ourselves looking at the various places of interest. No set timing was involved, we just had to meander around for endurance rather than range. Just before the briefing started, we were standing round in a small group and I was ribbed by Villiers who said that his main recollection of me on our previous tour was when I ducked to avoid the flak on our first trip to the Frisian Islands. Strangely enough, among my many memories of Villiers this remark stands out most prominently, but it was said in a friendly way and nobody enjoyed the joke better than myself. My leg was pulled on numerous occasions after that by various people who had been within earshot.

I have mentioned that the station commander at Kirmington was promoted to base commander at Scampton, and when the news of the Cook's Tour was received, Air Commodore Carter himself had his interest stirred. He too was determined to elbow himself on board, just as I had done, though of course he carried a little more weight than me! As Villiers was the senior pilot flying from Scampton, it was arranged that the air commodore would come with us, to the exclusion of a member of the ground staff who had to go with another pilot. All the other aircraft carried ground crew personnel, who were thus given the opportunity of seeing the targets for which they had toiled long and hard to prepare the aircraft for bombing. Take-off was at 11.25 hours, and we were in PA168. It was definitely like old times being Villiers's right-hand man as we became airborne, but as soon as we had levelled off after about five minutes, I had to vacate my position in deference to the base commander. I spent the rest of the trip either in my usual standing-up pose or sitting on the navigator's bench, and I had an excellent view of the proceedings.

Of all places, our first 'target' was Rotterdam, which I had seen recently at an even lower level, but this time we were able to spend more time circling round the war-damaged regions without having to search for a particular airfield. I cannot vouch for the exact order in which we visited the remaining places, but they were probably as follows: Arnhem, Dortmund, Osnabrück, Bremen, Hamburg, Hanover, Bielefeld railway viaduct, Möhne dam, Hamm, Essen, Düsseldorf, Cologne, Aachen, Brussels, Dunkirk and the Mulberry Harbour – a Cook's Tour par excellence! The Dortmund Canal, Bielefeld viaduct and Möhne dam were the targets of celebrated special raids; Arnhem needs no introduction, and neither does Rotterdam, which was badly bombed by the enemy. The German locations had all been heavily attacked by the RAF, and the damage had to be seen to be believed. Brussels was a bonus, a place with no obvious damage, and Dunkirk was the venue for the desperate British evacuation from France in 1940.

Throughout the length of this trip Villiers flew at a steady 170 knots, and maintained a mean height of 2,000ft, although we came down a bit lower where there was something of special interest to see. The engines behaved impeccably, with the temperatures and pressures rock steady (as proved by my logbook). Landing was made at Scampton at 18.15 – nearly seven hours of sightseeing without any alarms or excursions (and no corkscrews!), and we were tired but happy, with many memories to savour; indeed, I can recall most of the events of that flight quite clearly all these decades afterwards.

The squadron continued with the flying programme that I have outlined, and on the damage assessment flights many photographs were taken. I was fortunate enough to obtain some of these shots (legitimately), which were taken at 2,000ft, the same height that we flew at, and they show very graphically the damage that we saw, with Essen, Hamm and Osnabrück being prime examples.

It was an unreal situation at Scampton during the months of June and July leading up to VJ Day (Victory in Japan) in August, and to try to add interest to the daily life, numerous sporting activities were arranged. Cricket matches were played almost continually when the weather was fine, and these usually developed into 'test' matches between England and Australia. If the Aussies were short of a player or two, the Canadians were roped in. Whether one was any good at the sport or not was quite immaterial; it was almost like a Battle Order – if your name was on it, you played regardless, and to prove the latter point, they were hard-pressed enough to include me in the team for numerous matches! Quite often football matches took place at the same time, even though it was the summer, and on one occasion I recall finishing play on a cricket pitch and then going to the adjoining pitch to take part in football. I was quite fit in those days as it must be remembered that I did a lot of cycling, but there were still a lot of times when I almost had to be carried back to the mess at close of play!

On 2 July we had to undergo the rigours of an inspection by Air Vice Marshal Blucke, the air officer commanding (AOC) No. 1 Group. The idea of this inspection was obviously for us to remain on our toes and give us something to do to keep us out of mischief. It produced the required result, as the whole camp then became involved in a huge spit and polish exercise! My department set to with a will on our little garden, edging it with stones and generally making it presentable. The floor of our hut had to be cleaned and the door repainted; in fact the place had a real facelift for which I later received congratulations of the highest order.

On the big day itself, I had all my lads seated in neat rows wearing their best uniforms, and I was at the front giving them a technical lecture when the AOC strolled in, undoubtedly having been attracted by the garden. Of all people to bring along as his aide-de-camp, it turned out to be none other than Villiers, and I had an immediate worrying thought that my set-up may possibly pass the AOC's critical eye, but not Villiers's. I was proved wrong in this, though, for afterwards he took me on one side and said that it was a marvellous effort, which had made a good impression on the AOC. As it happened this was the last time that I saw Villiers, and I am glad we parted on such a happy note. Later in the day we paraded on the airfield for a grand-scale inspection by the air marshal and his retinue, closely followed by the senior station officers. The official photograph shows the general scene, and includes myself and most of the top brass, and is the only one I have of such a formal occasion.

It was two months after the Cook's Tour before I flew again, and this time I was a member of another scratch crew when, with Wing Commander Rodney, we went to Italy on 24 July on Operation Dodge, with the Lancaster being used in the humanitarian role of repatriating our soldiers who had been engaged in the North African and Italian campaigns. It had been known for some time beforehand that this operation was to take place, and we had had good time to be well prepared for it. The main consideration had centred around the fact that there were various diseases for us to catch in Italy, so a round of injections was administered to all concerned. At the end of June I therefore had three typhus jabs plus a smallpox vaccination. Naturally, like everyone else, I was not very keen to have these done but had to accept it for the good of the cause.

There was also a supposed issue of tropical clothing, but in the event Scampton only received a consignment of khaki shirts, and so a number of people didn't bother with them and wore their normal uniform. In my case I wore one of these shirts tucked into my battledress trousers. In addition to the squadron commander, who was anxious to sample one of these Italian trips, we were again honoured by the presence of

Air Commodore Carter. Not surprisingly, the base commander came fully fitted out in tropical gear, which was either his own from a previous campaign, or some that had been sent specially for him. Either way, the clothes did not fit him at all, because he had thin legs and wide khaki shorts that flapped about as he walked, rather in the Eric Morecambe style! I still have the memory of seeing him cut this ridiculous figure; he would have been much better off wearing his ordinary uniform with an open-necked shirt.

There were two destinations in Italy for Operation Dodge – Bari on the east coast and Naples on the west. Bari was reputed to be a pretty awful place, and so we were glad that we were being sent to Naples.

For some reason that I cannot explain, we started our journey from RAF Ludford Magna, some miles north-east of Scampton, which was the home of No. 101 Squadron who were also taking part. Another mystery is how we got there, for in my logbook I have no record of having left Scampton at all! Fairly obviously we flew to Ludford, because our aircraft NE113 certainly belonged to No. 153 Squadron, so I must have just forgotten to record it. There was a fairly extensive briefing before we left, during which we were given details of the route, height and speed at which to fly, what to do when we arrived, and how to position our human cargo on the return flight with regard to the centre of gravity etc. I can only think that we must also have got up very early that day, for we were positioned on the runway ready for take-off at 10.15 hours.

Once we were airborne, course was set almost due south, and we levelled off at 2,000ft, the height we maintained throughout except when over high ground. Soon after crossing the Channel coast, the Mulberry Harbour came into view, and then we were over France, passing Caen, Falaise and other Normandy battlefields. The aircraft was flying very smoothly, and after I had checked the engine synchronisation, George, the auto-pilot, was turned on and I tried out a balancing act; this was not a gymnastic display, but simply balancing a spoon on a pinhead on the navigator's table! The spoon remained absolutely still and was a perfect example of the steadiness of the aircraft and engines when not flying under battle conditions, and also gave a tribute to the excellence of the French weather. While on this leg over France, our prestige passenger, the air commodore, took over the controls for a spell, although

I must say that even I could have managed to fly the aircraft without any trouble in those conditions!

Our next destination was Toulouse, where a change of course was made to a south-easterly direction, taking us to the coast at Narbonne. This was a more interesting leg, with the Pyrenees to starboard (my side), but it was short and sweet and we were suddenly crossing the coastline again to go out over the Mediterranean Sea. My impression of the Mediterranean on this my first sighting, was that it did not seem much different to the North Sea, looking very grey and cold, but it soon changed to a very deep blue in confirmation of all that I had heard about it. At the same time, the air temperature became much higher, and we soon had the sliding windows open – another first for me as to do such a thing under British weather conditions would have given us all pneumonia. (Later on, when we landed in Italy, we could have done with an open cockpit, let alone sliding windows!)

On leaving Narbonne, we changed course to fly a more easterly route, which took us parallel to the French coastline, and we saw Marseilles in the distance and then Toulon. Early in the war, Toulon had been attacked by the Germans who had succeeded in sinking a large number of French warships in the harbour, but although we circled round once or twice we could see no evidence of this. We were somewhat rewarded, however, by the sight of a large warship at anchor, surrounded by a battery of smaller vessels. At this point, another change of course was made and we were now right out over the Mediterranean and heading for Corsica. The wireless operator had kept our home base advised of our progress from time to time (radio silence had ceased to exist!), and at this stage we were handed over to Pisa control. They welcomed us and informed us of the weather conditions (which we already knew!) and gave us permission to approach the Italian coastline. This we did by flying over Corsica and Elba, neither of which looked very inviting, appearing to be mainly rock and mountains.

Eventually the Italian mainland loomed, where we turned in a more southerly direction to follow the coast to Naples, having a good view of Rome on the way. Vesuvius, a volcano rising to a height of nearly 4,000ft and situated some ten miles east of Naples, was a splendid land-mark and we proposed to have a look at it there and then. We circled above it several times and I was quite fascinated; it was the only volcano I had ever seen, or was likely to see. There were no signs of any activity from it, but it was of course an active volcano, and it had erupted in 1944 causing contamination of the water supply, which was still unusable during our visit. When we had had our fill of this scenery, we ventured back on course and landed at Pomigliano airport after a journey lasting eight hours and fifteen minutes.

Pomigliano airfield had been brought up to heavy bomber standard during the latter stages of the war, by the laying down of metal tracks to form runways and hard standings for the aircraft, and when we arrived there were already a considerable number of Lancasters parked, so we lined up with a row of them. Transport took us to the administration block, where after a briefing of dos and don'ts there was a currency exchange when our English money was changed for Allied military currency notes printed in Italian lira. This was done at the airport as a precaution against our being duped by returning servicemen who were anxious to obtain extra sterling for their lira by quoting a false rate of exchange! We were also issued with yellow Mepacrine tablets, which together with our mosquito nets, helped us to ward off malaria. After an English-style meal, we were then whisked away to a large apartment block at Portici, a suburb of Naples. Here, we found the rooms were sparse but fairly comfortable, and had the inevitable balconies over-looking the street.

By this time we were rather tired and wanted no more than to lie down for a catnap, although we did not wish to miss out on the fun. A couple of hours later we summoned our reserves of strength and went out to sample the delights of Portici. It was fortunate for us that a religious festival had been celebrated that day, and we were just in time to join in the street dancing. The houses had been decorated and the people had donned fancy dress – it was just as though all this had been laid on to welcome us! The shops were still open, but I only remember the green-grocery ones, and these were mainly filled with melons and peaches, together with nuts of all descriptions. Melons were so plentiful that they were being used as footballs in the streets.

Eventually we staggered back to our billets, and this time we hit the hay well and truly, until we were woken up the next morning about seven o'clock by numerous street vendors singing their Neapolitan airs! We were allowed a free day in Naples before flying back, and we were determined to make the most of it, the result being a sightseeing tour of the city on a grand scale. Transport was no difficulty as a large Army depot was stationed at the Royal Palace, and they provided transport for all and sundry. This depot was so big that I think it catered for the whole of the Neapolitan area; some of the vehicles were buses, and they appeared to run a scheduled service throughout the city.

Anyway, we travelled to the Royal Palace (wherein was situated the officers' club), and starting from there the grand tour began. Obviously we could not cover the whole area, not even the city centre, as Naples proved to be a sizeable place, but we made sure of visiting the fashionable parts, and in particular the Via Roma, a wide and straight street almost a mile in length. Here there were shops of all descriptions, although many of them were closed owing to the war. No doubt in normal times this would be a dazzling place, but when we were there it was very bedraggled, and the main trading was done by the ubiquitous street vendors.

These people dealt mainly in filigree jewellery, watches, carved wooden boxes and other trinkets. There were also stalls where bags, carpets and clothing were on sale, and a good deal of buying and bartering was undertaken by the RAF contingent as we all wanted some souvenirs to take back. As in many other places, there were a lot of rogues operating, and we all had to be on our mettle to avoid being swindled. There were a number of articles that were suitable for barter such as cigarettes, shirts, butter and, best of all, bicycle tyres. Most of these things were almost non-existent in Italy at this time, and we had had advance information of the best items to take away with us. I 'obtained' some of the jewellery to take home for my mother; this was of surprisingly good quality and was much appreciated when I arrived back. I also bought one or two boxes and a few shopping bags that had been fashioned from raffia, but one had to be very careful when these were handed over, as they were often the nests of various large bugs and spiders! Other places that we visited were the Piazza Garibaldi, where the main railway station was sited, the Via Marina, where we went on to the beach to pick up pumice stone, and countless other arcades and avenues, occasionally resting awhile and frequently consuming bottles of lemonade to slake the thirst!

At the end of the day we arrived back at the Royal Palace after a very hot but most enjoyable time. By now my feet were in poor shape, but fortunately talcum powder was available at the Palace and I spent a fair amount of time getting myself back into a decent condition. After another night at Portici we were transported back to Pomigliano, on this occasion passing through a typhoid-affected area where the houses were marked with warning signs.

To say that the aircraft resembled a greenhouse would be a grave under-statement, for when the door was first opened, I was greeted by a heat barrier that intensified the further I went forward. By the time the cockpit was reached I was actually gasping for breath! Opening the windows seemed to make things even worse, so we had to live with the situation until we were airborne, when a beautiful stream of cold air released us from our misery.

The returning soldiers arrived about the same time as ourselves, and their kit had to be stowed in the bomb bay, presumably in the same panniers that we had used for Operation Manna. While at Pomigliano we discovered that some Lancasters from other squadrons had yellow circles painted on the floor to indicate where the soldiers should be posi-tioned, but our aircraft had not been marked, so we had to ensure an even distribution of the weight, mainly around the rest-bed area as this was the normal centre of gravity. (I am also inclined to think that we did not take parachutes on these trips but there were extra Mae Wests on board just in case we came down in the sea.) The soldiers themselves were then put in their appointed places, and last of all the engines were started, necessitating my clambering up in the nacelles again to operate the priming pumps. Fortunately the general heat meant that only a small amount of priming was required, and they were soon ticking over nicely.

Only a minimum of testing was carried out to avoid the engines over-heating, and we taxied out to the runway to take off as soon as possible. We had twenty passengers on board (excluding the air commodore!), and I circulated among the Army lads once we were airborne as we were all concerned for their comfort. The Lancaster aircraft was big enough when used for its original purpose, but with nearly thirty people crowded inside, it was a bit like the black hole of Calcutta, especially in the hot weather; but the lads stuck it out well enough, only too pleased to be homeward bound. They couldn't be connected to the intercom system as there weren't enough points available, so we passed notes to them giving them the distance left to fly and the airspeed etc. We also had each one forward in turn to see the view from the cockpit windows.

In great contrast to our leisurely progress on the outward journey, the flight back was made with some urgency in deference to the conditions experienced by our passengers, and we arrived back in six hours and forty minutes, a saving of one and a half hours, even though the route was substantially the same. Great was the joy and cheering when we crossed the English coast – very reminiscent of my operational days. A stop was made at RAF Glatton near Peterborough, to disembark the soldiers, and while there we came under the scrutiny of HM Customs and Excise! This took the form of our signing that we had nothing to declare, but one or two aircraft were searched and a few bottles of wine were unearthed (no duty free in those days), but nothing more serious than that. When Scampton was reached at 18.10 hours, it was the conclusion of three hectic yet exciting days. This excursion was also the last time that I flew from Scampton even though I remained there for several months to come, and in due course Wing Commander Rodney signed my logbook to confirm the entries I had made from January to July.

The next bit of excitement that we had was the commemoration of VJ Day. On 5 August, Hiroshima was laid waste by the Americans dropping the first atomic bomb, and this was followed on the 9th by the further atomic bombing of Nagasaki. These devastating blows were enough for the Japanese, and on 14 August they surrendered unconditionally to the Allies. In similar fashion to the end of the European war, two days of celebration followed, the first one being designated VJ Day. In comparison with VE Day, the rejoicing was half-hearted as Germany had always been the main enemy. Although there was much revelry in the United States, final victory went almost unnoticed in Europe, and the only manifestation I can remember was the placing of the letters VJ on the Stonebow in Lincoln, replacing the letters VE that had been there since May. There was little or no celebrating at the time, but I cannot escape the thought that we must have had a drink or two, for after all it meant the cancellation of Tiger Force (the attack on Japan) and our escape from the reality of operations once more.

Following the surrender of Japan, there was a steady run-down of the Lancaster units, and this was most apparent with regard to the Australian and Canadian personnel, who now went home. There had been an early exodus of some of the Commonwealth people after VE Day, when they returned to their own countries to prepare for Tiger Force, but this had only taken place on certain selected squadrons, and they had in the main stayed on at Scampton until the Japanese war had finished. I cannot vouch for the ground crews, but most of the aircrews flew their own Lancasters back, the Australians going via the Middle East and Malaya, and the Canadians via the Azores. There were many sentimental goodbyes, and they had a ceremonial send-off from the huge crowds lining the runways. I particularly remember Tom Tobin taking off with another pilot at his side in the place of the English flight engineer. After they had gone the mess seemed strangely silent, and it took some time for us to adjust to their absence. There were mixed feelings over this, as we had often cursed them for their rowdiness and lack of discipline, but my angle on this was that while they were often uncontrollable in groups of more than one, as individuals they could be charming.

It was a time of demobilisation for the British personnel too. Indeed, the whole squadron was in a state of flux, with numbers of people leaving and being replaced by new faces. Of course, it will be appreciated that whole units could not suddenly be disbanded and all the servicemen turned out on to the labour market, so consequently although many establishments were reduced, for most of us life went on as before. For those people who faced imminent demobilisation, lecture sessions were held and a large amount of literature was produced to help acclimatise them to Civvy Street. It also gave advice on the sort of jobs available to a lot of younger people who had joined the forces straight from school.

I was still sitting on the fence, waiting to see which way the wind blew, and although I glanced at some of the pamphlets, I saw nothing that inspired me to make a move. The aircrew training units were also affected but, as in our situation, training was still maintained although the schools were gradually run down. It was obvious to me that the aircrew training wheels were still turning when new crews appeared on No. 153 Squadron with pilots in place of flight engineers. This had been brought about not by a change of policy but because of the intensive drive that had been maintained to produce pilots over the years of war, which had now culminated in there being more pilots available than aircraft to fly. It was decided to put some of these pilots through the engineers' course and reduce the intake of engineers accordingly. Later, when the post-war situation settled down, this decision was reversed and flight engineers held their own again. Aircraft overproduction was another problem to be faced as there were very few losses on the post-war squadrons, coupled with the reduced establishments of these units. For the time being Lancasters and the new Lincolns (which were to replace the Lancaster in due course) were still being churned out, and we received an occasional new one to replace one or two of the older machines.

At about this time, a further award of campaign medals was made. Seven of these, fashioned as six-pointed stars, were issued to cover the different theatres of war. I was the proud recipient of the Aircrew Europe Star, which had a light blue ribbon with black edges and a narrow yellow stripe on each side; the colour blue represented the air, and the black and yellow stripes represented night and daylight operations respectively. Those who were eligible for the Aircrew Europe Star were flying personnel on aircrew duties who had completed sixty days on an operational squadron flying over Europe. They must have flown at least one sortie during the period 3 September 1939 (the outbreak of war) to 5 June 1944 (the invasion of Europe). Aircrews who operated over Europe after that date were awarded the France and Germany Star. I was also eligible for this decoration as well, but it was covered by the award of a clasp to the Aircrew Europe Star. The latter honour consisted of a bar of metal worn on the ribbon with the legend 'France and Germany'. As it was not practicable to wear this clasp on our uniform, a silver rosette was sewn on to the uniform ribbon instead. In addition to these stars, I also received the Defence Medal and the War Medal 1939–1945. As in the case of the 'Spam' Medal, only the ribbons were issued at the time and the actual stars etc., were distributed about twelve months later.

On 5 September I was sent to RAF Digby (a few miles south of Lincoln) to take part in a Junior Commanders' Course. This was a full-scale affair and I was there for a month. It was another example of the continuation of routine after the war, highlighted in this case by the fact that out of the hundred or so of us in my entry, a fair proportion of them were demobilised very soon afterwards! As the name implies, the object of the course was to give a good disciplinary grounding to junior officers, and to give them a preparation for future promotion. I did not take kindly to it at first as I was never keen on the 'management' side of the RAF, but I warmed to it as it went along and realised that I had nothing to lose and possibly much to gain by treating it seriously.

The course was of a similar nature to the one I had undergone at North Luffenham a year previously, but was much more comprehensive. I have kept a record of the syllabus, and I think it will prove interesting reading to repeat it here: Powers of punishment, Drill (of the energetic kind!), Service correspondence, Signals (paperwork not flags), Officers' and sergeants' messes, Messing and catering, Summaries of evidence, Courts of inquiry, Court martials, Airmen's documents, Equipment and stores accounting, Posting and promotion of officers, Parliamentary procedures, General accounting, Welfare, and WAAF administration. Most of these subjects are self-explanatory, but I will elaborate on a couple of them.

Ever since my Halton days I had been in constant contact with the RAF stores procedure without fully understanding it, and now at Digby it suddenly became clear. It was a fairly elaborate procedure with much paperwork, and I remember that when drawing an item from stores several signatures were needed. It may have seemed cumbersome, but it really did work well and was a model of its kind that presumably kept going until the computer age rendered it obsolete. Although I had no dealings with the system itself, one could not avoid coming up against it when, for example, an item was lost or stolen. Even if one broke a window, a piece of glass had to be drawn from stores and a further piece sent there to replace it. The value also had to be accounted for, and in the case of domestic items this meant a transfer of money from one's pay to the equipment branch.

The drill periods were used mainly for the study and practice of large parades rather than the simple 'square bashing' of which I had already had my fill. On one occasion, a large manoeuvre was to be made involving considerable numbers of men divided into three wings, and when a difficulty arose over the natural reluctance of anyone to act as parade supremo, I spoke up and was immediately accepted. Although it appeared to be a job to avoid, I believe I managed it rather well and shouted all the correct words of command. The main problem I had was to make myself heard as I do not possess a parade ground voice, but whether my instructions reached the persons at the back or not, they all made the right movements and I was able to report to the inspecting officer with the parade in good order! There was so much detail to study on the course that it was not possible to go outside the camp confines except at week-ends, when I used to visit the Moss family at Lincoln, and on one of these excursions I met Roy Taylor who informed me that the squadron was to be disbanded in the near future.

It was made clear to me how soon this was to be when I reported back to Scampton on 3 October after the Digby course had finished. Only three days were left before the squadron was to break up on the 6th, but as I was due for leave I went off home and missed the final fateful day. Before going, I had learned that I was to be posted to RAF Sturgate as their flight engineer leader, but no other details were available so I departed from Scampton for the last time in a very thoughtful mood. I had been with No. 153 Squadron for twelve months to the day, having been posted to Kirmington on 7 October 1944. During this period 1,041 operational sorties had been flown by the squadron.

Chapter Twelve

Sturgate

RAF Sturgate turned out to be another wartime station, and was situated a few miles south-east of Gainsborough. I had the pleasure of moving there with Harry Howling, who was to be the bombing leader, and Ron Stewart, the signals 'chief'. Another old colleague of mine from the Hemswell days, Eric Weaver, was also there as gunnery leader. The airfield circuit practically overlapped that of Hemswell, and their runways had been used by the trainee pilots from Hemswell for landing practice. It was a terrible blow for us to be sent to this station, for it meant exchanging the superb comforts of the Scampton mess for the grim conditions of a temporary camp. Naturally, I had arrived at the wrong time of year as usual, and the mud was waiting to greet me! I think that, all things considered, Sturgate was the worst camp that I experienced during my career; it may have been fractionally better than Faldingworth in one or two aspects, but it was much colder and a lot sparser. It was definitely gumboots only in the living accommodation area, and also had the same primitive washing arrangements as other stations of the same ilk. The only bright star on the horizon was a promise that the squadron would move in the near future to a more amenable camp, but we were very sceptical about this and were prepared to believe it only when we saw it happen!

No. 50 Squadron was one of the old originals, having been formed during the First World War, and throughout the Second World War it had been in No. 5 Group of Bomber Command, flying Lancasters for the last few years. The squadron code letters 'VN' had become very well known when, in 1942, one of their Lancasters, 'N' Nan, had given a demonstration in front of the press to show off the aircraft performance and handling qualities, and for the remainder of the war photographs of her appeared in books, periodicals and advertisements. Even the Germans used reproductions on propaganda leaflets!

In the aftermath of the war, the squadron was sent to Sturgate during June 1945, along with its sister unit No. 61 Squadron, and was now transferred to No. 1 Group and restructured at the same time. It took us 'new boys' a day or two to settle in before we became involved with the flying programme, which turned out to be an aimless repetition of that at Scampton, with cross-country flights and navigational exercises etc. With the war over, we were all living in a time of confusion, and there seemed to be very little momentum; throughout my RAF service I had been involved either in or with intensive training, or with actual operations, and this period was very disturbing and featureless. All things considered, it is no wonder that I looked forward with some concern. Incidentally, the tenor of life on this new squadron was forcefully conveyed to me on the very first day when, having dropped my kit off at the mess, I found my way to the flight offices with the intention of reporting to the CO, only to be told that he, together with a crowd of senior officers, were away for the day playing golf – peacetime had truly arrived!

The first event of any significance at Sturgate happened towards the end of October. It had been decided that a limited number of aircrew would have the opportunity to visit Berlin, with priority being given to those who had actually taken part in bombing raids on the German capital. This was a great idea, for it afforded a chance to actually set foot on German soil, whereas up to this time we had only seen the war damage from the air, and naturally I made sure that I was included in the visiting party. It was arranged that we would stay in Berlin overnight so that we could have a good look around and even do some shopping there; our currency would be exchanged for Deutschmarks on arrival, but it might be useful to arm ourselves with items to barter as we had done on the Italian visit. The outward flight took place on 23 October, and I flew in PP671 with Flying Officer Thackray and crew, taking off at 11.20 hours. The route took us to Helmstadt and thence through the air corridor over the Russian Sector to land at Gatow airport after three hours and forty minutes (there must have been a speed restriction in the corridor, as I had been to Berlin faster than that on a 'business' trip!). On the way, we had landed at Tibbenham (in Norfolk) to pick up some RAF ground crews who had been permanently posted to Gatow, but the time of the flight made allowances for that.

Gatow was used by us as it was in the British Sector, the main pre-war Berlin airport of Templehof being used by the Americans. On arrival we were ushered into a large hall to be briefed regarding our conduct and the restrictions we had to accept (no fraternisation for example), plus various other matters such as the currency and the limits of the British Sector. When an officer arrived to talk to us, I was amazed to see that it was Flight Lieutenant Wilkinson, the No. 12 Squadron gunnery leader while I was at Wickenby. He had been a bit of a comedian in those days, and he now made a most interesting speech with a laugh in nearly every line, ending up with tips as to how to get around the regulations that he had already outlined to us, with a request for us to forget what he had said!

We had a meal at the airport and also a currency exchange, and were then driven to an ex-Luftwaffe camp nearby where we found very comfortable quarters, complete with hot and cold water and all mod cons. The thought struck me that the Luftwaffe accommodation was of a very high standard compared with our lot at Sturgate, but it had to be remembered that it was a headquarters unit, and should therefore be judged on that basis; certainly it was adequate for our needs. By the time the preliminaries were over it was too dark for sightseeing, so we were taken to the officers' mess for the evening. The mess, also ex-Luftwaffe, had been converted from two large houses and was on the same grandiose scale as the living quarters, but there was little else to do but prop up the bar and listen to my old No. 12 Squadron colleague cracking jokes – still, it made a change to the routine back at base.

A tour of the British Sector of Berlin was laid on for the following morning, but first of all the aircraft had to be checked as take-off was in the early afternoon. Outwardly, PP671 was in good order, but on running up the engines, I found one of them to be overheating, and in calling in the ground crew this was diagnosed as being due to a faulty oil cooler. The aircraft was plainly unserviceable, and although we could have flown back on the remaining three good engines, it would have been impossible to guarantee a successful take-off, so there was no alternative but to wait a further day while a new cooler was flown out to us. The remaining crews eyed us with a suspicion that we were trying it on, but it was a completely genuine fault even if we were happy to take advantage of it.

Our sightseeing vehicles were single-decker buses, and there was a guide inside each one to give us a running commentary. The route we took would be impossible to describe, even if I could remember it, but we visited a number of important places commencing with the Olympic Stadium where the 1936 games had taken place. An impressive processional way led up to the stadium, and it was not hard to imagine this to be lined with storm-troopers, or even Hitler himself ranting and raving from the rostrum. One tangible reminder of the war were rusting flak guns near the entrance gates – during my Wickenby days, I could not have imagined myself living long enough to see this day. Although as far as I can remember it was in the British Sector, I can clearly recall a group of Americans playing baseball on the hallowed turf! Further on we stopped at the Reichstag, the parliamentary building that had burned down before the war. Although in ruins when we saw it, it had been partially repaired and later used by Hitler, only to be badly damaged again by the RAF. We were keen to have a souvenir of our visit, and rummaged about to see what could be found; many people had been there before us and anything of importance had already gone, so I had to be content with a coat hanger from one of the cupboards! Although only a lowly coat hanger, it had a specially long wire hook to accommodate the high military collars of those days, and had the name of a German tailor stamped on it. It is still in use today, and although it looks a bit incongruous with an ordinary jacket on it, it is a constant reminder of my day in the 'Big City'.

Before the war, the Unter den Linden was a very famous thoroughfare in Berlin and had worldwide acclaim, but when we arrived there on our tour we were not allowed to set foot in it as it was in the Russian Zone. It was all the more impressive as it led up to the Brandenburg Gate, which stood on the actual boundary of the British Sector. Warning notices in several languages were prominently displayed, and the boundary was being closely patrolled by Russian soldiers; all this, of course, being a prelude to the Berlin Wall. Not wishing to collect a Russian bullet, the only souvenir I was able to obtain was a photograph of the Brandenburger

Tor (as it is known in German), one of the only two snapshots I had left in my camera.

Throughout our travels of the British Sector there were scenes of devastation; whole rows of buildings had been razed to the ground, and even some of the streets themselves had disappeared and we had to make detours around them. It is no exaggeration to say that of those buildings that were still standing, no more than a quarter of them had roofs on. This damage was not entirely wrought by the RAF, as the city had been heavily bombarded by the advancing Russians, who had also waged a policy of destruction when they took up occupation. The German population who had to endure the terrible raids during the war, now had to face the problems of peacetime with little or no proper accommodation and very little food. I saw many families living under canvas amid the ruins, and some whose only home was a large drainpipe that had been left on the road prior to reconstruction.

It was rather fortunate that the suburb of Charlottenburg was included in the British Sector, for this was the most stylish part of Berlin, somewhat akin to Edgbaston in Birmingham, with the main thoroughfare, the Kurfürstendamm, being equivalent to Regent Street in London. Here it was that our crew were left during the afternoon, having returned to Gatow for lunch. Naturally we were not keen to wave the other aircraft off on their return to England, but preferred to make ourselves scarce! It was on the Kurfürstendamm that we met the German people, particularly a number of hawkers who were keen to sell any sort of trinket in an effort to make a living. There was really nothing worth buying, though, either from them or indeed from the shops. But I was rather tempted when I saw a shop that sold only binoculars; however, one look at the prices and back out I came!

We spent all afternoon in this area and thoroughly enjoyed ourselves; the trams were running and we made a couple of excursions (free to Service personnel). It was very noticeable that the Germans were very subdued and stood up to let us sit down, also giving us priority on entering and leaving the tram. During our perambulations we were approached by a group of German ex-Servicemen who had a number of medals for sale, and realising that these would make excellent souvenirs, we each bought some, under the impression that they were Iron Crosses. It was some years later that I found out they were actually the German War Service Medal, similar to our Spam Medal! We had been fooled because these medals were actually in the shape of a cross, but never mind. I come across them occasionally – together with my coat hanger and the photograph of the Brandenburg Gate – and they invoke as many memories as if they were the genuine article.

To round off the day for our little group, we paid a visit to the Femina Pusta, one of the higher-class nightclubs in Charlottenburg. Here one could drink, dance, or just listen to the orchestra, and determined to enjoy ourselves we needed little persuasion to join in the fun. To do this we had to fraternise on a temporary basis, as all the female element were Berliners. The German girls were no different to any others I had met previously, and most of them played an unwilling part during the war. We ended up sitting round in a large group having a most interesting conversation in pidgin English. We were given graphic descriptions of the air raids from the German point of view, and there seemed to be no embarrassment over the fact that we had taken part in them, and that we had been their enemies until a few months beforehand. It was a most stimulating and unusual experience, as had been the whole day, and it was a tired but happy band of airmen who retired to bed at Gatow that night.

Our new oil cooler had arrived during the late afternoon, and was to be fitted on the following morning. Another batch of crews had flown in, and we were told to be at the airfield after lunch in time to return to England at the same time that they did. As we had already been on the 'grand tour', we decided to wander around locally as we had seen various buildings in the vicinity that were worthy of exploration.

Little did we know that we were to stumble across such a fascinating complex as the German Air Warfare School, which had been established at Gatow in the early 1930s. The place can best be described in the words of someone who had actually been a cadet there, and I quote this description taken from a book that I read some years ago. Werner Baumbach who became General of the Bombers in 1943 at the age of twenty-six, gave details of his introduction to the Air War Academy at Gatow, Berlin, in one of the first cadet classes of the new Luftwaffe: 'The moment we entered the establishment, we had the impression that no trouble or expense had been spared. Our quarters, the sports ground, the gymnasium and swimming baths, the flying ground, halls and lecture rooms were all the last word of their kind. The whole atmosphere of the place breathed the spirit which animated Hermann Goring, Commander in Chief of the Luftwaffe, in building up the new arm. We swore by the Fuhrer and worshipped Goring as the greatest war hero of the First World War.'

No words of mine could better that! It was indeed a most comprehensive school, much like a university, and although I have not been to Cranwell, which would be the English equivalent, I feel that I am on safe ground in saying that it was far in advance of anything we had. That this school had not had universal appeal was obvious from the time we entered the doors, as it had been completely vandalised by the Russian troops. In the halls and lecture rooms, absolutely everything possible had been broken up. I saw scientific instruments and equipment worth thousands of pounds broken and bent, text books, maps and diagrams torn up, and the glassware smashed. All this debris was lying on the floor just as they had left it, and there were even some Russian helmets that had been left behind. The mind boggled over the senselessness of it, but from what I heard later, this act was typical of the Russian attitude. It can best be described as a pointless act of vengeance. We spent some time sifting through it all, but there was nothing that could have been salvaged – it was only fit for the junk heap. Even the gymnasium and swimming pool had been wrecked, but we could not understand how the living quarters (where we were staying) had escaped any damage; perhaps the Russians themselves were billeted there at the time.

It was soon time for lunch, and after having had our currency exchanged, back we went to the airfield where PP671 was now serviceable again. Take-off was at 14.50 hours, and we had more passengers on board, who were dropped off at Tibbenham, where we were also subjected to a customs check. The last leg of the flight, from Tibbenham to Sturgate, took place in darkness and, as it transpired, it was the last night flight that I made.

Back at base we were soon into the old routine of training, and I took part in this myself when I had a trip in PB821 on an air-to-sea flying exercise off Skegness. In this, targets were floated on the surface of the sea to simulate shipping for the gunners to aim at, but the logic for this

escapes me as it would have been out of the question for us to attack
shipping in a Lancaster bomber in any future war; perhaps it was meant
to be practice against a moving target in the absence of drogues.

It was not very long before another outing was laid on for us, helping
to break the monotony, and once again it was Operation Dodge.
Repatriating the soldiers from Italy had now been going on for four or
five months, and was to continue for several more. In all 100,000 men
were finally brought back home, some having been away for five years.
The main task had been entrusted to Bomber Command, and squadrons
had been sent to Italy in turn. Now No. 50 Squadron was at the top of
the list, and we were raring to go. Just for a change I was actually detailed
to take part, and so on 26 November I crewed up with Flight Lieutenant
Bill Lundy in RA591, and we were airborne at 07.40, an unheard-of hour
for peacetime! The journey was broken at Glatton, where some passengers were embarked, and then it was full speed ahead, taking substantially the same route as before, and Naples was reached after six hours.
It was another comfortable journey, and as the air commodore was not
present on this occasion, I was able to stay in my normal crew position
and enjoy the view. Before landing, the opportunity was taken to see a bit
more of the area, and we flew round the Bay of Naples passing over such
places as Sorrento, Amalfi and the Isle of Capri, all bathed in sunshine
and set off by the blue Mediterranean. What a difference to the grey
November morning we had left at muddy Sturgate!

Landing was made at Pomigliano, followed by lunch and the usual
currency exchange, but unlike the Berlin trip there were very few restrictions to be briefed about except for the obvious ones concerning
fraternisation and the typhoid no-go areas. Everything else was left to
our common sense, and we were allowed to go wherever we wished on
the understanding that we were back in time for the flight home.
Several people who, like myself, had been to Naples before, considered
the possibility of travelling the hundred miles or so to Rome, given that
there was plenty of public transport available. One or two of them may
have done so, but no doubt many others were put off by the tight time
schedule. While on this subject, a number of crews who went to Bari in
December were grounded by bad weather for up to three or four weeks,
so of course they made the most of it by travelling round the tourist

places, and were allowed to spend Christmas in Rome. (Until I heard this I thought I had done well getting an extra day in Berlin!)

Our accommodation was in Portici as before, and owing to our early start there was plenty of time to wander round Naples as soon as we had dropped off our travelling kit. On this occasion I had the hilarious experience of being accompanied by Eric Weaver, our gunnery leader, who, like his opposite number Flight Lieutenant Wilkinson, was something of a comic. Eric was determined to obtain a fair number of souvenirs at the cheapest possible cost, and his haggling with the street vendors had to be heard to be believed. I had my camera with me (this time with a new film in), and my photograph of Eric buying a watch shows it all! Central Naples was our main beat, but we did get as far as Piazza Garibaldi, the big attraction here being a magnificent funeral procession preceded by the coffin borne on a splendid black coach pulled by a team of horses. I well remember getting a lift back from the Piazza along the Corso Umberto to the Royal Palace in a flashy-looking American bus, and it was at this time that I realised how many Americans there were about; there seemed to be hundreds of them, considerably more than at the time of my previous visit. Like the British Army, their transport was open to all and this was a great consideration as it was much more comfortable than ours!

Our arrival at the officers' club in the Royal Palace coincided with a sudden tiredness of body and legs and dryness of throat, so our course of action was to slump down in a restful attitude and have a few drinks until it was time to return to our apartment. In retrospect there is one thing that I have always regretted not doing. Across the street from the Royal Palace stands the San Carlo Opera House; it is not tucked away in a side street as is our Covent Garden, but it is right out in the open and clearly visible when entering or leaving the palace. Moreover, even at that time there was a full programme of opera each evening of the week, including Sundays, and indeed there was a different programme daily including such favourites as Tosca, Aida and La Traviata. All this and I didn't go! It would have been easy for me to do so as I was at the palace on several occasions, and even just to see the inside of such a well-known place would have been of great appeal. My reasons for missing out are not very clear; perhaps I was among a crowd of people who were not interested, or I may have seen an advertisement for one of the unpopular operas, or even perhaps my fascination for the subject has developed since those days. Be that as it may, it was a splendid opportunity that I let slip by and unfortunately it has not presented itself again since.

We were woken up early on the following morning by the 'barrow boys' trundling along with their melons, peaches and large red tomatoes. We found that it had rained overnight, but the sun was now out and a group of us, including my pilot Bill Lundy, decided to go to Pompeii, which lies sixteen miles to the south-east of Naples. The journey presented no difficulty as we were able to hitchhike along the Autostrada, and were soon picked up by a British Army vehicle (no comfort, but it saved us the walk!) that dropped us right outside the ruined town. Pompeii, of course, needs no introduction other than to say that it is the most remarkable specimen of an ancient Roman town in existence. When it was over-whelmed by an eruption of Mount Vesuvius in ad 79, it was covered with ash to a depth of 20ft. It was the fact that it was covered in this ash, and not lava, that enabled it to be dug out in the eighteenth century to become the tourist attraction that it is today.

To the best of my recollection there were no guides operating at Pompeii when we were there, other than one stationed in one of the best preserved buildings (of which more anon), and so having bought a small guidebook at the entrance gate, we were left to our own devices. Another advantage to our being there so close to the end of the war was the scarcity of tourists, apart from a few Servicemen, which made for more comfort and an improved view of the buildings.

The town is approximately a mile square, and we made our way round looking at the simple things first – the streets, the forum, the amphithe-atre and the larger houses. Some of the 'houses' were just open ground with a few walls remaining, but others were much more elaborate and better conserved, retaining such features as bathrooms and kitchens. The streets were clearly definable, mainly through the ruts in the paving caused by the wagon wheels, which in some cases were as much as six inches deep. Most of them had quaint straightforward names, such as the Street of Fortune, the Street of Abundance (the main shopping area) and the Street of the Sepulchres, a very long street lined with tombs on each side (Pompeii was an ancient town before the eruption). We saw all the public buildings and the shops, as well as the bakery, and had our photographs taken sitting on the grinding mills.

Tiring at last of the paved grey solitude under the hot sun, we sought the shade and ate our packed lunches before doing the rounds again, this time exploring some of the houses with their attendant ghosts. In this way, we arrived at the special building that I mentioned above, and although the name escapes me its purpose was quite clear. It was a type of public bathhouse, lined inside with colourful murals that had escaped the ravages of time and disaster. Apart from the fact that these murals had survived, they were all of an erotic nature, and so was a star attraction! It was strictly 'men only' inside, and of course we all went in to have a look! The age of these paintings was really more fascinating to me than the subject matter, and the only picture I can really remember clearly is one where a man is balancing a certain part of his body against its weight in gold! Although these murals would be classed as pornographic by us, we were assured that they were quite normal to these people of so long ago, and indeed we saw one or two other examples painted on house walls as we wandered around. We had spent a most mesmerising and absorbing day, and ended up footsore and weary by late afternoon when we returned to the entrance gate, and departed for the modern town of Pompeii looking for food and drink.

A cafe appeared invitingly, wherein a waiter produced a menu which, being in Italian, was not very decipherable to Bill or me, but after a bit of sign language we settled for egg on toast, assuming this to be the least spicy item available. Unfortunately, my idea of egg on toast was at variance with what actually arrived, the toast being black and the egg hard-boiled, but as this transpired to be another quaint Italian custom we had to accept it with good grace. We were not prepared either for the violinist who stood by us and played throughout the meal, giving us a rather tinny version of some Strauss waltzes. It did, nevertheless, help to take our minds off the egg and toast and subsequent black coffee, and it was also a welcome change from the incessant Neapolitan songs to be heard at almost any hour of the day.

This cafe of surprises had one more to spring, and after we had paid off our violinist, we were immediately besieged by a crowd of boys with the usual souvenirs to sell. We were more disposed to listen and look while sitting in comfort, than we would have been out in the hot dusty street, and I had had orders from home for shopping bags and jewellery ('if you go to Italy again …'), which I had intended to pick up in Naples at the end of the day, so we thought it quite convenient to buy them there and then. The trinket and cigarette boxes were better than I had seen before, so I had one or two, together with some shopping bags, but the filigree work was not very brilliant, so I did not bother with it. Bill Lundy also bought some items and it was a good job that the transport park was nearby to save us an uncomfortable walk carrying our wares. We went back to Naples in the 'comfort' of an Army lorry, and persuaded the driver to drop us outside our accommodation at Portici. After our long day out in the unfamiliar sunshine, coupled with the necessity for an early start on the following day, it was prudent to rest for what was left of the evening, but I did wander down to the shops to buy a bag full of melons, which I took home on leave a day or two later.

We were awoken a lot earlier than required on the last morning by the usual clatter from the street below (I am sure there were no windows in that block!). The bus taking us to the airfield went by a somewhat different route this time, and we saw some of the squalor of Naples on the way, with backstreet slums and families living out in the open with no sanitation available. In view of these conditions it is hardly surprising that typhoid was so prevalent. We were rather glad to arrive at Pomigliano, as our journey had been one where it was far better to arrive than to travel! There was no trouble with the aircraft this time, except for the internal heat, and having packed the returning soldiers in, the engines were started and we were away with alacrity to the cooler regions a few thousand feet higher. It was a steady flight back, with the usual messages being circulated among the uncomfortable but otherwise happy passengers. Glatton was reached in just under seven hours. We had nothing to declare to customs, and after dropping off the human cargo we were off again on the short hop to Sturgate, where we landed in pouring rain. Surprise, surprise!

The weather in our part of England had now taken a turn for the worse, and we entered a period of cold east winds and driving rain. The flying programme was not affected too much, but the living conditions deteriorated as each day passed, with the mud becoming more churned up and even obliterating many of the paths. Inside our huts the situation was only marginally better as they were cold and damp. Had we still been at Scampton, the weather would have been hardly noticeable, and even the huts of Wickenby had a degree of warmth, which was sadly lacking at Sturgate. A single stove was kept alight continuously. It usually resembled a steel-works furnace, and we put hot bricks into the beds to try and relieve some of the misery. There was also a general shortage of accommodation, and we were overcrowded to the extent where protocol could not be properly maintained; I even had one of the flight commanders in the next bed to myself, a situation unheard of at any other camp that I had been to. The only bright note I can recall, was that I had several of my close colleagues with me, including Harry Howling and Bill Lundy, and at least we could console ourselves that we were all in the same boat and were suffering together.

Under the circumstances, it is little wonder that we looked forward to our promised move to a more permanent station, and three hearty cheers rang out when it was announced that we would be moving to RAF Waddington 'sometime in January'. Our spirits rose further when we knew that the move was imminent, and new life pervaded the camp, but we had to soldier on in the meantime and relieve the monotony with a few activities such as mess parties and outings to Nottingham and other points of the compass!

In this way passed the last days of 1945, a momentous year indeed, with the transition from war to peace. It marked the end of my eighth year of service, and although I could be reasonably certain that I would survive the coming months in the physical sense, my future in the RAF otherwise was very unclear. This position had been confounded further by a significant event, when on my previous leave I had met my future wife-to-be, Joan. This considerable happening had taken place at the Masque Ballroom in Sparkhill, Birmingham, which I used to visit occasionally while at home. At first this meeting simply led to a succession of 'dates' on my subsequent leaves, but our relationship soon developed further and was to have a far-reaching effect on my Service career.

Our waiting game at Sturgate eventually ended on 25 January 1946, when with great relief the squadron, together with No. 61 Squadron, made the long-awaited move south to Waddington.

Chapter Thirteen

Waddington

RAF Waddington lies on an escarpment of land about three to four miles south of Lincoln, and my posting there marked the first occasion that I had been stationed south of the city. The site was, like Scampton, a permanent camp of the highest quality, and was such an improvement over Sturgate that the only thing they had in common, except for the runways, was the legend 'RAF' in the title! The main blessing for us was, of course, the mess, which was laid out in the standard pattern of a pre-war station and was very inviting to us exiles from the wilds. As far as I can recall, the previous unit had recently moved out, leaving the mess empty except for the permanent staff, so we were able to get settled in without any problems. I had a room on the first floor that I shared with Harry Howling, and my first act on dropping my kit was to have a bath in the luxurious surroundings – the first proper one I had had since my previous leave! The squadron offices were on the same plane of superiority, being positioned in the front annexe of one of the hangars. I was even better off than I was at Scampton, now having a separate centrallyheated office and large lecture/crew room, instead of a Nissen hut and stove! My now veteran nameplate on the door just set the seal on it.

Most of us had flown over from Sturgate in the squadron aircraft, and so the training flights were able to be continued without interruption. I will comment on the programme later, but first of all I should mention the aircraft themselves. The imminent introduction of the new Lincoln bombers to squadron service was by now common knowledge, although it was early in June before they were supplied to No. 50

Squadron, and in the meantime we carried on flying in our old veteran Lancasters. A check on the records of the Lancs that I flew in at Waddington reveals that they had nearly all seen service on several squadrons before they reached No. 50, and one of them, PB583, had flown with no less than six squadrons before reaching us. Under these circumstances it is no surprise to hear that when I went up in it in March it was on an air test!

Why we were stuck with the old faithfuls when new ones were continually being made is not clear, but I can give an indication of what was happening to the new ones. A.V. Roe and Co. (designers and builders of the Lancaster) had a repair depot at Bracebridge Heath, a short distance from Waddington on the road to Lincoln, and our technical staff paid frequent visits there to obtain spares. We flight engineers were very anxious to see what went on there and I managed to organise a visit for a party of us to investigate. Naturally enough the site was littered with damaged aircraft that had been brought there from all over Lincolnshire for repair, and we were interested to observe the restoration procedure. Also on the site were a number of brand new Lancasters, which were being stored there. The answer to this apparent paradox of repairing old aircraft while new ones were deteriorating out in the fields was presumably to afford employment for the staff and to enable them to keep their hands in. Later, it transpired that a certain number of the new production aircraft were being converted for special purpose work and research, or to Lancastrians, which were the civil version used for passenger carrying. The remaining new aircraft were simply scrapped, and this applied to most of those at Bracebridge Heath as we were to see with our own eyes on a subsequent visit.

Coincidental with my arrival at Waddington, I, together with many other aircrew, received a formal notice of demobilisation, purely a Service term for redundancy. I was not really surprised as there had been a considerable amount of flux in the squadron for some time, and my name was certain to crop up sooner or later. There was an 'escape clause' in the document stating that a person of my status could apply for a permanent commission (which may have meant remustering to a different occupation), or that I could extend my period of service by six months with a possibility of extending it for a further six months at the end of that time. I could, of course, have taken both courses together, but I opted purely for the six months' extension to give me further time to see which way things were moving. For the time being I applied myself to the job in hand, and tried to forget about the more distant future. The flying plan was very desultory, ranging from cross-country flights and fighter affiliation, to mere circuits and bumps. I was nevertheless kept fairly busy, and had to attend endless conferences and flight briefings as well as ensure that there were always enough engineers available to fly in spite of all the comings and goings and sickness etc.

One of the flight engineers that I inherited was Sergeant Eric Oliver, a well-known motorcycle rider, who at that time was the world sidecar champion. Apart from being a superb rider, he was also a first-class mechanic, and made an ideal engineer who was able to effect any minor repairs in flight and diagnose any engine faults. On the other hand, when he wasn't flying, he was very difficult to locate, as he was usually tinkering with his motorbike somewhere on the camp. We were supposed to report for duty at 08.30 hours each day, but the number of times that Eric was there at that time was very few, and when he was present he was very scruffily dressed, with oily hands, and this naturally drew me into conflict with him. To keep faith with the rest of my charges I had to clamp down on him, and this led to a full-scale confrontation when I told him that his position in the motorcycling world cut no ice with me as far as his Service duties were concerned, and that I was quite prepared to charge him before the CO if necessary. This little diatribe was adequate enough to bring him to his senses, and thereafter he toed the line almost impeccably. To be quite truthful, I did not want to appear to be at odds with him, or to lose him if at all possible, as he was a celebrity and he brought a fair amount of prestige to the department. He was imbued with a great sense of humour, and in due course we got along with each other very well, so much so that I once had a ride in his sidecar, but that is another story to be told later.

I did a certain amount of flying at Waddington, but apart from two or three special trips, it was mostly of a local nature. On 22 February I did forty minutes' local flying in RA591, followed by an hour's circuits and landings in ME359 on 9 March, this being a dual pilot exercise with Wing Commander Coad, a visiting officer who wanted some Lancaster instruction. Some days after this I was up again on an air test in PB583.

At the end of April, the squadron was selected to fly the Bomber Command rugby team to Bordeaux to take part in a match against the French Air Force. I cannot remember exactly how many aircraft were involved in this flight, but it was probably around four or five. Bill Lundy was one of the pilots detailed to go, and as he was still without a permanent engineer, I selected myself to accompany him.

The rugby team were assembled at Waddington, and on 25 April we took off in yet another different aircraft for me, ME382, on the way to the French Air Force base just north of the city. The route was direct, and we took three hours. When we arrived it was a surprise to see that there were no formal runways on the airfield, but as the weather had been fine the ground was firm and presented us with no problems, except for a few dust clouds that blew up in the slipstream while taxiing to the parking area. We had been led to understand that we would be staying in a hotel in Bordeaux, and a coach actually turned up to ferry us there, but at this point we had our second surprise when we learned that just prior to our appearance, a party of nurses had arrived and been given our accommodation! We therefore had to lump it and make the best of life in a barrack room together with our French hosts. As things turned out we were not too inconvenienced by this as we were out most of the time, and really only had to sleep in the barrack room for the two nights we were there.

As a part compensation, our French friends took us out to a night-club in Bordeaux after we had sorted ourselves out and had a meal. This outing was enjoyed by all concerned, as much for the fact that it was something entirely different by way of amusement for us, as for the entertainment itself, there was a revue as well as dancing girls and vocalists (les Sisters Swing!). It all went on until 2am, but we were tucked up in bed and fast asleep long before this time.

Unlike our visits to Italy and Berlin, we were dependent on public transport in Bordeaux (although of course the rugby team were provided for), and consequently when we went into town for some sightseeing on the following morning we could be seen sitting on a tram rattling along a country road among the vineyards! The tram consisted of two coaches coupled together, with the conductor at the back with a whistle to direct the driver, and although I suppose these trams were commonplace in France, it was once again a novelty to us. The morning was spent wandering about, and apart for some shopping (I bought a film there), we paid a visit to Bordeaux cathedral and watched the shipping on the Gironde river. As usual the hours passed too quickly and it was suddenly time to watch the big match. The stadium was a short distance from the city centre and necessitated another tram journey. I tried out my meagre knowledge of the French language to ascertain which tram to catch, but although my query was understood I could not decipher the answer. In the end, though, we were led to a No. 12 tram standing nearby that quite clearly said 'Stadium' on the front, and within minutes we were inside the ground.

Although the match was the highlight of our visit, and indeed the raison d'être for our being there, it is the one thing that I can least call to mind. Not one incident of the play remains in my memory, except that we actually won the match against all the odds. Clearer to me was the stadium, a magnificent structure with a huge cantilevered roof, and also the fact that we British supporters, twenty to thirty strong, were heavily outnumbered by a ratio of several hundred to one. The 'spoils' of the contest were some cases of champagne consigned to the higher echelons at Bomber Command, and the nearest that I got to them was that they were transported back in our aircraft and I was responsible for stowing them to ensure their safe passage!

That evening, a party of us decided to go to the opera, the idea being partly inspired by myself to make up for missing out in Naples. Again, the Grand Theatre in Bordeaux was another splendid building, with a huge colonnade of pillars forming the frontage. Inside it was even better still, with marvellously decorated balconies and boxes, the scene being further enhanced by the bright hats and dresses of the ladies who, by tradition, seem to don their most colourful outfits for the occasion. Our little group had a box that was available because, disappointingly for us, the opera being performed was a rather obscure one called *Sigurd*, in Wagnerian style featuring Brunhilde and the Valkyries. As we had made a special effort to go we stuck it out until the end – and it must be said that there was a special atmosphere about the place, and there was also some very good music – but I am sure that most of us would have preferred to have been there on the following evening to see *The Barber of Seville*, which we saw advertised on the way out!

Our journey back to Waddington on 27 April was accomplished in the much shorter time of two hours and forty minutes, due probably to a headwind in one direction and a tailwind in the other. During the middle of May Joan came to visit me for a weekend, staying at the Great Northern Hotel in the centre of Lincoln. Having ensured that she was well ensconced in the hotel, I took her to lunch at the Glory Hole cafe on the river bridge, one of the few bridges in the country to have shops on it. In the afternoon we toured round the town before dragging our weary legs up Lindum Hill to visit the cathedral. A special treat was laid on for Joan on Saturday night – dinner at the White Hart Hotel. I had invited Harry Howling to be with us on this special occasion, and he duly arrived at the Great Northern in his Lanchester car, whereupon we drove to the White Hart in grand style. The highlight of the weekend for Joan was to be escorted into the poshest hotel in Lincoln by two RAF officers, an event which completely overshadowed the meal that we had come specially to eat! With the passage of time I can remember very little else about our dining out evening, but Joan has reminded me that we had lobster for the main course.

Another pointer to the insidious return of peacetime routine, was my involvement with a church parade on Sunday morning, in view of which Joan attended morning service at the cathedral by herself, but I was able to get to Lincoln just after lunch and we went for another stroll around before having an early tea at Westgate Court. As the name implies, this was another hotel within the boundaries of the old Roman town – near the West Gate in fact! The hotel had a deserved reputation for after-noon teas, even during wartime, and was usually crowded out at the weekend. Our visit was therefore a must, and Joan came away suitably impressed. Her train back to Birmingham arrived a few minutes after we reached the platform and we parted once again, fortunately not for long as I had a leave coming up in a few weeks' time.

Two or three days later, on 15 May, I was sent to RAF Lindholme near Doncaster for an air experience flight in a Lincoln bomber. No. 57 Squadron had recently been re-equipped with them, and they were in effect 'stretched' versions of the Lancaster with a new type of rear turret. The squadron was used for demonstration flights for personnel

from other units such as mine who were expecting the imminent arrival
of their own Lincolns. Travelling to Lindholme by road the day before,
I was, in RAF jargon, 'temporarily attached' to No. 57 Squadron for the
occasion, and my flight took place in RF405 at 09.20 hours on the
following day. I can say categorically that I took an instant dislike to the
new aircraft, even taking into account the difficult circumstances of the
trip. We performed twenty minutes of circuits and bumps, and had a
second pilot on board who at least stood behind me for a change. The
cockpit did not seem very different from the Lanc except for the addition
of fuel flow meters (which would have been invaluable on operations!),
but the whole machine seemed too big and unwieldy, and far from herald-
ing it as a worthy successor to our faithful Lancasters, I was not sorry
when the session ended and was glad to disembark. Perhaps I would have
changed my viewpoint if we had done a four-hour cross-country instead,
who knows? In any event, it was my first and last flight in a Lincoln.

During May we had a change of squadron commander when Wing
Commander Knyvett took over. Knyvett was a frosty sort of person who
would not have got very far if we had been operational, and to the
extent that I can recall he had done a fair amount of time in Training
Command and had not flown in Lancasters before. I was let off the
hook when he was converted to the type by one of the flight commanders,
but I have mentioned his name as it does crop up in my logbook.

Owing to the superiority of its airfield and its open position on high
ground, RAF Waddington was chosen to carry out some of the first trials
of Ground Controlled Approach and Landing procedures. Hitherto the
routine had been for us to inform the control tower of our position and
request permission to land, which was done without help from the
ground except in some circumstances when a radio beam signal was used.
It must be said that this was one of the more positive moves to give us
an interest in life, and of course we were very pleased to carry out some
of this pioneering work that was to lead to the sophisticated radar systems
in use today. While the squadron as a whole did a great deal of labour
on this project, my involvement was minimal and restricted to a short
session of landings with the aforementioned wing commander on
18 May. To fly with a pilot who knew little about handling the aircraft,

however, and who was being asked to have faith in an unknown voice to land it for him, was very unsettling for me to say the least, and I consider my contribution to the effort was much higher than my logbook implies!

We were given something else to occupy our minds on 29 May, when Waddington camp was opened to the public in aid of St Dunstan's, the charity for vision-impaired ex-Service personnel. A number of activities were planned to take place, and of course all departments had to buckle to and make the place spick and span. When I had been at Cosford, and later at St Athan, I had seen numerous mock-ups of aircraft systems, and I thought that it would be a good idea to have something along the same lines in my lecture room at Waddington. This would have the advantage of being an attraction on the open day, but would also give my group some employment when they weren't flying, in addition to it being instructional for new engineers to study. I put the idea to the engineers and it was greeted with enthusiasm, and it was decided to re-construct the Lancaster hydraulic and fuel systems (minus the tanks!), providing we could scrounge the necessary parts. I obtained official sanc-tion for the project on the understanding that no official spare parts from the station stores would be used, and also that no help would be expect-ed from the transport department. One obvious source for the parts we needed were the RAF maintenance depots where all the wrecked air-craft were taken, and two or three of us managed to get a lift to the one at Stafford. Although we travelled hopefully, we were disappointed on arrival as all the bits and pieces were stacked in several massive heaps and there was no chance of extracting what we wanted.

My next move was to contact the Avro depot at Bracebridge Heath, and they kindly offered me every facility to have a look around their scrapyard for the items we required. As previously mentioned, this depot was only a mile or so away on the road to Lincoln, and it was no trouble for us to get there on our tour of inspection. Unlike the situation at Stafford MU, Bracebridge Heath was like an Aladdin's cave; when we entered the main yard we were astonished to see almost brand new Lancasters being broken up for scrap, and we were allowed to have what we wanted providing we were able to dismantle the items ourselves. To cut a long story short, we went again the following day armed with tools and ended up with a full hydraulic system including the pipework, and even two electric motors to drive the pumps. The largest item operated hydraulically on a Lancaster was the undercarriage, but this was too big for us to handle so we settled for a pair of the hydraulic jacks that were normally coupled to the oleo legs.

Even the transport arrangements gave us no difficulty as we fell back on Eric Oliver and his sidecar. In effect his sidecar was merely a flat board and was ideal for transporting our conglomeration of parts, and he managed to get all the stuff to Waddington in about three or four journeys. I made the mistake of travelling with him on the first journey there, and it is no exaggeration to say that I have never been so frightened in my life as he set off at world record speed and hardly seemed to slow down at corners, merely leaning over in true sidecar style. I had to hang on like grim death and was never so relieved as when we reached Avro's. I swear he did the distance in just over a minute! Needless to say, when he was transporting the parts he had to drive with much more decorum, but he really was a tearaway, and with his sidecar technique plus the terrific exhaust noise he was quite a menace on the roads. As in the case of my flight in the Lincoln, it was my first and last journey with Eric!

It turned out that the fuel system idea was not practicable for reasons of space, but we mounted the hydraulic system vertically along the wall, and soon had it assembled in working order. At the touch of the various controls one could operate the undercarriage, bomb doors and flaps, and even feed non-existent hot air to the non-existent carburettors! We had to use some of the official hydraulic fluid from the stores, and also employ the station electricity to run the system, but in return they had gained a splendid piece of apparatus. It was viewed by not only most of the other aircrew types, but also by a large proportion of the ground staff as well, and was a star attraction on the open day. It had also fulfilled the original aim of providing employment for my staff and had helped to improve morale in the department. It took us somewhere in the region of three to four weeks to build and was ready some days before the open day itself.

In addition to our contribution, numerous other exhibits and areas had been prepared, and when the visitors arrived they were able to see the Link trainer, the briefing rooms, an array of bombs of all sizes, parachutes being packed, and numerous other items of equipment.

Undoubtedly the most popular attraction was a Lancaster that was open for inspection. For the best part of four years the people of Lincoln had seen and heard untold numbers of Lancasters droning in the sky on operational duties, but owing to the veil of secrecy many details of them and their equipment were unknown to these civilians, who now had their chance to see for themselves. There was a queue at the aircraft all day long. A flying display was also held, and the planes taking part included a Meteor (the first RAF jet aircraft), a Mosquito, several Spitfires and Hurricanes, and of course a Lancaster and a Lincoln, both of which made several runs over the airfield at nought feet! In the evening there was dance music played by the RAF Dance Orchestra, and the whole day went off successfully in reasonably good weather. The proceeds totalled £300, which was a tidy sum in 1946.

Many changes were now taking place in regard to the station personnel and routines. A number of the administrative officers who had been in the Volunteer Reserve had now been demobilised, and this situation, plus a change of policy, meant that we aircrew officers became more and more involved with station duties. I found myself taking part in numerous parades and inspections, and I also had to accept responsibility for part of a barrack block that had to be checked over at regular intervals. In addition to all this I was handed over the inventory of a hangar, the contents of which I had to monitor carefully to ensure that they did not vanish overnight! A move was made to bring in formal mess dining-in nights once or twice a month in pre-war tradition, and this was the thing that finally made up my mind, and that of many others, that enough was enough and that I would be much happier if I left the Service. There were other factors, of course, such as the fact that I didn't like the forthcoming Lincoln bombers, and in any case even if I had liked them, the future flying prospects were featureless in comparison with the frenzied operational activity that I had been used to. Last, but by no means least, I had been considering the possibility of marriage to Joan and this, together with the other things on my mind, led me to give formal notice of my intention to leave when my extension of service ran out in August.

I had been to London during April to see Freddie Prowse (my old rear gunner from No. 12 Squadron days), who had recently been demobilised.

I stayed at the Wings Club in Grosvenor Square, and the two highlights of the visit were my being introduced to Freddie's numerous relations and a visit to White Hart Lane to see Tottenham Hotspur play Portsmouth (most of the relations were there too!). Other outings now followed my decision to end my Service career as Harry Howling (who was also due to 'retire') joined me in a final fling before we were thrown into the melting pot of civilian life.

Not for the first time, Harry's car was very useful when we made another visit to Nottingham, staying overnight at the Flying Horse Hotel, commonly known by RAF types as the Airborne Nag! It was beautiful weather, and we spent the whole of one day messing around with boats on the River Trent. Towards the end of June we had a trip to Skegness, accompanied this time by Leslie Gray, one of the No. 50 Squadron pilots. Again, the weather did us proud and we decided to go in informal dress. My two companions, who were temporary reservists, had their old civilian clothes handy, but I who had not worn anything but my uniform for eight years, was at a disadvantage and had to make do with a borrowed shirt from Harry, tucked into my Service trousers, which were held up with a makeshift belt. This was a weekend jaunt and we stayed at a boarding house, spending most of our time lounging on the seafront. While strolling to the promenade, we were 'snapped' by one of the local photographers, and my copy shows off my makeshift outfit to perfection. It was also the first time for many years that I hadn't worn a hat, and it made me feel quite undressed!

I had not quite finished with flying yet, and indeed two days after the open day I had a short flight to Binbrook to help ferry an aircraft over, and returned with a different crew as a passenger. This was the only time that I flew in a Lanc with no duties to perform. Shortly after this the squadron was given another task, that of flying a programme of meteorological reconnaissances. These involved long flights, practically due north, and owing to the expected duration of them, two pilots were carried to share the workload. About ten aircraft took part on each of these runs, and I joined in the first of them with two flying officer pilots.

Take-off was at 13.15 hours on 16 June in ME359, which I had flown in on a couple of previous occasions, and as far as I recall course was set for slightly east of north so that we were over land for most of the way.

On we stooged for hour after hour with absolutely nothing to see as we were flying at about 6,000ft above unbroken cloud, until after what seemed an eternity, there was a clearance in the cloud cover and we saw the Shetland Islands below. During all this time the wireless operator had been sending back reports at half-hourly intervals. These were based on our observations through the windows, and must have been pretty monotonous with the amount of cloud about, although we would have also reported the wind speed and direction as accurately as we could determine it. Having reached a latitude of sixty-two degrees north, it was about-turn and back to base, but we did have an element of excitement when I had to feather the port inner engine because of falling oil pressure. As we were about two-thirds of the way back by this time there was no need for me to juggle with fuel tanks to ensure an even loading on either side of the aircraft; in fact throughout my period of Lancaster flying I (fortunately) never had reason to make use of the cross-feed cock. The whole trip took a wearying eight hours and twenty-five minutes to complete.

My next two flights are well worthy of mention as they both had unusual aspects to them. The squadron was warned of the possibility of it being sent abroad, probably to India or Malaya, and in view of this all the flying personnel had to be fitted up with tropical kit. It made no difference whether some of us had only a few weeks to serve – everyone was involved and quickly! The matter was apparently so urgent that some Dakotas were dispatched to Waddington to fly us down to North Weald on the outskirts of London so that we could be kitted out. I flew there in KP215 on 18 June, two days after the Met flight. The Dakotas were quite bare inside, except for a bench seat along each side of the fuselage upon which we were herded together to endure one of the most uncomfortable flights of our lives. The whole aircraft was a rattle trap and we felt most insecure, especially as we were not carrying parachutes. Mercifully we were at North Weald in three-quarters of an hour and were very grateful to tumble out, blinking, into the afternoon sunshine. It took us about an hour to draw the kit, and then we were subjected to the same miserable conditions on the return flight home. Needless to say, I never had to wear my tropical kit and to the best of my knowledge neither did any of my contemporaries on the squadron!

I went off on another Met reconnaissance on 21 June, this time in RA591, with Flight Lieutenant Haslam and Wing Commander Knyvett as second pilot. We were in trouble before getting airborne, for when tearing along the runway at full power, the aircraft suddenly swerved. Fortunately the undercarriage held firm, but we found ourselves bounding over the grass and across an adjacent runway at over 100mph. The engines were immediately throttled back, and by diligent application of the brakes the pilot just managed to pull up before any damage was done. I cannot give any explanation for this as I had certainly held all the throttle levers fully forward and the engines had not faltered. I had known this sort of thing to happen when a tyre burst, but our tyres were found to be intact, and I can only conjecture that the pilot's foot had slipped on the rudder bar. Whatever the cause, it was the nearest that I ever got to crashing. After a quick examination by the ground crew we taxied back to the runway and this time got off the ground without mishap.

The story of this trip is similar to the previous one, apart from the engine trouble, with unbroken cloud covering the ground for most of the way. Whether we saw the Shetlands this time is debatable, but we certainly saw nothing of Scotland even though our track covered the whole length of it. I had never been north of the border before these Met flights, and it was some thirty years later that I visited that delightful country for the first time and was able to say that I had seen it at last! Again, we turned about at sixty-two degrees north, and when we arrived back at base we had been airborne for exactly eight hours. The most significant point about this flight was that, although I probably didn't realise it at the time, it was the last one I ever made. No doubt later on, when I had left Waddington, I reflected back to this occasion with sadness, for I had got quite used to flying, and I think it must be said with fairness that I had done my share under almost every conceivable condition. The fact remains, however, that I was not at all keen to fly Lincolns, which by now had arrived on the squadron, and I don't really think that I would have taken kindly to have flown regularly in any other type of aircraft except my beloved Lancaster. 'Finis' was written quite literally when Wing Commander Knyvett signed my logbook for January to June 1946. It was the last entry in the book.

During the next six or seven weeks until my release, I continued to work conscientiously; there was more interest than hitherto and probably more flying as well as the crews converted to the new aircraft, but there were slack periods to fill, and to help the situation I organised a squash tournament within the department. I had previously played squash at several of the stations I had been to, and there was a very good court at Waddington, so with a bit of guidance the tournament prospered, giving a bit of healthy exercise as well as keeping minds occupied. Another idea I had was to obtain an old Stromberg carburettor so that we could section it and show the working parts. The carburettor was quite a big object, five or six times the size of one in a motor car, and kept us busy for a fair length of time.

Inevitably the time for my leaving Waddington approached. Knowing well beforehand that I would have to journey to Wembley to finally sign off, I was kindly invited by Tommy Thompson to stay a few days at his flat while I was in London; Tommy himself had left the Service in July, and the idea appealed to me so much that I had no hesitation in accepting. Of course, I had to clear myself at Waddington before leaving, and first of all I put my spare uniform up for sale. I had only worn this uniform once or twice, as although it had been made to measure it didn't really fit me, and I had toted it round from camp to camp for use in an emergency. I was able to describe it as 'new', and I had no sooner put up a note on the mess noticeboard when I was approached by the junior medical officer, who bought it on the spot. I handed my tool kit, flying helmet and boots back into stores, and had no problem in getting my clearance chit signed by all the appropriate departments. With a final drink with my cronies and my mess bill paid, I was ready for the off.

I left Waddington on 11 August, comfortably seated in Harry Howling's car on the way to the station in Lincoln. My thoughts on leaving can well be imagined, as I had completed nearly nine years' service and had known no other life since leaving school, but my reverie was interrupted at the end of the short journey to Lincoln, where we had to wait about half an hour for the train to arrive. Whiling the time away over a cup of tea, we had a short, rather unreal, conversation, and I was quite pleased when the train eventually pulled in as it was a moment for action rather than thought. I had a fair amount of luggage with me as I was taking home the bulk of my Service dress, including my greatcoat, raincoat and battledress (which were to complete their service many years later!), and I suspect that Harry was pleased to give me a hand with it to keep his mind occupied also. Soon it was time to go, and as we pulled out of Lincoln station Harry's final words were ringing in my head: 'If you want a best man when you get married, you know where to apply!'

Things had improved a little on the railways since my epic wartime journeys and, particularly as we were on the main line, King's Cross was reached in respectable time and I was able to partake of a little lunch in the station buffet before the next stage of my journey across London. Tommy had a flat in the stockbroker belt at Snaresbrook near Epping Forest, which necessitated a journey on an Eastern Region steam train from Liverpool Street station, and well do I remember this station as being the smokiest and noisiest of all that I had been on. I am somewhat of a steam enthusiast and no doubt some people would have revelled in being able to spend the day there, but for me it was as quickly in and out as possible. (Snaresbrook and beyond are nowadays reached from the Central Line of the London Underground.) The flat was in the luxury class, which was so vastly different to the Nissen hut at Wickenby where I had first met him! Tommy had returned home early from his office so as not to miss me, and I had an enthusiastic welcome when I finally arrived, rather tired and weary. After a meal I was quite content to sit and talk until the late evening, whereupon I retired to my luxurious bedroom and found sleep very easy.

On the following morning, 12 August, I made my way to the Wembley Dispersal Centre housed in a small hut by the station, to complete the final details of my release and to collect my civilian clothes. This demobilisation outfit was a gift from a grateful government for services rendered, and consisted of a suit, shirt, raincoat, trilby hat and shoes. All of these items, together with the aforementioned Service dress, were to form the nucleus of my civilian attire, and although they were very austere, they were fashionable for the age and I was not too proud to wear them until they became unserviceable. The remainder of the formalities consisted of form filling and rubber stamping until I ended up with a final clearance certificate and a rail warrant for the journey home. That was it, and for all practical purposes I was now a civilian again, although

I was on eight weeks' 'demob' leave until my last day of official service on 7 October. I spent a very happy three or four days in London, and was very grateful to Tommy for his hospitality and understanding at this emotional time. I travelled home from Paddington station, the very last of a long series of railway journeys, during which I again had plenty of time to reflect back on my years of service in peacetime and in war. Memories flooded in, and I recalled that beyond the din of battle and the loss of friends, I had had many times of pure happiness when life was joyful and rosy. It would take a long time and much effort for me to settle down to civilian life again.

Appendix

The Nine Wing Commanders

Wing Commander Wood (Wickenby)
Wing Commander Craven (Wickenby)
Wing Commander Roberts (Wickenby)
Wing Commander Donaldson (Faldingworth)
Wing Commander Campling (Hemswell)
Wing Commander Rodney (Scampton)
Wing Commander Villiers (Scampton)
Wing Commander Coad (Waddington)
Wing Commander Knyvett (Waddington).

Index